Praise from Job Seekers for the *Knock 'em Dead* Books

"I got the position! I was interviewed by three people, and the third person asked me all the questions in *Knock 'em Dead*. I had all the right answers!"

— D.J., Scottsdale, Arizona

"I just finished writing the letter I have dreamed of writing for three years: my letter of resignation from the Company from Hell. Thanks to you and the book, *Knock 'em Dead*, I have been offered and have accepted an excellent position with a major international service corporation."

— C.C., Atlanta, Georgia

"Thank you for your wonderful book! I read it before attempting to secure a position in an industry that I had been out of for fourteen years. The first company I interviewed with made me an offer for more money than I had expected."

— K.T., Houston, Texas

"My previous employer asked me to resign. Your book got me through my depression, and in only four weeks, got me four job offers. This is the first time in my career I have this many options to choose from."

— D.H., North Canton, Ohio

"I credit you as being the number one source of information on this issue, and recommend you every time I hear that someone is in the job market. The cost of the book is the best money I've ever spent."

— T.S., Atlanta, Georgia

"After college graduation, I searched and searched for a job, and ended up taking a few low-paying ones I was overqualified for. Finally, I read your book and have been offered *every* job I have applied for since."

— L.E. (no address given)

"I followed the advice in *Knock 'em Dead* religiously and got more money, less hours, a better hospital plan, and negotiated to keep my three weeks vacation. I start my new job immediately!"

— A.B., St. Louis, Missouri

"My job search began a few months ago when I found out that I would be laid off because of a corporate buyout. By following your advice, I have had dozens of interviews and have received three very good job offers. Your excellent advice made my job hunt much easier."

— K.C., St. Louis, Missouri

"I found your book to be absolutely invaluable during my recent job search. Since then I have had a chance to speak with my interviewer, who informed me that it was my strong interview that landed me my job offer. He went on to outline what had turned him off about other candidates, and it was some of the very same mistakes I used to make before reading your book!"

— D.D., Houlton, Maine

"Every time I've used your book, I've gotten an offer! This book is incredible. Thanks for publishing such a great tool."

— W.Z., Columbia, Maryland

"Just a quick note to let you know how much your book has helped me. I was chosen for my job out of over one hundred applicants! I later loaned the book to a friend and circled the things that had helped me. She interviewed on a Thursday, and she was offered the position that Thursday night! Thanks for writing such a helpful book."

— S.G., Sacramento, California

"Your book is simply fantastic. This one book improved my yearly income by several thousand dollars, and my future income by untold amounts. Your work has made my family and myself very happy."

— M.Z., St. Clair Shores, Michigan

"Thank you for all the wonderfully helpful information you provided in your book. I lost my job almost one year ago. I spent almost eight months looking for a comparable position. Then I had the good sense to buy your book. Two months later, I accepted a new position. You helped me turn one of the worst experiences of my life into a blessing in disguise."

— L.G., Watervliet, New York

"I was out of work for four months—within five weeks of reading your book, I had four job offers."

— S.K., Dallas, Texas

"Yesterday I received two job offers in the space of fifteen minutes. I am now using the 'Negotiating the Offer' chapter to evaluate these positions."

— W.B., Thornhill, Ontario

"I read every page in the book and, after a two-month search, got ten interviews with top-performing companies and six offers (five of which I declined)."

— M.V., Millington, Tennessee

"I was sending out hordes of resumes and hardly getting a nibble—and I have top-notch skills and experience in my field. I wasn't prepared for this tough job market. When I read your book, however, I immediately began applying some of your techniques. My few nibbles increased to so many job interviews I could hardly keep up with them!"

— C.S., Chicago, Illinois

"I read the book, cover-to-cover, and then flew to California to complete fourteen intense interviews in a two-day period. Although I was interviewing for an entry-level position with a high-tech firm, I faced few technical questions. Most of them were behavioral questions, exactly the types your book prepared me for. I had the enviable position of making a choice of which job to take!"

— S.T., San Jose, California

"I got two job offers within a twenty-four-hour period. The information you've provided is as valuable as the air you breathe."

— J.M., Greensboro, North Carolina

"I will always remain a student of yours. Since the first edition to the last, I got every copy, and with each I learn more. I have had several interviews, all of which were generated by the tactics of your book."

— M.R., Beaumont, Texas

"It was as if the interviewer had just put the same book down! After being unemployed for more than a year, I am grateful to say that I've landed the best job I've ever had."

— E.M., Honolulu, Hawaii

"I read and used your book, *Resumes That Knock 'em Dead,* as I searched for a job. I was called for an interview and was up against ten applicants. To make a long story short, I interviewed on Monday morning, and by Monday afternoon knew I had the job."

— E.H. (no address given)

"I just received the offer of my dreams with an outstanding company. Thank you for your insight. I was prepared!"

— T.C., San Francisco, California

"After reading your book, *Resumes That Knock 'em Dead*, I rewrote my resume and mailed it to about eight companies. The results were beyond belief. I was employed by one of the companies that got my new resume, and received offers of employment or requests for interviews from every company. The entire job search took only five weeks."

— J.V., Dayton, Ohio

KnOCK 'em DEaD BUSINESS PRESENTATIONS

Martin Yate & Peter Sander

Adams Media Corporation
Avon, Massachusetts

Published by Adams Media Corporation
57 Littlefield Street, Avon, MA 02322 U.S.A.
www.adamsmedia.com

ISBN: 1-58062-760-9

Printed in the United States of America.

J I H G F E D C B A

Library of Congress Cataloging-in-Publication Data
Yate, Martin John.
Knock ’em dead business presentations /
by Martin Yate and Peter Sander.
p. cm.
ISBN 1-58062-760-9
1. Business presentations. I. Title: Business presentations.
II. Title: Knock 'em dead business presentations.
III. Sander, Peter J. IV.Title.
HF5718.22 .Y38 2002
658.4'5—dc21
2002009992

This publication is designed to provide accurate and authoritative information with regard to the subject matter covered. It is sold with the understanding that the publisher is not engaged in rendering legal, accounting, or other professional advice. If legal advice or other expert assistance is required, the services of a qualified professional person should be sought.

—From a *Declaration of Principles* jointly adopted by a Committee of the American Bar Association and a Committee of Publishers and Associations

Rear cover author photo by Ariel Jones.

This book is available at quantity discounts for bulk purchases.
For information, call 1-800-872-5627.

Contents

10 • Build on Your Excellence 233

1 Speak up, Speak Well, Speak Often

Speaking is a major cornerstone of your career and professional life.

Were a fortune-teller to spy this book in your hand, she might surmise that you intend to be successful in your professional life—that you have made the commitment to develop your professional skills. As this describes just about every reader who comes to the *Knock 'em Dead* books, that assessment is pretty much a no-brainer. All the fortune-teller had to do was connect the dots.

Knock 'em Dead Business Presentations will connect some dots for you too, dots that will help you harness your communication skills and advance your career. In this particular *Knock 'em Dead* book, you will develop powerful core competencies that will make you stand out in your profession. Your interactions will become more profitable as you increasingly sway others to your point of view. You will become a more competent professional, with an ever-increasing sphere of personal influence in your professional world. These enhanced skills will unquestionably aid your professional growth over the years, but they will also be of assistance in other facets of your life.

You want to be successful in your career. An integral part of success is the personal fulfillment that comes from the respect you receive in your profession. When people know who you are and respect what you do, your commute becomes less stressful, that workday never stretches to the horizon, your meetings go more easily, and support for your projects is often more forthcoming. This happens because you are a known and respected individual, not just a business "commodity." You have credibility and visibility in your work life. Developing "Knock 'em Dead" presentation skills is a solid, almost guaranteed, path to this end.

A Consummate Professional

Here's how it can work for you. All journeys start with a single step, and your speaking career will start with a single presentation. You may make one particular presentation a number of times over the years, or you may make presentations on many different topics. But no matter how many presentations you make, or how many different types, they will all share similar schematics, foundations, and building blocks. Your topics may change—the context and the audience most certainly will. However, you will learn that every presentation has a fairly finite number of building blocks. You lay them, one on top of the other, just as you would to build the wall of a house. The design and purpose of the house may change, but the building process remains consistent.

It is the same with business presentations. Even the busiest professional can learn and apply these techniques. Each of these building blocks requires an existing knowledge of the subject matter, a message that is strengthened with research and quality content, and proven delivery techniques. We'll show you how to maximize acceptance of your message. You played with building blocks as a kid; this can be just as much fun and almost as easy!

What's more, with every presentation you make, you will become more knowledgeable, effective, and respected in that topic area. Not only will you enhance your credibility because you know more, you will enhance your visibility because you are seen to know more by a greater number of people. Don't overlook this "collateral" benefit!

You may have come to this book because you recognize that becoming a better communicator will dramatically improve your professional growth. If not, know that this is exactly the way this book is intended to impact your career. Credibility and visibility go hand in hand. Together, they lead to greater job success, promotions, and greater earning capabilities.

A World Thirsty for Knowledge

We live in the Information Age. There is an almost unquenchable thirst for people who can communicate ideas and strategies in a public forum. All of our metropolitan areas have convention centers; almost all hotels have meeting rooms and depend on business meetings as an essential revenue stream. Meetings have become a multimillion-dollar business.

There are meetings going on every day to share information, discuss issues, evaluate alternatives, and plan strategies. Companies run meetings all the time for people at all levels and with all kinds of titles. For every one of the thousands of meetings being planned today, there is a desperate meeting planner looking for people with something relevant to say and the ability to share their thoughts in an engaging manner. That could be you.

Once you have your chops down within your company, the outside world will be anxious to hear your message at venues such as professional associations, industry conventions, in the press, and on radio and television. Your professional world, along with the opportunities it offers, expands exponentially as you increase your sphere of personal influence with the visibility you generate making presentations. These same presentation skills will also add immeasurably to your self-confidence and know-how in all business and social situations.

Enhance Your Employability

Building business presentation skills will add to your overall employability because employers in all industries look for certain core competencies in those they hire and those they promote onto the fast track of the modern corporate world. Amongst the most desirable core competencies are communication and presentation skills. This is true whether you are in sales, finance, management, administration, technology, human resources, or any aspect of nonprofit or government work.

Success comes down to being a consummate professional in your field, always striving to improve and to become that little bit better than your colleagues and competition. Then, it is a matter of finding something to say and taking your message to a greater audience. Finding something worth talking about will happen naturally. Your topics will come from the challenges your department and company face on an ongoing basis. Your topics will also come from your personal pursuit for professional development. It is a safe bet to say that any skill you have mastered, anything you have learned to do better than your colleagues or the competition, is something others would be interested in hearing about.

When making presentations for the first time, you may start with familiar topics that make you feel an immense confidence and certainty. That's fine! Making presentations on familiar topics will improve your competency even further. How so? Building and preparing the presentation will undoubtedly give you new ideas, information, and approaches. The very process of presentation development will hone your critical thinking and, thereby, your understanding of the topic. Preparing business presentations just makes good sense when it comes to being on top of your professional game.

Making the presentation and verbalizing it to a group of people will clarify your expression. If you are like many speakers, you will be surprised and pleased to find yourself connecting the dots in ways you had never before considered. The audience questions that arise during or after a presentation will also give you new depths of understanding, new approaches, and new ways of expressing your expertise. The more you do, the more you grow.

Most professional speakers will tell you that no matter how many times they make a particular presentation and share their wealth of knowledge, that they always learn something new from the experience. They may add to their body of subject matter expertise, or they may learn something new about human nature and behavior, or they may glean an insight that illustrates a particular point better than before. Keep your eyes and ears open as you present. By deconstructing the event afterward, you will invariably learn something new.

Improving your business presentation skills will bring rewards throughout your career. It increases your perceived value in the eyes of colleagues and in the chain of management in your organization. Most bosses and business leaders take a hierarchical view of employee contributions. The "base" level of employee competence is the ability to do the job. Come to work. Do the job. Do it well, do it professionally. Go home. The next, or second level of achievement, is represented by the ability to teach, or show others the way. If you know your job, or your topic, well enough to teach it, you start to contribute above and beyond the call of duty. The third level is the ability to foster change—to make a progressive contribution to the company or to the profession itself. The ability to communicate your skills and effectively present your knowledge is obviously important to teaching and to leading change. What should be equally obvious is that as you move up the hierarchy to the top two tiers your value as an employee grows dramatically.

The Department of Labor, in its ongoing analysis of jobs in the American workplace, recognizes that in the modern world of work, speech is essential in seven out of every ten occupations. This analysis encompasses all jobs, including somewhat solitary occupations—like forest rangers. Forest rangers, you may say?! Well, have you been to a national park lately? Forest rangers lead tours, conduct hikes, run children's programs—and have to talk to all manner of audiences—foreign and domestic, young and old, friendly and hostile. Presentation skills required? You bet. It is fairly safe to say that communication skills are essential to every professional in every aspect of the modern business world. If communication is one of the critical standards of entry into the business world, it therefore stands to reason that enhancing those skills is equally critical for promotions and intelligent career management.

If you expect to succeed over the long haul of a fifty-year professional work life, you simply must develop your communication and presentation skills to be the best they can be.

The Arguments of Persuasion

Through making business presentations, your communication skills take on a finer focus and clearer intent. You'll not only want to share ideas and approaches, you'll want to persuade your audience to agree with you, to understand things in a new light, to see things in a specific way, and, usually, to take action as a result of being persuaded by your arguments. This is the case regardless of the type of presentation you are making: program or project proposal reviews, status updates, management summaries, launch presentations, business strategy reviews and summaries, sales presentations, skill development, interviews with the boss, client presentations, contact with journalists, radio hosts, or news anchors. Whatever the presentation situation may be, your goal is to persuade others to adopt your point of view.

In the new working world that the Information Age has ushered in, the most consistently successful professionals share the common key behavior of superior communication skills. They listen well, analyze carefully, and express themselves succinctly and persuasively. These professionals have a developed ability to crystallize ideas and share them with an audience who, in turn, is validated by the information. The audience hears, understands, agrees, and acts as a result. Professionals who achieve prominence in their careers do so as a result of conscious effort. The ability to consistently persuade others to a specific point of view is not a God-given gift; rather, it is a carefully developed professional competency.

There are tens of millions of people in the professional workforce, all of whom have the basic communication skills necessary to gain entry to the white-collar world. Yet very few of their number ever realize the enormous positive impact that consciously developed personal influence skills can have over a fifty-year work life.

A very small number realize such a skill is a career booster and, accordingly, strive to develop it over time and apply it one-on-one in their professional lives as they meet with clients, the boss, or their colleagues. Of course, there are those who decide to advance their presentation and communication skills—and thereby enhance their employability and their promotability. However, it never occurs to them to take their hard-won skills and apply them to larger audiences. An even smaller number, a miniscule number in the context of the professional workforce, realize that if they apply their business presentation skills to larger audiences, their sphere of personal influence will expand, as will their opportunity for professional growth. The very few that do get it become the people who are seen, listened to, and agreed with. Their message is acted upon. They become respected, sought out, remembered, and quoted. They become the leaders, coaches, and champions in the modern world of work.

These anointed ones of the professional world are the very same people who took the time to develop their persuasive influence skills by seeking opportunities to make business presentations within the context of their day-to-day professional work lives. They achieve their goals because they embody the following characteristics:

- They are committed to becoming consummate professionals in all aspects of their professional lives.
- They have something relevant to say.
- They have committed themselves to sharing their views and applying their skills to groups of people rather than merely one-on-one.
- They have learned the skills of public speaking, and they apply them whenever the opportunity arises.

Speaking effectively in public takes time to learn. It is generally regarded as one of the scarier propositions in the lives of most professionals. Yet it really isn't brain surgery. If you are working in the professional world, you already have the basic skills you need. You can build on these skills over time, but you will see results almost immediately as you learn the preparation, structure, and delivery techniques that underlie any successful business presentation.

2 Hot Air vs. Hot Stuff

Different strokes for different folks—and different business presentations for different audiences.

It can happen in any number of ways—an invitation, a mandate from the boss, or your own self-directed drive and initiative to get things done. You find out that you need to make a speech. You will be on stage, responsible and accountable for everything you say. You're in the hot seat and the audience is your judge, jury, and—just maybe—the benefactor. Whether it's a success or a failure depends entirely on you. Your project, your program, your budget, your whole *department* might depend on you. The meeting to which you've been invited to speak may depend on you . . . on you . . . on you.

Is that pressure? Well, yes, of course. Even the most gifted actors get butterflies before they hit the stage or when the red camera light goes on. The most gifted presenters get butterflies every time they sign up for a speech. It's natural, an inevitable part of human nature. As a *Knock 'em Dead* presenter, you will not only learn to deal with pressure but to make the most of your opportunity. If you take the right approach to preparing and delivering your speech, those butterflies will fly in formation. You'll channel all that uncertainty and nervous energy into achieving your objective. You may even have fun doing it!

Your approach, preparation, and thought process make all the difference. Approach your speech incorrectly, skimp on preparation, or fail to organize your thoughts, and you are likely to fail. Not only do the regular "jitters" come into play, but extra ones emerge as you start to sense imminent failure. Presentations either start out good and get better, or they start bad and get worse. The outcome is either "hot air" or "hot stuff," and you have total control over which way it goes. The rest of this book is aimed at turning your presentations into "hot stuff." Chapters 2 through 5 describe how to *build* the presentation; Chapters 6 through 8 discuss how to *deliver* it. In this chapter, we cover the foundations of your presentation, including situation and audience assessment, research and preparation, and how to develop your presentation idea.

You and the Audience

When making a presentation, you and the audience are both playing a role. You are the portrayer, actor, leader, teacher, informer, instigator, inspirer, and the persuader. The audience is the listener, follower, student, informed, and the convinced. The common bond between you and the audience is communication—verbal and nonverbal. If you fail to communicate with the audience, the audience won't be able to play its role. Everyone's time will be wasted.

The more effective you are in your role as presenter, and the more you fit the role the audience expects or wants, the more effective the communication will be. And the more natural and comfortable both you and the audience are in playing those roles, the better things will be for your presentation overall.

Ever notice that when you're being introduced to someone, you have a tendency to forget his or her name almost immediately? It's a consistent phenomenon explained by the fact that during the brief moment in which you are shaking that person's hand and hearing that name, your mind is going a mile a minute wondering if you look all right and how you'll respond. Guess what happens? That name is lost—forever, if you decline to embarrass yourself a little by asking again.

With audiences, it's sort of the same thing. Our ability to communicate with the audience is hampered by the little insecurities and brain lapses that occur during presentations. Likewise, the same happens to the audience. While focusing on some aspect of you, your slide, *or themselves,* something important goes right over their heads. Here's the point: when you're standing up there with the *right* presentation—well-researched, well-organized, and well-tuned to audience needs—those little stumbling blocks are less likely to get in the way.

Your success depends on your frame of mind, mental preparation, and the preparation of the material in the pitch. We're going to keep hammering on this point throughout the book: your success depends on *preparation.* Following are a few guidelines that will help make this happen successfully.

Above All: Be Yourself

When you are in front of an audience giving a project review, a launch, or sales presentation, that audience is asking two questions: Are you credible? Is your message credible? If people find you believable, it is much easier for them to buy your message. Here are three pieces of excellent cautionary advice:

- Be yourself.
- Never give a presentation without understanding your audience.
- Never give a presentation without preparation on the topic.

Audiences, and people in general, have an incredible ability to sense when something isn't right—when you are acting, rather than representing the truthful you. When you aren't being yourself, audiences get nervous and skeptical. You need to give a talk you believe in, one that sounds like you—that is consistent with your work, your personality, and your previous presentations.

The False Pretense of Perfection

An inexperienced speaker can fall prey to a temptation to mimic a news anchor or some other well-known figure in the business world by adopting their tone, voice inflection, or mannerisms. This will always end in failure. Tone of voice, inflection, and physical mannerisms are unique to the individual; a speaker's stage presence is an outgrowth of his or her own personality. You don't have to copy anyone else. Who you are is quite good enough if you know your subject, your audience, and if you prepare the subject matter with the audience's needs foremost in mind.

An audience is gathered to learn something. They want to make decisions on ideas, subjects, and approaches. The audience is there to improve their skills and their lives by learning something new. Those are the concerns foremost in their minds. If you are believable as a human being and as a professional in your field, it doesn't matter if you make a few mistakes or if your presentation wasn't the best ever delivered. No one will mind if your jokes weren't drop-dead hilarious, if you were a little nervous, or if you lost your train of thought. (That does happen, but later in this book we'll show tricks to recover without missing a beat.) These are all small issues if the audience gains something from your presence in front of them. The audience expects small imperfections. They are also generally on your side, as long as your message is clear and your intentions are good.

One of the hardest things to remember is that the audience doesn't know or care about what you *didn't* say. This has a lot of implications in both the construction and delivery of your presentation, but in this context we advise you to stick to what you know and what you're comfortable talking about. Don't tell jokes if you aren't good at telling jokes, and don't make analogies to Einstein or his theories of relativity if you don't understand them. If you aren't sure about it, don't talk about it.

Conversation—On Stage

The days of booming orators with formal language and declarative gestures have gone the way of silent movies; it's only some of our public officials who haven't gotten the message yet. Writing today is less formal and more personal because speech has become more casual. Business presentations have followed much the same path, as they combine both the spoken and written word. Modern business presentations are mixed-media events. To make them successful, they need a rock-solid foundation.

If you want to be successful in front of professional audiences, be professional, but also be personable and informal. Talk *with* your audience—not *at* them! Think of a presentation as a natural, normal conversation between two people. If you aren't concentrating on becoming someone else when making a presentation, you are much more likely to get your ideas across, sway people to your point of view, and stimulate the action you desire from the group. We'll talk more about developing a stage presence that complements your personality in Chapter 8.

Understanding the Audience

A marksman cannot hit his target unless he sees it clearly. The same applies to your goal with a business presentation: you won't reach your goal unless you understand the people you are trying to influence. Like a business that must understand its customer to sell a product, you as presenter must understand your audience to sell your message.

To maximize the impact of your presentation, you need to create a profile of your general audience. First figure out who you are building this presentation for to help ensure your presentation is targeted appropriately. We'll start that now. In Chapters 3 and 4, we'll build on the idea as we create content and the presentation around it. Later we address how to get to know the people in the audience who will be sitting in front of you on the day of the performance.

Understanding your target audience is the first concrete step you take in building a business presentation. A careful analysis of your proposed audience will affect everything you say and everything you do in your presentation; it will keep you from talking above people's heads, talking down to them, or giving them irrelevant, useless information. Commit any of these sins and you lose credibility, and with it your ability to move people to action.

Getting your message across comes down to answering one simple question: Why should they listen to you? Your audience members aren't there for your benefit. They have a single overwhelming need: to get something out of the experience that will help them—whether that means help them personally, or help them do their job. Understand your audience—get inside their collective head to find out what you can offer that could help them—and you generate and build presentation ideas that are likely to be welcomed.

Effective and Efficient

Building effective business presentations on any topic takes time. Some topics take more time than others do, but they all take time to do well. Good presentations are *effective* at communicating the message and achieving desired outcomes. Good presentations are also *efficient*—they achieve their objectives with the least amount of work on your part and on the part of the audience. When you understand your audience, you'll understand what makes a presentation effective and efficient for *them.* If you present to the same audience over and over again, you'll learn what works and will communicate more effectively. The same approach is likely to work with similar audiences. If you make a successful presentation to a group of stockbrokers in Dallas, more or less the same approach (perhaps using different jokes or football analogies) will work for a group of stockbrokers in San Francisco. However, your pitch to the stockbrokers may *not* work for a group of female executives. If you understand the communication and productivity needs of a particular audience, you can build presentations that remain effective over the years. Successful formats and structures can become valuable, reusable templates.

This practice applies to nearly all types of presentations. Practically speaking, when a new need arises for a particular type of presentation, you can dust off the template, use what you can, and develop the content further as the needs of the occasion dictate. In using the template from an earlier presentation, you will recall how the presentation worked—or didn't—and immediately come up with ideas to make the next one even more effective. Do it well the first time, and you will never have to start from the beginning again.

It all comes down to understanding the different audiences you will face over time. When you move your focus from audience member to your audience as a whole, your role is reversed. You need to understand their professional needs. As much as possible, you need to understand their collective frame of reference.

Audience Composition

Audiences come in all shapes and sizes. Audiences can be internal (employees of your company) or external (professional colleagues, customers, or students). Audiences can consist of peers, superiors, or subordinates—or, as is common, a mix of the three. Audiences can be large or small, even as small as a single individual. Audiences can be physically present or they can be connected only electronically with the presenter. There is usually a common bond or thread of interest among all audiences, but occasionally even this is not the case. Your job, before even starting to work on the presentation, is to assess audience composition and then to figure out how it influences your presentation. At the risk of overusing this analogy, the audience is like your customer base. You, as a presenter, are building a product that you must sell to them. To do this effectively, as in any marketing situation, you must understand the customer/audience base and what it is that they need. Fail here, and you won't get the sale; you may not even get their attention.

If your audience is focused by means of similar professional occupation, you can use this unifying bond to build the illustrative points of your presentation. If your audience is comprised of many different functional areas, awareness of that will help you be sensitive in the structure and delivery of the presentation, the illustrations you use to make your main points, and in your introduction and closing.

Finally, an assessment of audience demographics and tastes may be helpful, especially if it is an external audience. For example, if you're addressing a group, and you know that the chair of that group graduated from Yale and is president of the local historical society, chances are you're dealing with a highly educated, sophisticated audience. Look at educational levels and position on the corporate or socioeconomic ladder—and what someone in that position might *need.* Good marketers profile their customers. They develop stereotypical models of what their typical customer might need. Good presenters do the same, especially with unfamiliar audiences. (Yes, stereotyping is legal in marketing and presenting—just not in employment or career advancement!)

When presenting to an internal audience, deep audience-profiling may not be necessary when everyone is known and familiar. But if there are attendees from other parts of the organization, it's a good idea to research in advance what their department does and what their roles are in the department.

Audience Knowledge and Background

Audiences come to your presentation with all levels of expertise and experience in your topic. Find out what they've seen and what they know. No matter what you choose to talk about, you can rest assured that it has been addressed before. Find out what the audience is likely to have heard or heard *about.*

The first person to speak to about this is the meeting planner—if, that is, you are building a presentation as a result of an invitation. You can ask for past attendee lists, which will often give you the names and titles you need. If it's an internal audience, refresh yourself and learn the history of the topic you're presenting—what presentations were given last week or last month, what meetings have been held, and what decisions have been made. Seek out potential audience members. Become a bit of a sleuth. Investigate and discover the history of your topic or issue; understand how the past affects the present (and your presentation!).

You also need to get a handle on what your audience knows about your subject. Why would it interest them? How can you tie your message to the immediate needs of your audience? Will you be using industry, or professional slang? Will the audience understand it, or will you have to explain and maybe give attendees a handout with a glossary of terms? Do audience members already perceive themselves to be experts on the topic?

If there are likely to be experts in the audience, it is best if you can identify them ahead of time. If you know who the experts are beforehand, you can gather information from them and develop ways to use them when you speak. Allying yourself with acknowledged experts will not only give you greater credibility, it will help you co-opt those experts as your allies. Experts love to be heard. Acknowledging your experts can short-circuit a major potential problem, as the expert in the audience who is not your ally usually enjoys getting his jollies by proving you wrong!

If you know what your audience already knows, you avoid talking down to them or over their heads. That knowledge gives you a foundation for your presentation. It shows you how much background and introduction is needed to get everyone focused and on the same page—*your* page!

Audience Needs and Objectives

As we stated previously, good presenters are like good marketers—constantly aware of customer needs and how those needs should be met. As in the marketing world, it's hard to be certain what those needs are. However, it is easy to find out. Just ask! When it isn't *obvious* what an audience is looking for, it is best to simply step forward and ask them. For an internal audience, do a little informal survey, and ask a few key audience members beforehand. For an external presentation, ask the meeting planner or your contact in that organization for a few pointers. Not only will you make a more accurate presentation, but the audience members that you poll are likely to be glad—and impressed—that you took the time to do it! Here's how you proceed.

Tell them about your topic, then ask them:

1. How does this topic affect your professional life?
2. What would you most like to see addressed?
3. Have you seen presentations on this topic before?
4. What stands out positively or negatively from your recollections?
5. What are the biggest challenges you face in this area?
6. Do you have any personal insights on this topic?

All of these questions are self-evident in their intent. Question 6, however, has a collateral benefit. Above and beyond the knowledge you will gain, you can also use this person and their insight during your presentation to great effect (assuming of course that they have something of relevance to say):

1. *You can quote them,* which gives depth to your presentation.
2. *You can ask them to comment,* which gives variety to your presentation. It also gives you a minute to regroup and glance at your notes while they take the stage.
3. When you seek someone's advice, this person is flattered and *becomes your ally* through the entire presentation.

Just as in marketing, the members of the potential audience that you survey also become your personal focus group. Questioning them gives you the information and focal points you need to target your presentation. For both internal and external presentations, you can also ask your personal focus group about other speakers they may have seen on the topic and any notes and handouts they may have saved.

Additionally, you can speak with other *presenters* who have spoken to this or similar audiences. Ask them what worked, what didn't, and what they might do differently. If you are working far enough in advance, it is a good idea to attend meetings addressed to your audience. The topics may be different, but you'll have an opportunity to watch your audience in action, as it were, and to look at the presenters from a new and different perspective.

A word of caution: Don't take audience research *too* far. There are writers on public speaking who will have you gather far more information than you will ever need. They'll have you analyzing the audience for every detail of age, sex, education, socioeconomic background, religion, ethnicity, political affiliation, and even marital status and sexual persuasion. Now, while there are instances when each and every one of these details could be relevant to your speech, they are patently *not* relevant to most speeches. In fact, in a professional environment, you need to be sensitive to all, and inclusive to all, but blind to many of these issues. Treat people in a group just as you would on a one-on-one basis in the workplace. The main line—let's say, 80 percent—of your presentation should be what's best for most. You may create some special highlights—20 percent or less—to address the needs of specific audience members, like the vice president or chief financial officer in the back of the room.

The goal of your analysis is to gain a greater understanding of the needs of your audience; some understanding of the arguments they will be most responsive to; the illustrations they will resonate with; the people you should quote; and the statistics you should use. The more you know about your listeners, the better you can serve their needs with relevant information and advice. Address their needs, and you will hit your mark.

The Wide World of Business Presentations

Just as audiences come in all shapes and sizes, so do business presentations. Whether you're an invited guest or regular performer; whether you were volunteered or you chose to speak; whether it's an external or internal audience; whether it's a new proposal, a project review, or a financial review; each presentation requires somewhat different applications of your "speechcraft."

Odds are that you are reading this book for one of two reasons. Either you already know that making presentations is a good professional move to increase your credibility and visibility, or you got *assigned* to make a presentation. If the former is true, you are excited but nervous about whether you can pull it off. If it's the latter, you are probably in a panic.

Relax—you have more control than you might think.

The Happy Volunteer

If you volunteered to give the presentation, let us first of all stop to say bravo! By taking it on, you'll learn more about yourself as well as your topic, and others will learn more about you. You'll get a chance to determine if it's a pitch or topic that has "legs" for the future. And if you volunteered, you're on good footing from the onset. That meeting planner came to you for two reasons. First, he or she is desperate to fill an agenda, and finding people prepared to speak in public is easier said than done. Typically people are chosen because they are perceived to have expertise in a particular area. If the general topic area is something in which you have a modicum of expertise, but you don't like the way you have been asked to speak about it, you can probably refocus the request to everyone's benefit. The meeting planner wants the meeting to be a success, so the topic ideas are rarely more than broad areas for discussion.

There is a reason for every meeting. Let's take an internal example: the annual company conference. As a meeting planner, you are going to need to address certain topics to give the meeting wide appeal. You'll need special-interest sessions for management, technical, sales, administration, and finance teams. You'll need general sessions, and you'll need entertainment. Having defined the broad areas, the discussion then moves to, "Okay, now what the heck do we present to each of these groups to fill up the time and have some kind of beneficial impact?" This is how your topic area came up, and, subsequently, your name as a potential subject matter expert. As a presumed expert, the planner will be eager for any suggestions you may have that will make the meeting better. Further, you will be accommodated in any way possible to avoid having you back out—thus putting the meeting planner back to square one with a time-slot to fill and a vacant meeting agenda.

Sometimes the topic is predetermined; other times, it is up to you to choose one. When it is up to you, what you choose to talk about is very important. A good place to start is by looking at your strengths and weaknesses. What challenges do people in your profession, with similar responsibilities, face on an ongoing basis? These areas are replete with good speaking topics, both from a skill development viewpoint (how to do what you do more efficiently and effectively), and from the meetings that regularly occur in the normal course of your business life.

If you are searching for a topic, first develop a list of ideas. Then, choose the most energizing topic from your list, using the following criteria:

- What do you do well that can readily translate itself into a presentation?
- What skill sets could you improve, and in the process build a presentation from your learning experience?
- What do colleagues talk about as an area of need or ongoing concern?
- What presentations have you already seen that made you think, "I could do that"?

When You're the Chosen One

Depending on your position and situation, chances are greater that you were "volunteered" to give the presentation—by a manager, coworkers, or a set schedule for sharing monthly financials with the rest of the organization. These involuntary situations are different. The audience will be more critical, and there's a greater need for precision and sticking to the assigned task. We're entering the wide world of day-to-day business meetings.

Business meetings come in all flavors. By and large, they consist of regular planning and review meetings and the project or program meetings to discuss the merits and progress of specific initiatives. Of course, some meetings will include elements of both. It depends entirely on the nature of the organization and the preferences of the people in charge. These meetings spawn all sorts of presentations: strategy reviews, management summaries, launch presentations, project and performance status updates, program proposals, reviews: the list is almost endless. Here are a few of the more commonly "assigned" presentations:

- **Strategy reviews and summaries.** You as leader or manager must define your objectives and propose your strategy and tactics for the coming business period, including prior results, new programs, results expected, and resources required.
- **Launch presentations.** You, again as leader or manager, are launching a new product, program, or project. Your goals are to remind those involved of the benefits and upcoming requirements, inform those not previously involved of what will happen and why, and signal to the "troops" that you are indeed moving forward.
- **Performance updates.** How is the business or business unit faring? Above or below committed goals? What course corrections are necessary? Monthly financial or project reviews are examples of this type of presentation.
- **Proposals.** You and your team have a new product, project, or program you would like to launch. Your job is to give background and persuade those in the audience that your "thing" is a good idea. These presentations have to be particularly well crafted. In this case, the audience, even if on your side, will be playing devil's advocate and looking for the weaknesses in your argument. Obviously, topic selection is less important for these meetings. The topic is known and has likely been discussed before. Your role is usually to add some knowledge and frequently to develop alternatives and come to decisions about future actions. You generally aren't there to "fill a meeting planner's

agenda"—if anything, the agenda is usually tight and the planner (usually a manager) would just as soon get you *off* the agenda if he or she could! (And he or she will, next time, if you blow it!)

The good news? Audience interest is already there. What you are going to talk about is probably important to them, their jobs, and their careers. So you won't have to do as much to capture audience interest. However, while audience interest is important, audience learning and *action* are usually more important. Since the topic has already been defined, spend time deciding what to say about it and how to say it most effectively.

Sales Presentations

Sales presentations tend to be a hybrid of the voluntary and assigned presentation. They are voluntary in the sense that you, as presenter, probably initiate them. Some creativity will be required of you to find an area of mutual interest to open the discussion. Here, the audience *really is* the customer, and the audience assessment is even more similar to traditional marketing customer assessments. Establishing rapport is important. Many of the techniques employed in the voluntary presentation do just that. But the sales presentation is also like the assigned presentation—the *proposal*—in that the topic is defined, and both you and the customer are there for a specific purpose.

Getting Started

You have some idea of what you have to do. The question now is where do you start? The beginning point lies in different places for different people. We'll share a few ideas and approaches to getting the presentation ball rolling.

You don't build a presentation chronologically, by searching for a good opening line and then working through the process is a clear linear fashion. It would be nice if the process were so straightforward, but the creative process doesn't work effectively that way. Why doesn't it? Your opening statement sets the stage for the meat of your presentation. If you don't know what the body of your presentation will contain, you can't possibly come up with the right opener. You have to come up with the content before you can come up with the introduction.

Here is an analogy to help you get in the right frame of mind as you develop your subject. A sculptor starts with a block of marble and chips away until some great work of art is revealed. With intellectual matters, such as creating presentations that share information and ideas, you can't see the physical "block of marble" sitting in front of you. But you start in a similar way with a "rough" set of raw material with which to begin your crafting process. The raw material is information, and like the sculptor, your first step is to choose and examine the information. At first, you will create a pile of information on your topic, which you will subsequently sift and sort, arrange and rearrange, until you too have a work of great beauty and real value.

Good Stuff in Ten Steps

You may rightfully be saying to yourself, "This is well and good, but where do I get started?" If you're like most people, getting started is the hard part—once a project is underway, momentum builds and thoughts crystallize more rapidly as confidence takes over. Businesses use ten-step methodologies for developing business plans and strategies. Figure 2-1 outlines a ten-step approach to building your presentation.

Step One: Take Audience Inventory

We've already discussed this step, and we'll touch upon it again and again as we build content, openers, closers, visual aids, and delivery style. Step back and think about your audience—who are they, and what do they need? List all participants if possible, key participants if you know only a portion of the

Ten Steps to Building an Effective Presentation	
Step 1	Take audience inventory
Step 2	Assess the situation
Step 3	Get organized
Step 4	Get your thoughts on the table
Step 5	Do the research
Step 6	Enrich the research
Step 7	Build the body
Step 8	Build the presentation
Step 9	Add visual aids
Step 10	Prepare, practice, and present

Figure 2-1. Ten steps to building an effective presentation

audience in advance. Identify their departments and organizations. Understand why they are there, and think about—and write down—what they might want to get out of your presentation. If it's a voluntary presentation where you select the topic—say you've been asked to say something at the community business forum or for a voluntary presentation—think through what they might *like* to hear. Obviously, if this is a simple one-on-one presentation, this is a simpler step.

Step Two: Assess the Situation

What is the situation and context of your presentation? Are you presenting something new and curious to the audience? Or are you trying to rescue a once-thought-important program to keep it from going belly-up forever? Is the audience likely to gasp in awe at your exciting new ideas? Or are they about to beat the hell out of you for being late yet again? Are you presenting a rosy financial picture to reward your colleagues, or are you telling of a disaster that requires immediate action? Are you reviewing, informing, or persuading? Your task here is to decide what you need to accomplish and the *desired outcome* of your presentation. (We talk more about "desired outcome" in Chapter 3.) Again, think it through, and write it down.

Step Three: Get Organized

This apparently basic step is left out by so many! You start work on your presentation, and by the time you're ready to build the slides, you find yourself covering the same point twice. And that beautiful "gem" you discovered early on is gone altogether—forcing you to cozy up to the finance manager *again* to rediscover it! The solution: get organized. It's hard to keep track of facts. When you can't do it effectively, key facts disappear, and it's harder to get your brain around the logic and sequence of the ones that are left—which compromises your presentation and delivery.

One common solution: get a stack of index cards and a folder or box to put them in. These are the tools of choice for writers in all fields, from Hollywood screenwriters to speechwriters, novelists, nonfiction writers, and poets. The index cards are a proven medium for intellectual creativity for a number of reasons. Anyone can a jot a few words or a sentence or two down on a small card. The index card fills up quickly, and even a couple of words don't look like a sad attempt at creativity; they have the appearance of creative genesis succinctly captured. (Well, that's what we working writers tell ourselves.) They aren't intimidating the way a large blank sheet of paper can be, where a single line looks lost and makes you feel daunted by the task: "How can I write a whole presentation when I can't even fill two lines on a notepad?" Also, it's hard to resequence material written down on a notepad.

Remember that cards aren't just for original thoughts—they are also handy ways of organizing *references* to other material, such as articles, Web sites, and similar materials. Write down the source and a brief description of the content.

Once you have collected all your ideas and are ready to start arranging and sequencing them, this is where index cards really come into their own. You simply clear the desk (or kitchen table) and lay them out in what you think is their logical sequence—we'll be addressing organizing your material in more detail a little later—then you can easily rearrange that sequence to your heart's content. They are as easy to manipulate as a pack of playing cards, with each card containing its own succinct thought. For capturing and organizing your thoughts, index cards rule!

Step Four: Get Your Thoughts on the Table

Clear your head—chances are, you already have a lot of good ideas and pent-up thoughts you can use for the presentation. You're most likely already familiar with the topic. (You work with it daily; whoever asked you to give a speech thinks you are, anyway!) So before those thoughts sprout wings and fly away when you need them the most, take inventory of what you already know and what's already in your head.

Get it out and start jotting those thoughts down. It's a one-person brainstorm. Don't edit your thoughts at this point; editing will only stunt your creativity. At this stage any idea is a good idea. Use index cards or whatever memory and organizing tool you choose to adopt. What do you know about the topic that really works? What bad advice have you had? What jokes, stories, and quotes come to mind that illustrate this topic, either in a positive or negative fashion?

Step Five: Do the Research

Identify sources and resources. Ask your colleagues and your boss what they know about the topic. Ask them to recommend books, articles, or Web sites. Ask them for any notes they might have taken on the subject at a prior meeting. Ask them the most important lessons they have learned in this area and how they learned those lessons. Talk to professionals who are known to be experts in the area. Ask them about how they got there and what were the most valuable lessons they learned along the way.

Think through the kinds of resources you'll need, and think through where you might find them, both internally and externally. In the external world, the

Internet has become the fastest and most direct way to access content of all types. Good libraries and bookstores, as well as newspapers and periodicals, should not be ignored. On the internal side, it depends on what you need. Make contact with your marketing, market research, and finance departments. Look at internal Web sites set up by other departments in your organization. Ask around.

The Internet is a fabulous repository and reference to the world's knowledge. There are, most probably, sites built around the exact topic you want to present. Portals and search engines provide the key to open the door to this information. We recommend a quick search on Yahoo! (*www.yahoo.com*) before starting any research, using the topic as a search key. Of course, if your presentation consists entirely of internal subject matter (e.g. financial results) such a search probably doesn't make sense. Other search engines provide still deeper searches on topics, including "Google" (*www.google.com*) and "Dogpile" (*www.dogpile.com*). And of course, if you already know of an industry trade organization or other resource organization with a Web site, you should take the time to check it out. There may be late-breaking news on your topic, and even if you include nothing from the site, you'll be prepared to answer questions from the audience about something *they* may have seen on the site. (Yes, there is such a thing as *defensive* preparation—preparing for what may happen during a presentation, even if you don't *intend* it to happen!)

Step Six: Enrich the Research

As you do your research, you want to add the subtleties and intangibles that add color and differing points of view to your presentation. Collect everything you can from your colleagues, previous presentations, audience members, and meeting planners or management. Remember—it's brainstorming. You can use it to add depth to your presentation and demonstrate that you really have a wide frame of reference in this area. In your presentation you can talk about what some people say or advise and why it is incorrect or inadequate. Then, follow up with a better approach: "Ladies and gentlemen, there is some conflict among authorities when it comes to [blah]. Some advise [blah, blah], others advise [blah, blah, blah]. (Cite your sources if it isn't going to cause offense to attendees, otherwise leave them anonymous.) I've noted these areas of conflict and discussed it with so and so (now you name an authority known to your audience), and we are in complete agreement that [blah, blah, blah, blah]." Remember that it's important to be able to answer the questions and consider the audience point of view. Always think offense *and* defense (but don't use *too* many sports analogies!).

The Use of Opposing Views

As you generate ideas with these steps, sometimes you will jot down a thought and a little voice in your head will say "Yeah, but what about," or "Says who? I've always found . . ." Don't let these thoughts stop the creative process. Instead, harness them to your purpose. Opposing views and counterarguments will do all of the following for you:

- **Help you refine what you have to say**. If the opposing views ultimately strengthen a point in your argument, use the argument to enrich your presentation.
- **Give you new input** that might take your presentation in a new and more powerful direction. It is often through addressing opposing views that we are led to real breakthroughs in business practice.

Your willingness to address opposing views demonstrates your objectivity, speaks to your wide frame of reference on the topic, and increases your credibility.

Think about citations. As you proceed with your information-gathering, always identify your sources so that you can cite them in your speech. Citations from your research add color and help prove and clarify your points. They give depth, add credibility, and make your presentation memorable. And you may have to return to them. Citations and references help support a point of view or make it clear, and they can make it more memorable.

External references and citations you will use can come in a number of flavors, all of which add credibility to your presentation. But also be aware that it isn't necessarily the case that "the more citations the better." Citations can include quotations, statistics, definitions, stories and anecdotes, professional opinions, and visuals (more on these "devices" in Chapter 3). Remember that citations must be relevant and useful, not there just for the sake of citing someone or dropping names. The audience came to hear your point of view, not someone else's.

One more idea is to identify the mistakes. What mistakes have you made, and what mistakes have others made? Mistakes are learning opportunities. Screwups are always good fodder for presentations, as they give everyone an opportunity for a good laugh. They are also useful in identifying an area where people make mistakes, observing the walking wounded around you, and analyzing what it is they are doing wrong. When you identify problem areas, you have a focus on helpful information that the audience will readily accept. Some of the best material might be right in your own personal "dust bin"—your own mistakes!

Step Seven: Build the Body

No, don't worry—you're not going to set all those index cards down and head off to the gym! In this step, you develop a "content" game plan in which you sort and organize the facts you just collected to support the message you want to deliver. This step is covered in more detail in Chapter 3.

Step Eight: Build the Presentation

The body isn't "it"; there's more work to do. Once the body—the message and supporting information—is complete, proceed to add an opener and closer to the body, as well as effective transitions throughout the presentation. This is the main subject of Chapter 4.

Step Nine: Add Visual Aids

Once the content and flow of the presentation are established, then (and only then!) is it time to think about how you will support the presentation and delivery with the right visuals. Visuals can make—or break—a presentation. Good visuals add memorable images and illustrations to support your points, and they help both you and your audience stay organized and on track. Bad visuals are distracting and waste time during the pitch. They also draw on valuable time and resources that could be better invested in better development of the presentation itself. We "look at" visuals in Chapter 5.

Step Ten: Prepare, Practice, and Present

If you do a good job organizing and building the presentation, the rest becomes much easier—but you're far from done. It's time to switch focus from the presentation package itself to the delivery. Investigate the venue, that is, the physical meeting room. Get to know the equipment, the acoustics, and even the position of the audience. If there is special audio or visual equipment, get to know that. Many a presentation has been tripped up by inept handling of a projection system or a teleconferencing phone. Figure out what the distractions might be, and develop a game plan to deal with them. Then develop a practice routine and practice your pitch. You'll be surprised at what adjustments you'll make even after hearing just yourself one time! Practice,

Do's	Don'ts
• Always be yourself. • Understand audience mix, background, needs and objectives, and what will "bond" you to them. • Treat your audience as a customer. • Target to 80 percent of the audience; have material available to meet needs of the other 20 percent. • Follow a process and stay organized.	• Don't "BS" the audience. • Don't try to be perfect. • Don't overanalyze the audience. • Don't build the opener first—build content first. • Don't overuse citations or external references. The audience came to hear you.

Figure 2-2. Do's and don'ts of effective presentations

adjust, practice. Try a few verbal devices, such as anecdotes and bits of humor. Lock down the delivery and check to see if they work. Chapters 6 through 8 explore delivery in greater depth.

In Short . . .

Effective business presentations start with a tight grasp of the situation, the audience, your role, and what's expected from you. From there, successful presenters use an organized, structured approach to developing content and delivery.

3 Finding Your Magic Bullets

Starting point: Find your message and the facts to support it.

"Just because you can speak doesn't make you intelligent."
—Qui-Gon Jinn to Jar Jar Binks, *Star Wars Episode I: The Phantom Menace*

Let's examine a couple of possible presentation scenarios.

Scenario One: The Emperor Wears No Clothes

There you are, in front of a large, diverse audience, going through Slide 23 of your presentation. Killer slide, you thought. One audience member rests head in hand, pushing his cheek up to eye level. Others start talking to each other, fiddling with laptops or PDAs, looking at watches, rolling up sleeves, reading e-mail, or whatever. Your chief audience "adversary" asks a question totally irrelevant to anything except possibly a detail you mentioned way back in Slide 5, then returns to his pile of printed e-mails. The next presenter shuffles through her slides and handouts. The parade of relevant questions and affirmative nods is long gone. Your boss chimes in ever more frequently, making points, summarizing *your* points, doing anything conceivable to revive interest in an obvious attempt to salvage. You begin to feel like the contestant on ABC's *Who Wants to be a Millionaire,* who when asked what it was like to be up there, answered "It's sort of like sitting on the toilet, with no walls and everyone watching." Discomfort, exposure, embarrassment—and no remedies available. What went wrong?

Scenario Two: Trash Talk

This time you're in the audience. In fact, you've been sitting there awhile. Slide after slide comes up—really neat stuff, cool pictures and colors. All offering lots of facts, great stories. Every bit of it sounds like stuff you needed to know. But it goes on and on: one more spreadsheet, one more flowchart, and a few more stories. On . . . and on . . . and on. Your mind begins to wander, first to this afternoon's day care pickup assignment, then to the party you're hosting this weekend, then to that beach in Hawaii. What did that ad say about reduced airfares? Aren't the airlines having a price war? Better check it out. Oops, back to reality. The presentation continues. Here's a two-page timeline, along with more "tech talk." Impressive research, great detail; it must have taken hours to put this thing together. Then suddenly you wonder—what was it exactly you were supposed to get out of it? Better get an extra copy of the handouts, just in case someone in your department asks you to summarize what you saw. Because you can't, not on your own. Not without thinking hard, and even then maybe not at all. What seemed like a great pitch to start with really didn't get the point across at all. You feel the urge to ask the presenter to start all over again, from the top. What went wrong?

What *did* go wrong? Was it bad slides? Poor delivery? Um's and ah's? Too little time? A stiff, humorless presenter? Boring subject matter? Projection problems? The reality is that "None of the above" is probably the right answer. What is the magic formula for a successful presentation? One that makes the point, with such clarity that it knocks them dead?

The reality is that most presentations fail. They fail not because of the delivery or skills of the presenter but because of poor content and organization. There simply was nothing there, or *not enough* there, or if it was *there* it was so hidden by superfluous material that the audience simply couldn't grasp and internalize it. Any communication becomes uncomfortable when it stops working—when the two communicating parties fail to grasp, then wonder why they can't grasp, then finally give up.

The concept of preparation—the most important investment you can make in a business presentation—appears regularly throughout this book. But perhaps nowhere is it more important than in the development of the *content.* Content includes the base message that you're trying to get across—what you want your audience to *do,* to *think,* or to *know.* But it also includes the supporting material that backs and *enriches* the message. Getting to the right message—and crafting the right supporting material—is what this chapter is all about. In Chapters 4 and 5, we move further into how to *organize* and *present* the content most effectively.

Content and Context

It's a mistake to dive headfirst into content. Like any successful business that recognizes customer needs before developing products to meet them, a good presenter will step back and take a close look at the situation—at the context—of the presentation. Who's the audience? What do they need from me? What is the situation in which I deliver it to them? What's the win-win situation—where I get the point across and achieve my objective, with the greatest degree of ease and confidence on the part of the audience?

Yes, that's right—whatever is easy and comfortable for the audience will, in turn, become easy and confident for you. But don't always assume you know what makes it easy and comfortable. Most especially, don't assume that whatever you usually do is right. Every *situation* is different, every *audience* is different (yes, even the *same person* can be different depending on the topic, the day, and the alignment of the planets). Thus, every presentation is different. Your job—and a big part of this preparation business—is to *understand* the situation first, then create and organize the content, then finally design the delivery in the manner that works best.

A Good Game Plan

We believe that a successful business presentation starts with a well thought-out presentation *game plan.* The game plan is really a *strategy* that shapes the content, organization, and delivery of that content before the first slide or note card is prepared. Without a good game plan, you run a big risk of getting lost, whether in preparing the presentation and/or during delivery of the presentation itself. The essence of the pitch won't be clear to the audience, or it may miss the mark altogether. The objective or desired outcome won't happen. You'll get frustrated, dig yourself in deeper trying to recover, and lose confidence in yourself as a presenter. This will cause inevitable problems down the road.

The game plan provides a framework, like a checklist, of tasks and considerations vital to achieving your presentation objective. The game plan includes a clear understanding of the intent or desired outcome of the presentation, a contextual analysis of audience and situation, development of a clear message, and, finally, the creation of content to support the message—your "magic bullets." Too often, presenters jump to content creation, designing slides before they even know what they want to do or have considered whom they're doing it for. The result is often neat slides or wonderful supporting data—but an objective that goes unachieved. Don't fall into this trap.

While it's true that a good game plan goes beyond content—thinking through concepts like delivery style and "on stage" presence—in this chapter we'll take aim at identifying the intent of your presentation, understanding the context, formulating the core message, and developing supporting points. Once these three objectives are accomplished, the "magic bullets" should drop into your presentation like ripe apples. Chapter 4 moves forward to the topic of effectively organizing and developing the presentation itself for delivery once the content and core message are clear. As a clarifying analogy (more about those later), think of this chapter as dealing with creating the product and the next two chapters as creating the packaging and delivery for that product. No marketer—or presenter—can survive for long without a good product.

In this chapter we're concerned with the following issues:

- The intent—desired outcome.
- The context—audience and situation.
- The message—what you want to say, a single theme in a single sentence.
- The position—the key points supporting the message—the "magic bullets."

What Are Your Intentions?

A seemingly obvious—though often forgotten—step in building your presentation strategy, or game plan, is to figure out the *desired outcome* of your presentation and then to build a presentation approach best suited to achieving this outcome. It sounds simple, but many great presenters either forget this step or make the naive assumption, "Oh, I know what I want to do." They then get lost in the weeds over this seemingly simple thought step.

What's the Desired Outcome?

Before jumping into the presentation, it is important to step back and lock in on *just what you're trying to accomplish.* Think through the *desired outcome.* Ask yourself out loud: "What do I want to have happen"? How should the world—my world—be different after this presentation is over? Do I want to effect change? Agreement? Make money? Create support? Close a sale? Sell a product? Sell an idea? Sell myself? Build enthusiasm? Maintain enthusiasm? Share bad news? Share good news? The list of possibilities is endless and depends entirely on your job, the business situation, and the audience you're working with. Your intent will likely be different with colleagues than it will be with executive-level management. There are no magic formulas—other than to establish, in the best possible scenario, what will happen—what will be the outcome—if your presentation *succeeds.*

And what happens when you fail to think through the desired outcome? It makes it harder to build and structure the presentation, and it makes it harder to *deliver* it. You'll flail and wander all over the place, failing to make the point, and either lose the audience or encounter their wrath when they realize your presentation *had* no point. Our advice: avoid that!

Building a "Desired Outcome" Statement

At its very essence, a "desired outcome" should include one or more audience actions. As a result of your presentation, they should be inclined, or at least more inclined, to do something, think something, or know something. (See Figure 3-1.) If your presentation doesn't get "lift" in one of these three areas, it most likely wasn't successful. Keep in mind that the audience probably *wanted* or *expected* "lift," otherwise they wouldn't have invested the time and energy to listen to your show. Remember—an expectation unmet is one of the hardest things to overcome in the business environment.

At the end of the presentation I would like the audience to:
• **Do ______________________________ (act, change)** • **Think ____________________________ (agree, support)** • **Know _____________________________ (understand)**

Figure 3-1. Desired outcome statement structure

Another thing to remember—enough is enough, but too much is too much. Too many desired outcomes are too hard to achieve and are more likely to cause confusion. If it takes more than a sentence or two to articulate a desired outcome, you're probably reaching for too much.

Examples of Desired Outcome Statements
• "I want management to fund my market research project" (DO) • "I want my department to understand our precarious financial position, and take actions to reduce costs" (KNOW, DO) • "I want my colleagues to agree and support the new call management strategy to avoid possible funding conflicts later" (THINK) • "I want this company to hire me" (DO)

Figure 3-2. Desired outcome statements

Indeed, the spectrum of desired outcomes is quite broad when you think about it. Business situations require a broad range of actions on a broad variety of topics. The following table may help you put together more precise desired outcome statements. Note the use of *action* verbs.

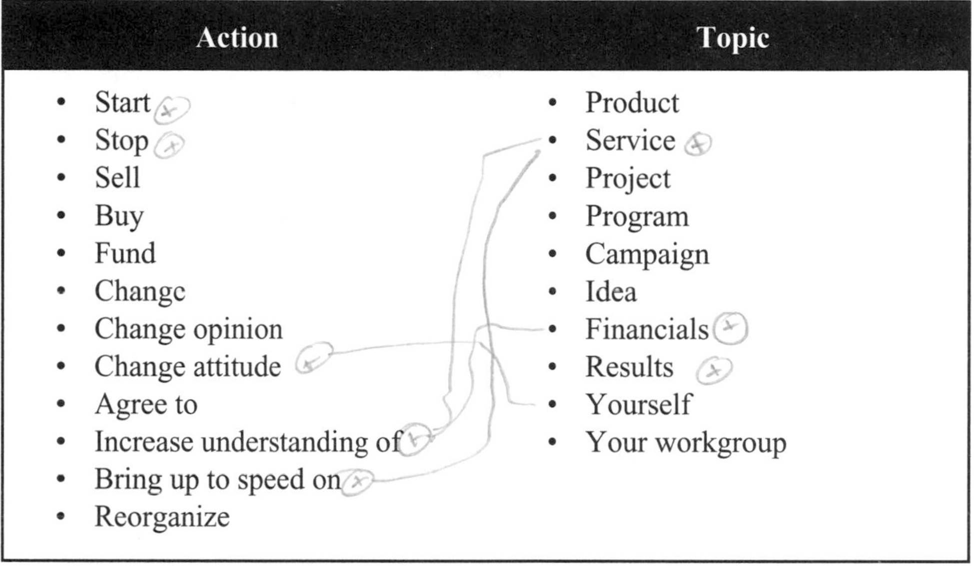

Action	Topic
• Start	• Product
• Stop	• Service
• Sell	• Project
• Buy	• Program
• Fund	• Campaign
• Changc	• Idea
• Change opinion	• Financials
• Change attitude	• Results
• Agree to	• Yourself
• Increase understanding of	• Your workgroup
• Bring up to speed on	
• Reorganize	

Figure 3-3. Additional words for desired outcome statements

Obviously, not every action works for every subject—"Stop your Workgroup" is something we hope you wouldn't have to give a talk on. With that understood, you can most express the desired outcome using words like the ones listed above.

Consider the Context

Misreading or failing to read the situation is another major "flailing and failing" point encountered by every business presenter. Failing to properly assess the context causes you to aim high, low, or wide almost every time. Too much detail for time-pressed decision-makers; too little detail for technical colleagues or customers; too strong a "push" for the skeptics—these tactical errors will derail your intentions every time. Understanding the situation—and the audience is a *big part* of the situation—often determines the course between success and failure. Different things are done for audiences that are internal or external, knowledgeable or unknowledgeable. Situation assessments include not only the audience but also the venue (location), time, formality, and familiarity.

Audience

One of the most important steps in establishing the desired outcome, and everything that follows, is to assess the audience—and what the audience is looking for. Audiences come in all shapes, sizes, and levels. We covered audience analysis in Chapter 2; suffice it to say that whom you're presenting to, and what it is they are looking for, will greatly influence the content of your presentation.

Audiences have different levels of knowledge, interest, listening skills, and tolerance for detail. Furthermore, audiences are usually mixed—that is, you must decide whether to go for the "lowest common denominator"—the most that the most will comprehend—or for select members who might hold the keys to what you want to accomplish. You as presenter must assess the nature and the mix of the audience. You must decide how to direct the presentation to those members who will most help you achieve your desired outcome.

Audiences come in all different sizes. Certainly the size of the audience affects your delivery, use of audio-visual tools, and so forth. Additionally, audience size can affect content. Typically, large audiences can absorb less detail than small audiences can. With a larger audience, it's easier to lose someone on a point less familiar. In a large-audience setting, it's also more difficult to ask clarifying questions. Details are harder to see to begin with in your presentation. We'll talk about "keeping it simple" later on, but this rule applies especially to large or very diverse audiences.

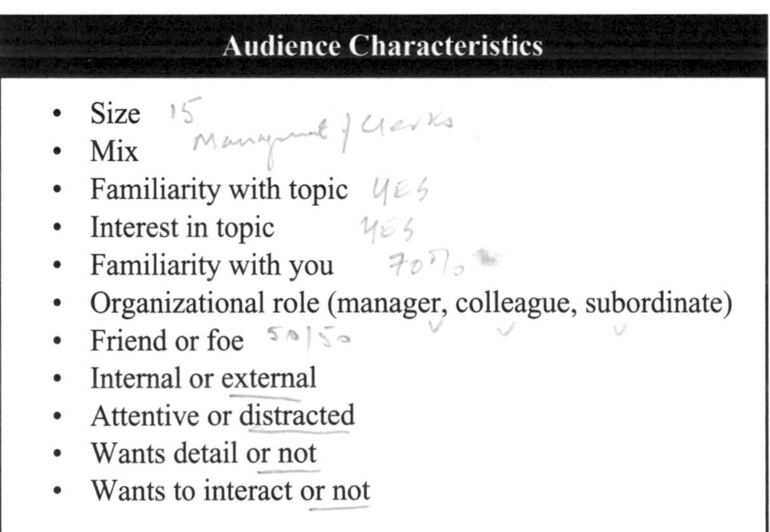

Audience Characteristics

- Size
- Mix
- Familiarity with topic
- Interest in topic
- Familiarity with you
- Organizational role (manager, colleague, subordinate)
- Friend or foe
- Internal or external
- Attentive or distracted
- Wants detail or not
- Wants to interact or not

Figure 3-4. Audience parameters affecting presentation content

Audiences come with different levels of "need to know." An audience of technical colleagues will want more explanation and detail, while an audience of high-level managers want only the key decision points without the background. ...hat happens when you "miss" in *this* critical area.

...ations, you will know your audience ... in that audience. With external ...esentations, you may *not* know the ... at just what they are looking for. That ... a desired outcome—get the sale or

... audience needs into your presentation ...essage and supporting points—as well ...should be geared to the audience and

...larger discussion, which is included in ...ent should consider location, or venue. ...the audience, for the audience is part of ...one with your boss in the quiet confines ...ntation in a hotel ballroom to a large, ...etail you bring and the amount of ... differ.

...nore than time. If you have ten minutes, ... when you have two hours or a whole day. ...inute version and the two-hour version. ... version and add on, while others start with the two-hour version and chop. Either way, going through this exercise will improve your own clarity and understanding of your pitch—and will prepare you for both situations. Many business presentations are given more than once, with different amounts of time allotted.

The rule of thumb: Don't give the two-hour version when assigned the ten-minute job! You'll go over time (count on it) and/or leave key components out. And never underestimate the downside risk of rambling on too long with a presentation—it gets harder to stop, the audience gets impatient, and other presenters—who may influence your career or desired outcome—are disagreeably forced to modify their pitches. That's not a win-win situation.

Time management is an issue for both content and delivery. Many presenters feel that time management is a matter of delivery. Wrong. Time management it starts at the very beginning, with the construction of content. The amount and depth of content presented depend greatly on the time allotted. Modifying delivery to compensate for poorly constructed content in order to meet time goals or constraints usually doesn't work. Points are missed. Some points take too long and interrupt the flow. Your talk doesn't match your slides, and you look unprepared. The audience may even think you're leaving stuff out on purpose—for some other reason besides time. Trust us on this one: it pays to make sure your content is created appropriately for the time allotted.

Formality

Your degree of formality in relating to the audience will influence both your content and delivery. Some audiences and situations call for a rigorous, highly formatted presentation of the facts, background, supporting evidence, assumptions, return-on-investment, and similar issues. Presenting in a court of law is an extreme example. Many managers or business environments have a set structure (such as a department project presentation format) for delivering presentations—you must adopt and use them. Some people just can't handle information presented any other way from what they're used to—still others find this boring and want to see creativity.

Other presenting situations call for less rigorous treatment—where the topic and players are familiar, where decisions to be made are less critical, or where earlier presentations have already laid the groundwork. The personality and attitude of the audience also plays a part. Some people simply prefer formal, rigorously organized, substantiated information, while others are better at reading between the lines and developing their own conclusions. If you know the audience participants in advance, you can use some judgment. If you don't know, find out or be prepared with different kinds of content available just in case. Know why lawyers carry large briefcases? So they have everything available, just in case.

Decision-Making Imperative

Does the audience—or the key players in the audience—need to come away from your presentation with a decision? Or is your presentation merely laying groundwork for another presentation or other supporting work? If a decision needs to be made, be sure to give the audience enough information to do make it. This includes telling the audience what you *don't* know and what is assumed but not known for sure. And in most cases, the audience is looking for your recommendation—you're the expert, after all—so don't leave this out! It is a borderline disaster when a decision is called for, but can't be made based on what you present. A careful assessment of the audience—including asking them beforehand—will provide you with valuable clues into the recommending and decision-making imperative.

You, Known or Unknown

And last but not least, there's *you.* Are you a "known quantity" to the audience? Audiences will treat you differently depending on whether you're known or unknown. "Known" audiences can be more forgiving and more likely to give you the benefit of the doubt—but they can also be more difficult or discerning (as in that old saying, "familiarity breeds contempt"). We've seen it both ways. The best thing to do is create the best, most concise content and content flow, and watch how the winds blow as you speak. A well-constructed message and position will almost always overcome the burden of unfamiliarity where it exists.

A Question of Style

Business presentations come in as many sizes, shapes, and colors as the clothing found on today's teenagers. You feel like you've experienced them all—the external sales pitch, the internal business proposal, the project review, the job interview, the executive summary, the media spot. Yet we find this broad assortment to boil down into the following three essential kinds of messages delivered in the business world:

- Persuasive/informative message (something you *want* to happen)
- Review/status message (something that *already* happened)
- A combination of the two

A persuasive/informative message concerns something that you want to happen, such as a project proposal, advertising campaign, equipment purchase, budget request, or a new job or responsibility. The message objective is to give the audience—and especially the decision-makers—enough information to take an action, which you hope to be the action you propose.

The status/review presentation is designed to give a progress report on something that you're already doing or *has already happened.* The goal is usually to maintain *continued* support of constituents and to refresh or remind key players of what is new and what might affect *their* jobs.

Many business presentations are a combination of the two—you present the current status of a project or a business situation, then work from that situation to propose business alternatives to solve problems or enhance the business.

Part of the preparation process is to figure out which approach, or style, you want to choose. It depends on the situation, the history, your role, and the audience. A monthly status report or financial review has a different objective and requires a different approach from a persuasive/informative presentation to "sell" a new idea. A presentation that is strictly informative, educational, or awareness-building falls somewhere in between, but it is actually more similar to the persuasive presentation in its logical flow. The chief differences between the informative and persuasive presentation are usually *length* (informative can be longer) and *intent.* The persuasive pitch has a stronger *call to action,* especially in the closing.

So what is the game plan so far? What preparation steps have we taken? We have a desired outcome, suitable to the audience and context. We've decided on the approach—persuasive/informative, a review presentation, or a combination of the two. The result should be a clear, declarable intent, something like: "This presentation will convince our management team to okay and fund an investigation of a new line of business." Or in a mixed-intent presentation addressing mixed audience needs, the intent might be: "This presentation will give cooperating departments a better understanding of our business and strategy, and convince the management team to okay and fund the investigation of a new line of business."

Later in this chapter, we'll provide additional guidance on how to craft and structure facts and positions for these different situations. We're not quite to that stage yet: there is one more step. We know our own intentions, we've sized up the audience, and we've decided what kind of presentation we should give. Now we need to switch focus from our needs to audience needs to carefully craft the *message we want to deliver to the audience.* We need a theme, in other words, a clear, concise, understandable audience takeaway that boils down to a point or set of points we're trying to get across. That message provides central framework for building the core points—the magic bullets—and the presentation itself. As we'll see, the core message should be *stated in a single sentence.*

Get the Message, Loud and Clear

Regardless of the type of business presentation, and regardless of what you're trying to achieve, there's no getting around it—the *message is key.* Like presentations lacking a clear desired outcome, those devoid of a clear message are doomed to fail before they start. No degree of fancy slides or brilliant, humorous delivery can rescue a failed or unclear message. True, you might entertain your audience, but you won't achieve the intent of the communication, and whatever it is you're really trying to say is likely lost. From a one-minute interview to an eight-hour seminar to a large audience—if you don't know what you want to say, then it's harder to find the right facts and content to support it. And your delivery will often fail because you stumble over your own lack of clarity with the subject matter.

Absence of a clear message is a glaring flaw. It shines straight through to the audience. The audience is confused because *you're* confused. The result—once again—is stone silence, off-track comments, and questions that throw you further off course. Worse yet, you'll find yourself having to give the same presentation all over again to get the message across—if you get the chance. That's not a win-win situation.

Many presenters fall into the following trap. You get a presenting assignment (presenting opportunity!), and the first things you think are: "How many slides? What opener and closer do I use? What quotes and stories? How can I make this entertaining or interesting?" Of course, those elements all figure into a successful presentation in their own way. But you're putting the proverbial cart way before the horse. If you haven't settled on a message and set of supporting content, all of the "dog and pony" acts in the world won't save you. You won't be able to create the "envelope" to deliver the message, and the point—and the opportunity to get it across—will be lost.

State Your Theme in a Single Sentence

Once you decide what kind of message you're "on the hook" for, it pays right away to start shooting for clarity. Otherwise, you'll "miss the fairway" and play from the weeds throughout the rest of the development and delivery of the show. You'll waste time researching irrelevant facts, creating irrelevant materials, tweaking, fixing, deleting, rebuilding, and otherwise overworking the whole production. And you'll be less confident and crisp in the delivery, which, at the risk of repeating, is usually apparent to your audience.

How to prevent this inefficient, nerve-wracking scenario? Follow the first rule of thumb of business presentations: *State your theme in a single sentence.* No matter what the topic, no matter what your "twist," boil it down to one sentence. With the one-sentence platform, you can then build the discussion and add the magic bullets, the most effective and *right* magic bullets.

Oh, how we've all been there! We know what it's like to be a captive audience to fully-loaded, fifty-slide presentations, replete with flowcharts and spreadsheets and numbers galore. We've heard the lengthy dissertations on "feature sets" and "user benefits" of some nameless piece of software. We know the shaggy-dog stories from beloved family members about the high school exploits of some distant cousin. What's the point? What do I need to know? Must be in there somewhere. Where? How can I get a handle on what I really need to know?

Put yourself in the place of the audience. What do they really need to know? *What is it that you want to tell them?* Figure *that* out, and you have the beginnings of a single-sentence theme, the vital *essence* of your message from which the rest of your presentation is built.

A single-sentence theme tells what you're trying to show, what you're trying to do, or what you've already done. Detach yourself from the detail, back away from your own in-depth knowledge of the subject, put yourself in the audience's shoes, and belt it out. Heard of an "out of body" experience"? Sometimes you need an "out of mind" experience to clear away the clutter and capture the essence.

You can change "Last quarter we improved profits by reducing cost of goods sold through implementing a new inventory control system, providing better training and expense management…" to "Through greater efficiency and cost control we improved profitability." That becomes your single sentence theme. The rest is detail. Good detail, to be sure, for it helps explain "why" it happened and what good decisions and efforts were taken. People will want to hear about the major and important reasons.

These "major and important reasons" become the magic bullets. But if you don't properly set the stage, both for yourself or the audience, the essential message is muddy, and the bullets will miss their target. They will fly all over the place, and futile attempts to aim them after you've gotten started can only cause further movement away from the message.

To illustrate, a few more single-sentence themes can be found in Figure 3-5.

Style	Single-Sentence Messages
Persuasive	• To beat competition and reduce costs, we need to implement XYZ system to interact with our customers.
	• To reduce customer wait-times and get a higher return on our technology investment, we need to combine our two call centers.
	• To find out how customers perceive our products and learn more about what future products they want, we need to do a market survey.
	• Due to lagging orders and deteriorating financials, we need to reduce travel and meeting costs by 25 percent.
	• If your company were to become our client, you would gain access to new, exciting ad designs while reducing your costs.
Informativc	• Thcrc arc four stcps to pcrsonalizing customer interaction: identify your customers, differentiate them, interact with them, and customize your products.
	• The competition started a new advertising campaign undercutting our price and service advantages—there are three alternatives for dealing with it.
Review	• Despite slowing sales, our financials last month were slightly better than expected, due to reductions in operating expenses.
	• Our project continues to move forward on time, but in response to unanticipated complexities, we have made a few priority changes.

Figure 3-5. Messages stated in a single sentence

Note the clarity and crispness of the preceding statements. Not only do they have a point and get it across, but you can also see that the following things about them:

- **They are audience-focused:** they define what the audience should take away from the presentation.
- **They include not only a declaration but also a reason why.**
- **They are stand-alone statements,** easily understood without further embellishment.
- **They leave the audience hungry for more** (supporting facts, supporting reasons, other impacts and effects on the business—or on them).
- **For the most part, there are no numbers.** A single, high-impact number is good if it further clarifies the message. In general, numbers provide too much detail and are too complicated to put in the message statement.

Do It in the Elevator?

Your presentation just might not be that simple. You have complex technical or business topics, mixed audiences, numerous and complex alternatives, lots of numbers, facts, opinions, and history. Now what? A single sentence? Yeah, probably a good idea still, but you might want to go further—into an *elevator speech*.

The "elevator" or "pocket" speech is a favorite tool of many presenters. It's an especially good tool to have in your back pocket in the business world. Simply, the idea is to craft a few short sentences describing and supporting your position that could be delivered in a short elevator ride (hence the name). When you can state a broad theme in a single sentence, and you can communicate the entire meaning of your presentation in a short, thirty-second elevator speech, you have achieved clarity. The rest, really, is downhill sledding. You have your theme and main points, and now you can get on with constructing the presentation.

It works differently for different individuals. What works best for us is to build a single-sentence theme or message in the beginning and then create a short elevator speech from there. Move forward with constructing the content of the presentation, then come back and try to *refine* the elevator speech. If you find that easy, chances are your content is relevant and to the point. If you *can't,* or if you find it difficult, chances are you missed the fairway or tried to hit the ball too far while you were still building the content.

Incidentally, elevator speeches are not only a helpful and useful tool in presentation building, they are also handy devices to have in normal business life. Yes, you may share an elevator with your manager's manager, or even a company vice president someday! When they ask what you're doing, or how your part of the business is doing, boy does it help to have that thing in your back pocket! You never know when you'll get that unexpected phone call or impromptu speaking opportunity. From personal experience, we strongly advise you to always carry your most important business activities in your brain in the form of an elevator speech. You'll make better presentations, but you'll also impress others in the "know your stuff" and "think on your feet" departments.

Always Think "Audience Benefits"

Put yourself in *their* position. They have to listen to you, your message, and all the material you'll present to support that message. That requires time, mental energy, maybe resources from their department, too. What's in it for them? Why should they spend the time? Why should they listen?

More successful presentations happen when it's clear to the audience what they get out of something—how they will get lift or *benefit* from it. If the concept you're presenting will make them money, save them money, save them time, or allow them to be more successful—you get the idea—it will help you as the presenter. Remember—the audience is the customer—and like any other customer they are looking for their benefit. We're not accusing them of selfishness—this is the nature of the beast.

Your message, whenever possible, should always stress the benefit of what you're advocating or communicating *to the audience.* If they will profit financially, if they will know more, be able to do more, or be able to make better decisions—*or whatever*—make that clear in your message. You'll get more attention and start off on the right foot—with an audience hungry for more. To repeat: Look for audience benefits, and where possible, make them part of the message.

Now, Take Your Position—and Support It

The message statement is really the central message of a broader theme or position taken on a topic. The rest of this chapter is about building out, or *supporting,* your position. The "build-out" is done through presenting facts and logically constructed conclusions—the magic bullets—that get your message across. And remember: It is hardly enough just to present a few facts. If it were, your job could be done by a computer and a well-designed database! Instead, your audience will require you to *use* the facts to weave them into a conclusive discussion that truly supports your message. Beyond just the facts, it's the structure or the flow, mix, and presentation of supporting evidence, that will make or break your show. The next few sections deal with "tricks of the trade" for constructing and presenting your supporting material.

Building a Story

It isn't enough just to present the facts. You must create a viable story around those facts, a flow of material to substantiate the facts and answer the obvious questions that the audience will have. That flow must do the following:

- Keep the audience interested.
- Strengthen the message.
- Answer obvious questions.
- Lead the audience to the desired action.

Presenters have successfully employed many structures to build a position and the presentation around it. We'll share three frameworks that are fairly easy to use and that get the job done. The first two are more appropriate for the persuasive or informative approach (what you want to happen), while the last is more suited to a review presentation (what has already happened). The three frameworks are as follows:

- Situation, alternatives, recommendation, rationale, requirements, timetable (SA3RT)
- Five Questions: what, why (how, when, how much)
- Results Comparison: what was, what should have been, difference, action

Each of these frameworks organizes and presents facts and conclusions in a logical flow and proactively answers the likely questions. We'll take them one at a time, briefly describing each element in the framework. Please note that these frameworks are intended only to construct the content—*not the delivery*—of your presentation. Proper openers, closers, and transitions are not included here but as part of the outline and delivery of the presentation itself. This material becomes the *body* of your presentation. For a more complete treatment of organization and delivery, refer to Chapters 4, 5, and 6.

Situation, Alternatives, Recommendation, Rationale, Requirements,Timetable (SA3RT)

The SA3RT framework is a very mainstream, straightforward way to construct a presentation. With this framework, you lay a background, explore alternatives, make a choice, substantiate the choice, and answer questions. The audience is left with your recommendation, how you got there, how it will benefit them, and what it will cost them. In the cleanest deliveries, each of these subsections is one slide (sometimes even less), to help achieve clean delivery and facilitate audience recall. The following sections describe each element.

Situation

SA3RT begins with a summary of the current situation, how it relates to the audience, and what has changed or is changing. The situation statement should draw the audience in, provide a common understanding of the issue or problem being solved, and reinforce the importance of the issue and decision to be made. The situation description may bring in key facts and assumptions being made.

Alternatives

Most audiences like alternatives. They don't like to be railroaded into a single proposal or solution. These audiences don't consider the work complete until alternatives are considered—perhaps what you're recommending does the job, but was there something *better*? When building alternatives, chances are you'll cast a wide-enough net to capture the alternative that *your audience* was considering, thus neutralizing objections. (If you fail to do this, the rest of your presentation comes off the tracks when you try to deal with their new alternative!) Finding out what alternatives the audience has in mind is part of your preparation process.

SA3RT Framework Example	
Situation	The XYZ Corporation has launched a new product newspaper ad campaign designed to capture market share in the superstore channel. Unless we respond, we could lose critical market share as the holiday season approaches. Today, our share is 25 percent, and with this campaign, it could drop to as low as 20 percent, according to retail buyers we've talked to.
Alternatives	• Do nothing. • Create a newspaper ad campaign to counter their ads. • Create an ad campaign using other media. • Hold a sale (lower prices) to reduce effect of their ads. • Work through existing customers to ensure repeat sales and get referrals.
Recommendation	Create a sales referral campaign to build sales through our existing customer base. Use direct-marketing techniques and a small promotional campaign to deliver this message. Reinforce the brand and lasting value of our company in this campaign.
Rationale	• Over time, a $2-per-customer investment should yield $5 or more in net profits. • It costs seven times as much to acquire a new customer as it does to market to an existing customer. • A $200K customer base campaign is cheaper than an ad campaign, which could cost upwards of $500K, with a lower "connect" rate. • It will work better than a "Me, too" counter to XYZ, and avoid the margin erosion and brand damage possible in a price war. • Doing nothing may also be viable since it's unclear that the XYZ campaign will work. But better to be prepared, and to take care of our existing customers.

chart continued on next page

SA3RT Framework Example—*continued*	
Requirements	• Identification of our most valuable existing customers and creation of a marketing piece. • A month's worth of IT time to identify customers. • A month from Advertising to create the promotional material. • Total investment: $2 per customer.
Timetable	• Develop next month, deliver at the end of second month. • In place October 31. • Customers identified and campaign designed Sept 30. • Checkpoint progress review meeting September 15.

Figure 3-6. Sample position built using SA3RT framework

Recommendation

Here—after proper audience preparation through situation and alternatives, you present your position or recommendation—what the audience needs to do, think, or know. The recommendation you choose to make is really your message.

Rationale

Now comes the challenging part—substantiating your choice! You already started this process through outlining the alternatives. Now it's time to return to the scene and tell the audience why you've chosen the alternative you have. Your rationale can be structured something like this: "Given Assumptions and Facts x, y, and z it makes the most sense to choose Alternative B because of Reasons 1, 2, and 3. . . ." It's a good idea to reinforce the important assumptions and facts employed in the decision or recommendation. Where possible, drive to a "bottom line," a return-on-investment that resonates with the audience. In your delivery, you may also choose to reinforce why the alternatives *aren't* a good idea. (Although be careful—most audiences prefer to hear why your product is good, not just why the others are bad. If they hear *only* what's wrong with the others they might be left to wonder whether yours might be just as bad!) Delivery of your rationale should be short, succinct, and crisp.

Requirements

You've probably seen this scenario. Someone is making a "killer" presentation, conveying a great understanding of the situation and problem, with a wise presentation of alternatives, then a recommendation, and a scintillating rationale. The presenter gets lots of affirmative head nods; it's going great. Then, suddenly, it's over. Within a few nanoseconds of the projector's being turned off, a hand shoots up in the audience, usually from the person with the most authority. "How much will this cost, and when will it be done?" says the voice attached to the hand. Suddenly the rest of the audience chimes in with, "Oh, yeah, what *about* that?" Audiences—particularly audience members who are responsible authorities—will always want to know what something will cost, in time, money, personnel, discontinuance of other programs, and the like. That represents their price tag, or "opportunity cost." Even if you covered this during your presentation of alternatives, recommendation, and rationale, it's a good idea to summarize the costs or investments that are required so that the audience can easily take them away.

Timetable

The timetable, or at least a summary thereof, is another one of those little details that's sometimes left out or buried in another part of the pitch. (Don't *ever* try to present an entire Microsoft Project or similar project management worksheet!) Advise or remind the audience of the target implementation date and key milestones (don't forget these) toward achieving your goal.

SA3RT Summary

The SA3RT framework as described mainly fits a persuasive presentation style, but can be adjusted for a straight "informative" presentation. In that case, the "recommendation" becomes facts the audience should know or thoughts they should think, not necessarily a recommended action. The rationale is the explanation and embellishment of those facts or thoughts. The SA3RT framework works both for internal and external sales presentations. Again, there are many variations of the SA3RT framework suitable for the situation, but it's a good standard core framework to keep in mind.

The "Five Questions" Framework

Another good framework for building your content or "business case" is the "five questions," or the "what, why (how, when, how much)" approach. This straight-up, direct approach is designed to answer the exact questions your audience will have about your message or proposal. You can play with the sequence a bit, but here are the main elements:

- ***What* is what you want to do**—your proposal, your strategy, your idea
- ***Why* is why you want to do it**—the business reasons for the audience to act on it or to buy it. This equates to "rationale" in the SA3RT framework. It includes tangible and intangible reasons, return-on-investment (ROI) data and the like. Note that, for situations or background unfamiliar to the audience, there can be a "why" element before the "what" as a situation statement. "What" and "why" really follow in the footsteps of your *message.*

The rest is supporting detail. Whether you explore each of these areas depends on the nature of your proposal and the nature of your audience. This approach often works well for an audience including a mix of high-level decision-makers and others. The high-level folks can get what they need in the "what, why" part, and others can stay on or pay closer attention to the tactical details—the information regarding how, when, and how much. Essentially, this framework packages the material to start at the top and "drill down" to the details when and where it is necessary to do so. This format also works well where the presentation will be given to a variety of audiences. You can slim down to "what and why," perhaps adding a brief summary of "how, when, and how much" for high-level decision-makers. For mid-level colleagues, you can build up the "how, when, and how much" sections. Here are some examples:

- ***How* is an explanation of how your proposal or strategy will be accomplished**—the tactics. Here you explain who will be involved and how, what steps are required and why, what resources will be needed and where they will come from, and so forth. "Where" can also be part of "how" if geography is involved. Your audience, having accepted the rationale, is now eager to know how the proposal will be brought to life.
- ***When* details the time schedule** and is analogous to the "timetable" section in the "SA3RT." Detail the completion dates, milestones, and checkpoints.
- ***How much* summarizes what investments are required**—dollar investments, personnel investments, and other resource investments. Detail the resources and investments required, where they come from, how they will be funded, and reiterate the ROI for the owners of those resources.

"Five Questions" Framework Example	
What	Create a sales referral campaign to build sales through existing customer base to maintain market share and fend off a new XYZ ad campaign aimed at the superstore channel.
Why	The XYZ Corporation has launched a new product newspaper ad campaign designed to capture market share in the superstore channel. Unless we respond, we could lose critical market share as the holiday season approaches. Today, our share is 25 percent. With this campaign, it could go as low as 20 percent, according to retail buyers we've talked to. Five alternatives have been explored: • Do nothing. • Create a newspaper ad campaign to counter their ads. • Create an ad campaign using other media. • Hold a sale (lower prices) to reduce effect of their ads. • Work through existing customers to ensure repeat sales and get referrals. The last alternative is recommended for the following reasons: • Over time, a \$2-per-customer investment should yield \$5 or more in net profits. • It costs seven times as much to acquire a new customer as it does to market to an existing customer. • A \$200K customer base campaign is cheaper than an ad campaign, which could cost upwards of \$500K, with a lower "connect" rate. • It will work better than a "Me, too" counter to XYZ, and avoid the margin erosion and brand damage possible in a price war.

chart continued on next page

"Five Questions" Framework Example—*continued*

- Doing nothing may also be viable since it's unclear that the XYZ campaign will work. But better to be prepared, and to take care of our existing customers.

The following "how, when, and how much" sections are at a management or decision-making level:

How — Use direct-marketing techniques and a small promotional campaign to deliver the message.

- Pull customer names from our database.
- Identify the most valuable customers.
- Deliver a promotional message with rewards for referring our products to other customers.
- Reinforce the brand and lasting value of our company in this campaign.
- Place occasional ads building the value of our brand and recognizing our existing customers and their product experiences.

When

- In place October 31.
- Customers identified and campaign designed Sept 30.
- Checkpoint progress review meeting Sept 15.

How much

- A month's worth of IT time to identify customers.
- A month from Advertising to create the promotional material.
- Total investment: $2 per customer.

Figure 3-7. Sample position built on "five questions" approach

The "five questions" format is most suited to persuasive presentations where decisions and actions are required, but it can also be used for an informative presentation. If you're doing a training pitch or seminar, you can organize your points in just the same way—except the "what" represents a fact, attribute, or characteristic that you're trying to get across, not a proposal or a choice.

Results Comparison Approach: Was, Should Have Been, Difference, Action

The final framework we'll share is the "Was, Should Have Been, Difference, Action" framework (WSDA for short). This framework is more useful for the review presentation, where you're sharing and analyzing *actual results* of something. It's fairly straightforward:

- **Was** represents what actually happened—whether that's a financial result, a business program or project result, a sale or no sale, or some other anticipated action.
- **Should have been** is what was supposed to happen—the stated objective, target, or goal.
- **Difference** simply captures the difference between what occurred and what was supposed to occur, with your interpretation/analysis of why that difference occurred, and whether that difference is favorable or unfavorable.
- **Action** is the course of action you recommend, if any, to change the course of business to achieve stated or desired goals, or perhaps change the stated goals themselves.

In this framework, the action, or "what," is saved for last, because you need first to review what's actually happened and what it means for the business. In effect, the "why" comes before the "what." After that, the how, when, and how much elements of your recommended action can follow.

Business Result	Was	Should Have Been	Difference and Reason	Action
Result #1				
Result #2				
Result #3				
Result #4				

Figure 3-8. "WSDA" Comparison Table

These frameworks are useful for defining the content you want to incorporate into the presentation and the logical flow of that content. Now let's take a look at the content itself—what it is, where it comes from, how it's presented, and what may be the most important task of all—how to keep it simple.

Getting the Facts

By now, you have a pretty good idea of your presentation "game plan" and which content structure you want to use. Recognizing again that every situation is different and that there is no magic formula for pulling the facts vital to your pitch, we'll throw out a few tips and concepts useful for building content.

Internal and External Research

Most effective presentations mix information from internal and external sources. External sources include the media, Internet, industry publications, textbooks, and authorities in your subject area. Internal resources include company data, previous studies and analysis. They also include your coworkers—don't forget about them. Your coworkers can be a rich source of information, and the fact that you utilize their knowledge can help gain audience support at presentation time, too.

But don't rely *too* much on internal sources. That may lead to presenting too much material that your audience already knows. At the same time, too much reliance on external sources can cause the audience to question your knowledge of the internal information that they're familiar with. It may make you seem threatening by disregarding their knowledge base, and it may also make you look speculative. The best presentations blend the known and unknown, internal and external information, to draw conclusions. This is a question of balance, dictated in part by your situation and what works best for your audience.

Hard Facts and Intangibles

The world doesn't all revolve around hard facts and numbers. Some things simply can't be quantified. Most effective presentations blend a few hard facts and findings with a few intangibles—things that are probably true but can't be quantified. Market share can be quantified, but market perception can't—and to say something about both in a presentation on marketing strategy is probably a good idea. Again, it's balance: too many or too few facts will cause some in the audience to think something has been left out.

Mix in Facts, Supporting Opinions, and Anecdotes

Too many facts can be dull and boring and may leave out the more intangible interpretations or experiences with the facts. It's good to "color and flavor" your facts with opinions and anecdotes from customers, other employees, or others with whom you may discuss your message and proposal. The audience is human—and it's always good to add a human—and sometimes humorous—element, to relate your presentation to them, to tell them what others like them might think. But again, don't overdo it—too many anecdotes turn your pitch into storytelling and can distract and dilute your main points.

Elaborate Alternatives, Downside Risks, Upside Potential

In most business presentations, the audience wants to make sure they know the alternatives to what you're presenting, and what, in the absence of certainty, might happen if they do or don't follow what you're saying. It's always good to explore the alternatives and talk of the advantages and disadvantages, the upside and downside, of whatever you're presenting. You may not need to make this part of the "mainline" presentation, but always be prepared to deliver this information if called upon to do so.

Emphasize Truth and Accuracy

"The truth, the whole truth, and nothing but the truth"—make sure what you're presenting is correct and accurate. In the early career of one of the authors, his manager would sit in the back of the room during detailed production-planning presentations and then start asking questions about the derivation of a single number in an entire worksheet. There would be a slight arithmetic error (this was in the days before computerized spreadsheets), and this manager would make the author stand there, in front of the audience, and figure it out. When approached later after the presentation about why he was being so "picky" about this detail, the manager simply answered: "It isn't the number itself, *per se.* You must learn to be accurate, for if anyone catches any inaccuracy, no matter how small, they begin to doubt the credibility of the entire presentation." This lesson stuck through the years—accuracy, no matter how seemingly unimportant—*is important.* And whatever you do, don't "BS" the audience. Sooner or later they'll catch on. And it may take years to repair your credibility.

Give Numbers and Dollars

You'll find that in most situations, people want to hear the story both in numbers and in dollars stories. They want to know the answers to the questions how many, and how much. Always "dollarize" your facts where you can and where it makes sense, even if you have to make some assumptions. Dollars are still the main yardstick used to measure business performance, and a "bottom line" orientation will help your career.

Assembling the Facts

Research can be one of the most challenging and yet rewarding parts of the presentation-building process. Turn over those rocks, inside and outside your work group, and see what crawls out. Look for pertinent facts, experiences, anecdotes, professional papers, or other presentations on your topic. The list is endless.

The main challenge is to keep it all organized, so you can indeed "find your magic bullets," and build out the position. Presenters use different tactics—index cards, binders, folders and so forth—to track individual facts and references. We'll leave that up to you, but we strongly recommend building an *outline* once the facts are collected or as they are being collected. Remember doing those outlines way back in grade school, with all their Roman numerals, capital letters, numbers, lowercase letters, and small Roman numerals? That's what we mean. Outlines serve multiple purposes, as the following sections describe.

- **Collecting and Organizing.** Outlines serve as a single repository for all of your information in the following ways:
- **Sequencing.** Outlines are useful in determining the presentation sequence.
- **Prioritizing.** By properly using the indents, you can decide which facts stand out and which are subordinate to other facts. This is especially useful for filling your delivery with enriching information and in crafting more- or less-detailed presentations for different audiences.
- **Designing.** Once your outline is together, your presentation materials (and handouts) can be drawn directly from it. Many successful presenters simply use chunks of their outline to build their slides. Outlines help the audience organize the information, too, and many audiences remember an outline best.

The practice of outlining comes straight from grade school; we won't change it any here. The outline can be as complex or as simple as is appropriate for your topic and the kind of information you're presenting.

Enriching the Facts

As pointed out earlier, a presentation built entirely on facts, without interpretations, opinions or anecdotes, can not only be dull but may also reflect a lack of understanding or internalization on your part. If you're a dull fact-head, or if you appear not to know the topic, you'll have a hard time getting anywhere with most audiences. Make sure you add some value to your facts. Your bullets usually don't become "magic"—and they may not even be credible—until you consider and include some enrichment tools.

Assumptions

Now, assumptions aren't usually very exciting either, are they? Usually not—but a presentation where you fail to declare or describe your assumptions can be exciting, especially when key audience members start pinging you with "How did you get to *that*?" questions. Business life is full of unknowns and intangibles, and it's usually a good idea to declare the *important* assumptions you make about those unknowns and intangibles. If you're assuming a "normal" customer acceptance rate of 25 percent, *then say so.* At the same time, audiences will bore easily if you rattle on with small, picky assumptions of little consequence. Put yourself in the audience's place, and from that perspective be the judge.

Examples

A picture is worth a thousand words, but an example may be worth more than that. Examples serve to illustrate the concept you're trying to present. For example, you can drone on for hours describing how poorly your Web site serves customer needs. Here's a better idea: go through the experience yourself and build a storyboard example, going from one page to another to solve a problem. Time how long it takes, and record the time. Show pictures of each screen and choice, with load times next to each, and show total time for the session. That story, as an example, works a lot better than a bland description of steps and screens. Similarly, instead of just "reporting" negative customer feedback about the site, give some examples. Paraphrase two or three quotes and put them into your presentation. It's more interesting, and your audience will catch on much more quickly.

Analogies and Metaphors

It's possible to go nuts with metaphors and analogies, but in moderation they do work! Comparing computer systems to plumbing, or inventory systems to bathtubs, or project development to house construction or recipe cooking or airplane flights are all analogies that work. Just make sure the analogies are logical, tasteful, and familiar to everyone in the room. Make sure, as you would in your writing, not to *mix* the metaphors and analogies. Don't be building a house on one slide and baking a cake on the next. Be careful about using too many sports analogies—being "in the ballpark" and "doing an end run" are illustrative but are perceived by some female audiences as male-centric and by many international audiences as total gibberish. Shooting analogies (such as "lock and load" or "pull the trigger") may cause self-inflicted wounds. And be careful about using the many "dating" analogies we hear used in business—it's easy to get carried away and offend someone.

Quotes and Anecdotes

Quotes can add an enriching personal or human touch to content. "Famous" quotes are fun, and can often enlighten or serve as a good opener, so long as they're relevant and not overused. They can warm an audience to a topic and get them in the mood, and they can link your presentation to famous people or events. Stories can serve the same purpose, and they can be used as examples to illustrate your point. But watch out—this too can be overdone. Remember that the audience is there to hear you—not every figure in American history. And they aren't there to hear you tell stories—they want to get your point. Stories are more effective that emphasize your own personal experience, a customer experience, experience with a competitor, or a relevant success or failure. Humorous or surprising stories are better. Remember that stories are a tool, a sidebar, an illustration, a rest break—not the presentation itself.

Comparing and Categorizing

Comparisons can be drawn using metaphors and analogies, but another important tool used in good presentations is the "internal" comparison—finding relationships between your facts and comparing them to common standards, such as time, quality, and the like. The idea is to relate your facts and findings to something meaningful to the audience, and then to present it that way. "Before and after" comparisons are a good example. Others include "high, medium, and low" and "most and least." Tables are often the most effective ways of presenting these types of comparisons. In the next chapter, we'll talk more about tables and other forms of relating data.

Advantages and Disadvantages

Whenever making recommendations or presenting alternatives, it's a good idea to analyze the advantages and disadvantages, or upside and downside, of whatever it is you're talking about. In the interest of brevity, it may not always make sense to present advantages and disadvantages, but it's a good idea to have them thought out—and in your outline—to whip out quickly if questions come up. Audiences frequently test you to see if you've thought through your material. If you can present advantages and disadvantages, that shows indeed you have.

Solutions, Not Just Problems

Many audiences—especially managers—get frustrated if all you do is point out problems or unfavorable events. A good way to enrich your data—especially if the situation is negative—is to pull together a positive side or a solution. The audience is more likely to feel like you're on their side and support you.

Timing and Dollars

Business runs on time and money. At the risk of being repetitive, it is always important to be able to tell your story in time (when it will happen, what the major stages and milestones are) and in money (the cost and the return, in dollars). Talking in terms of time and money makes your case more practical and real. While it may not come up, it's important to be prepared in case it does.

Keeping It Simple

Now that we've run this long-winded discourse on collecting and organizing your content, it hardly seems fair at this point to be talking about keeping things simple! But we'll do it anyway. The reasons to keep your presentations as simple as possible are fairly obvious. First, it will help you keep from losing your audience. Second, it can help you avoid getting lost yourself! Simple presentations are the easiest to do, the easiest to remember, and the most likely to achieve desired outcomes. Here are a few pointers for organizing your content in "Keep It Simple Style" ("K.I.S.S.").

Stick to the Message

A fact, anecdote, or other presentation element must support your intent and message. If it doesn't—or it isn't clear how it does—leave it out.

Three to Seven Points

Numerous studies of human memory and behavior all conclude the same thing: the human mind is capable of absorbing between three and seven major points at a time, no more! So if your audience hasn't nodded off by your thirteenth point, they probably aren't "getting it" anyway! Build and outline your content in such a way that the major points stand out and stay inside these parameters. It's a good idea, once the presentation is built, to go back through and test—what are the three main points? Are they clear? Are they memorable? Too many points, or points that don't stand on their own clearly, will defeat your purpose.

Logical Sequence

There are many ways to organize and order your bullets. The order you choose will depend on the situation. Chronological order works well for many presentations, while others build facts in steps toward a conclusion. For a persuasive presentation, we've found it best to present the strongest points both at the beginning (to get attention) and at the end (to get more impact), while putting the smaller or "softer" points in the middle. People are more likely to remember the first and last things they see or hear, while what's in the middle is more likely to be lost.

How Much Detail?

This is the age-old dilemma in making presentations. Those of us with extensive presenting experience feel that if you leave detail out, audiences will ask you for it, seemingly miffed that it wasn't there in the first place. If you include it you get slapped on the hand for including *too much,* or end up running way over your time limit. What's the right balance? We can't offer any specific guidelines, as it varies by audience, situation, and the nature of the topic. But in our experience, it usually works best if you have a "main set" pitch with the high-level points presented in three to seven bullets, covering the what-why-how information or something similar. Then you would also prepare a second body of materials—*backup* slides—to supply additional material on demand. Make your audience aware that this information is available. The "parking lot" sidestep technique—where you handle a specific question requiring a time-consuming detailed explanation by offering to do it later "in the parking lot"—is a useful technique for staying away from too much detail (as long as you're careful not to appear evasive).

If all of your information is on your main slide set and you have nothing left for a backup, *look out.* You may have too much detail on your main set. The best advice: make sure the detail is available in some form, but not in such a way as to clutter your main pitch or message.

In Short . . .

Once the audience "market" is understood, good content is vital to any presentation. Content should be designed to support a well-stated desired outcome and message. There are many ways to develop and structure content effectively to achieve the desired result.

Do's	Don'ts
• Think "audience benefits." • Be clear about the desired outcome, and build a desired outcome statement. • Understand the influence of location, time, formality, and audience knowledge on content. • Decide early if it's a persuasive, informative, or review presentation, and build accordingly. • State your message or theme in a single sentence. • Use an outline to develop and "flesh out" content. • Build an elevator speech. • Enrich content with the right quotes, anecdotes, analogies, and citations. • Make detail available—but don't present it all. • If the topic is familiar, stick to "what's new." • Keep it simple: three to seven main points.	• Don't start building content before desired outcome is understood. • Don't overlook audience and situational clues into level of detail: you need to persuade, need to decide. • Don't rely too much on either internal or external sources. • Don't use tired analogies or clichés. • Don't present problems without solutions. • Don't omit alternatives, positives and negatives, or benefits the audience may be looking for. • Don't forget to give the "dollar" picture.

Figure 3-9. Do's and don'ts of content design

4 Get Your Ducks in a Row

A great set of facts alone won't do it. Structure them to make your message clear and memorable.

It's a warm, steamy evening, and your detective team has searched high and low. Finally, a shout from the murky depths of the woods: "We have a body!" You, the district attorney, breathe a sigh of relief—no, *you're thrilled*—knowing full well that while the first big hurdle in the case is overcome, there's still a lot more work to do to develop the case. But at the very least, you have a body. You can't get anywhere without that. Now you may logically wonder, what does *this* have to do with building presentations?

If you pardon the heavy-handed analogy, you also must *start with a body* when making a presentation. Once the body, or the content, is created (as described in Chapter 3), you can continue to build out the presentation. Just as you can't show only a body to the jury, you must also show more than a body to an audience. The audience needs to know what you're trying to show with the body and why. They need you to point out useful evidence besides just the body itself, and they will need your help to determine what conclusions to take away. They need to connect emotionally with the situation, and you need to get and keep their attention. Critically, they need the complete, start-to-finish pitch, done in logical, easy-to-grasp order, to help them get the most from the presentation. That's your job, and they need you to do it. This chapter shows how to move from a "body" of facts (sorry) to a complete start-to-finish presentation.

A Guided Tour

We'll risk switching analogies to use an example most of us have actually experienced. The ideal presentation is like a guided tour through the facts. As the presenter, you're the tour guide. You give a little monologue at the beginning of the tour to create rapport with the tourists and tell them what they're going to see. In presentation parlance, this is an *opene*r. During the tour, you help them get the most out of what they're seeing. You build in time for enriching explanations and answering questions. When moving from one place to another, you explain or remind them where they are going and what they can expect when they get there. For presenters, that's a *transition.* Finally, at the end of the tour, you sum up what they saw, answer questions, make a few parting comments to make everyone feel good about what they saw, and—who knows—you might try to sell them on another tour. This is the *closer.*

The best presentations, like the best tours, have just the right amount of direction and assistance from the presenter, or tour guide. A tour guide that talks too much or spends too much time answering questions detracts from the essence of the tour itself. Likewise, a tour guide who stays stone silent while tourists try to decipher just what the heck they're looking at probably tips the other end of the scale. Keeping the opener, body, transitions, and closer in balance and flowing smoothly is a vital part of the presenter's "game plan"—and is one of the true tricks of the presenter's trade.

"Shaping" the Presentation

We'll explore the objectives and techniques of openers, closers, and "body parts" shortly. But since a picture is worth some large number of words, it might be useful to offer an illustration. Figure 4-1 shows a presentation diagram used by many presenters to structure presentations.

You can see each of the "parts of the speech"—the opener, body, and closer, in logical sequence. The shapes and how the shapes are connected say a lot. In the opener, you start broad, connecting with the audience, bringing them in, and hitting them with your main *theme and message* just when they're ready. The body is a logical, orderly presentation of each main point and the supporting evidence. At the close, you hit the message again, reinforce it, and broaden out to address audience concerns, make the audience feel good about what they saw, and set the stage for whatever is next.

Tell Them, Tell Them, Tell Them . . .

Besides the presentation diagram and the "parts of the speech" concept, many presenters use another useful and related "rule of thumb" model. This model is pretty simple, but it is surprising how often these basics are ignored and to see

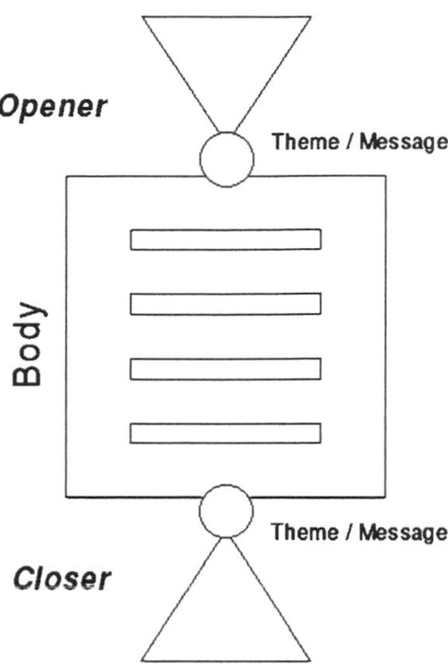

Figure 4-1. Presentation diagram

how many presenters fail as a result. This model applies to almost all communications, whether that means a speech, a telephone call, or a conference with your spouse or children. The objective is to help the audience listen to your presentation and get the most out of it. Since you know what you want to say, but the audience doesn't, they need some help! Audiences have a great many things competing for their attention and mental "bandwidth." The easier you can make it for the audience to prepare for and absorb what you say, the better.

Tell Them What You're Gonna Tell Them

The listener must form expectations of what they are going to hear and how they're going to hear it. A few words to introduce the topic and to indicate how you plan to discuss it and for how long goes a long way toward setting expectations and fostering effective listening. This also means improved communication between you and the audience. Naturally, this occurs in the opener. It's a good idea to introduce your topic and tell your listener how long you plan to talk about it, what the presentation format is, what types of visual aids and examples they will see, and so forth. The audience gets a little "roadmap" of your tour before beginning, and they are far more prepared to take the tour. Naturally, you want to give a brief overview. You don't want to use your entire time allotment telling them what you're gonna tell them!

Tell Them

This is the straightforward delivery of your content, your body, point by point.

Tell Them What You Told Them

Your objective, of course, is for the audience to take away as much as possible from what you presented. So the closer provides a good opportunity to "set" points put forth in the body into audience minds. Thus, in the close, you want to review the message, key supporting points, actions, inquiries, and so forth—or whatever you want the audience to walk away with. It is a review of your pitch sharply focused on the points you want the audience to remember as they walk out of the room or hang up the telephone.

By now you should have a grasp of the overall framework or flow of an effective presentation. From here, we go deeper into the purpose and specifics of building a presentation, the do's and don'ts of preparing the opener, body, close, and transitions.

The Opener

Let's look at a couple of different opening scenarios.

Scenario One

Once again, you're a member of the audience. The door opens, and the presenter flies into the room. She slams her laptop down on the table, plugs in, hooks up, and turns on. The first slide hits the wall: a big pie chart showing market share for one of your products in the southeastern United States. She starts to talk, pointing at the large blue pie slice in the top left. You're still staring at the title of the chart and fumbling through your papers desperately searching for your copy of the agenda. What is she talking about? What is she supposed to talk about? She drones on, but for you, it's just mumbling noise. You don't pick up a word of it. You're still trying to figure out who she is, what she's talking about, and why. By the time you catch up with the pitch, you've already missed the point. Now you're doomed to thirty minutes of wondering what you're supposed to get out of it. She had some pretty slides, wore a nice navy-blue business suit, and had a couple of good bits of humor—that's about all you'll remember.

Scenario Two

It's the same day, same agenda. The next presenter stands up from his seat in the third row and heads for the podium. He straightens his shirt, tightens his tie, and paces the floor a couple of times. He starts apologizing for the fact that having been asked just the night before to do this pitch, he wasn't able to give it his best efforts. Then he starts talking about last Sunday's football game and how your city's team could have won had they only kept the ball on the ground. Then a few joking, self-deprecating comments about how the new members of the audience "will get used to me sooner or later." Next a story about his last trip to the southeast and then a barroom joke shared (clean, at least) that he picked up on that trip. You glance at your watch. Your neighbor shuffles some papers. The guy in back of you boots up his laptop ("ta-taaaa" blares out Windows loudly and obnoxiously). First slide goes up, but the golden moment of interest has long since passed, and you're not sure what he really intends to talk about—nor do you care.

The Analysis

What went wrong—in both of these cases? In both cases the problem was the same: lack of a compelling, precise opener. And what happened? The golden moment we all have to rivet the audience tightly onto our program was lost. The audience is lost. The presentation—and what it was trying to accomplish—is lost. The horse not only did not drink—it was never led to water. The message didn't come through, expectations weren't set, and reasons to listen or pay attention in the first place were never given. What are the chances of recovery? It is possible but difficult. A poor opener can be overcome, but it's an uphill battle. Unless you're Alan Greenspan, to whom everyone listens intently regardless of opener or any other presentation structure, you'd better work on the opener. (If you are Alan Greenspan, your position and stature is opener enough!)

What Should the Opener Accomplish?

A good opener will accomplish the following four things:

- Capture the audience.
- Put yourself at ease.
- Set expectations.
- Convey your theme or message.

With these points in mind, let's explore each one further.

Capture the Audience

An audience not listening is an audience not getting it, and that means a communication failed. If you don't win audience interest in the beginning, they usually won't develop interest on their own (exception again, Alan Greenspan). You want to establish yourself and give the audience a reason to devote themselves—and their time and attention—to what follows. The following sections describe what good openers should do.

Break the Ice

Good openers should get audience attention focused on you and your topic. They should make the audience more comfortable. Entertaining or funny openers—stories or jokes—often work, but they must be used carefully. Sometimes a funny picture or cartoon will do it. The audience stops what they're doing, eyes and ears point your way, and the moment is yours. If there's tension between you and the audience, caused by the topic or merely fear of the unknown, a lighthearted opener will work. But beware—a humorous opener that misses the mark will turn *off* the audience and make your task that much harder.

Build Rapport and Credibility

This works especially well for an unfamiliar audience. Tell them who you are, what you do, and how you came to give a talk on the topic. Even for a familiar audience, it may help to review what you've been doing for the past few weeks or months that make you a more knowledgeable expert on the topic. And most audiences—even if familiar—have a few new or unfamiliar faces in them. It's a good habit to introduce yourself for their benefit.

Acknowledge the Situation

Where appropriate, thank those who invited you. Reflect on what a great opportunity it is to be there. Acknowledge any previous speakers who did a good job of laying groundwork for your pitch.

Acknowledge the Knowledge

When the audience has already heard something, or when they bring their own knowledge or familiarity into the room, acknowledge that. "You saw a presentation last week on the benefits of the new tax law. Most of you are already familiar with the new rules. Today I am going to add to your base of knowledge and explain how our company will benefit specifically from the changes." This empathetic tactic shows your awareness of the audience and is a good rapport builder.

Put the Audience at Ease

There is some anxiety in the beginning of almost any communication process resulting from the natural unknowns. The more unknowns you can remove—from who you are, to what you'll present, to how long it will take—the more the audience will be on your side. And that's very important—you *always* want the audience to be on your side.

Provide a "Hook"

Most of all, the audience, if they are to listen, wants a *reason* to listen. You need to captivate them. You need to show them the importance and impact of what you're about to say. You must demonstrate how it affects their business or affects them personally. There may be multiple "hooks" in the opener. Early on there may be a bit of humor to establish attention, relieve tension, and make the audience more comfortable. Then there is a second hook—often your theme or message—supplying the compelling business or personal reason for staying "on board" with your pitch. Remember that everything you say, especially in the opener, should leave the audience hungry for more.

Put Yourself at Ease

At the same time your opener puts the audience at ease by establishing rapport and setting expectations, the opener also serves to put *you* at ease. A well-tuned opener serves to get your internal speaking machine warmed up and running, just as it warms up the audience. As a speaker, you need to get comfortable. Like a performer, you need to establish a rhythm and pace. You need to get the proverbial butterflies to fly in formation. Once that rhythm and pace are established, confidence builds at both ends of the room, and your task becomes easier.

Set Expectations

Most of the time, an audience that knows what's coming is better than an audience that doesn't. It's human nature to wonder about the unknown, and many listeners will subconsciously get caught up in the game of trying to guess what's next—while failing to listen to your presentation. It's a good idea to "tell them what you're going to tell them," and provide a few clues as to what they will see. When you lay a proper foundation in the minds of the audience, it's easier to "build" your message.

Provide a Road Map

Good openers answer questions proactively, that is, in advance, about who you are, what you will talk about, how long it will take, how you will convey the message, what they will see along the way, and what will be important to remember. As with our "tour guide" analogy, the tourists don't need to know everything, but a few clues about where they're going and how they're going to get there come in handy. Here's an illustration: "Today we are going to talk about customer acceptance of our new multicolored widgets. Along the way, I will show you pictures of the latest products. Then I'll explain preliminary findings and statistics, by region, from our first round of customer research. At the end of the presentation, I'll share a few customer testimonials." Now the audience knows what they'll see. When they see it they'll know how it fits, and will be able to concentrate on the content

Do "Housekeeping"

If there are any housekeeping issues, such as when and how lunch will be served or where the bathrooms are, this is the time to get them "onto the table," as it were. Otherwise, someone inevitably will ask just as you are about to launch your strongest point of all. Let the audience know whether there will be breaks and if so when they will occur. A rule of thumb when presenting: know the possible distractions and avoid them.

Present the Situation

Although in Chapter 3 we presented the "situation" statement as part of the body, it can also become part of the opener. If you don't review the situation in the body, you should do it in the opener. But be careful not to become too bogged down in facts or numbers—it shouldn't take too long to get to the message and the body of the presentation. Some presenters will give a situational overview in the opener, then come back and add detail in the body. The amount of information and detail provided in a situation statement is, of course, geared to audience familiarity and relevance to your message.

Convey the Message

If the message of your presentation doesn't become clear somewhere in your opener, just when will it become clear? Will the audience wait patiently for you to wander through the woods until they finally hear the message? Worse yet, will the audience construct their *own* message in the absence of yours? Obviously you want to avoid these scenarios.

The message should be a simple, declarative sentence. It is usually best placed towards the end of your opener. You've provided background, established audience rapport, gotten yourself comfortable, and set some expectations—now it's time to come forth and declare your message, that is, your intent or your theme. The early part of the opener should lead the audience to your message statement. Some presenters will state the message then expand a little to set audience expectations with a road map: "The new tax laws will reduce our taxes by 5 percent and cost us less to administer. I will demonstrate that first by reviewing the text of the new laws, then by showing, line by line, how they apply to our business. Finally, I will share a few comments from the folks in our financial reporting department."

Familiar vs. Unfamiliar Audiences

If you know the audience and the audience knows you, your opener tactics will be different from a situation where neither you nor your topic is familiar. If you present on the same topic every month—as in a project or financial review—there is hardly a reason to introduce yourself and go to great lengths to build credibility and audience rapport. But that doesn't mean you shouldn't *warm up* the audience. By the way, it's good to warm yourself up at the same time. A funny story from today's *Wall Street Journal* or the latest cover story from the *New York Times,* especially if relevant to your topic, could be a good icebreaker or warm-up. But don't do a fifteen-minute essay on your background. You may not even need to set expectations or do a road map—if the presentation is regular and routine. You should take care to recognize new audience members and bring them up to speed—but make sure you let the rest of the audience know what you're doing so they don't wonder why you're "going there." This is one place where it helps to know your audience—including who is new—in advance and during preparation.

Figure 4-2 summarizes differences in opener tactics for familiar versus unfamiliar audiences.

Familiar Audience	Unfamiliar Audience
• Shorter opener. • Shorter warm-up. • Briefly review earlier presentations. • Tie presentation to other presentations or knowledge previously gained. • Briefly summarize situation.	• Longer, more formal opener; establish credentials and rapport. • Explain your background and history with the topic. • Introduce the situation, with a more complete description of situation and background.

Figure 4-2. Opener tactics—familiar and unfamiliar audiences

Opener Techniques

The tools, tips, and tricks presenters use to build openers—particularly to capture audiences—are as wide and varied as presentation topics themselves. The techniques presented in the following sections can be used—and mixed together—to achieve your desired opening "outcome." The choice depends on your own creativity, the topic, and the needs and nature of the audience.

Conversational

Simply start as if you were having a one-on-one conversation with a single audience member. "Hello, my name is Joe. Glad to be here, and I hope you're doing well. Remember last week when we discussed the roll-out of our new multicolored widgets? Today I would like to bring you up to speed on how the campaign is going and answer any questions you might have."

Significance

Appeal to the audience early on with the significance of your topic. "We're at a critical, go/no-go juncture with the roll-out of our new multicolored widgets. The success of our division rides on this new product line. Today I want to share the latest developments and, with your help, make a decision about where we go from here.

Quote

Quotations from famous people are interesting and sometimes fun, and they can help the audience put things in perspective. They work well as icebreakers and can help establish your credibility as knowledgeable and well read. The key is relating the quote to what you're talking about. Otherwise, the audience is left to wonder. "Civil War cavalry officer Nathan Bedford Forrest once said the secret to winning is to 'get there firstest with the mostest.' Wise words, those were, and we think we've succeeded in capturing the multicolored widget market by doing just that. I'll show you where we are with the new campaign, and now that we've established our market position, where we will go from here."

Rhetorical Questions

Questions get the audience thinking along with you. "Our competition is responding to our multicolored widget campaign by launching an advertising campaign and selling direct through their Web site. Now, why would they do that? Today I'll show why that won't work, and what we plan to do as we move forward with our campaign."

Stories

Done right, but not overdone (as illustrated in Scenario Two of this section), stories can be powerful, especially if they relate to the topic and audience experience. Customer experience stories can be especially powerful. The secret is to establish relevance and make the stories interesting or entertaining. Avoid stories about your family (unless especially relevant), and please, not too long!

Facts or Statistics

Share a surprising or particularly high-impact fact. "Did you know that customers on the West Coast prefer our multicolored widgets at a rate almost twice that of the rest of the country? Today, I'm going to explore this phenomenon and share a few other facts that I think you'll find interesting about our new product campaign."

Historical Analogy

Relate your topic to something significant or interesting that happened in the past. "Remember back in the 1920s, when General Motors bucked the trend and started selling cars in multiple styles and colors in response to customer preferences? Well, we've now started doing that, and our customers are just as pleased with us. Today I'll share the status and show the latest findings from the multicolored widget roll-out."

Event

Share an important event, either internal or external to the company. "Last week, market surveys showed our widgets to have just surpassed XYZ Corporation's widgets in market share. Let me share how the new campaign is going, and where we plan to go from here."

Visual Aid or Demonstration

If you're talking about something physical, bring it in and show the audience! Demonstrations can be fun and a welcome break from dry talk-and-slide shows—a good icebreaker. They get attention, and they can help the audience better understand or appreciate what you're talking about. If you're selling new multicolored widgets, bring some in to look at or test. "I know you've all heard about our new multicolored widget campaign. Today I'm going to show you what they look like and how they work—and then we'll talk about how the campaign is going and where it will go from here."

Audience Game or Quiz

This is a favorite, for both familiar and unfamiliar audiences. Play a little trivia game, or have them guess something relevant to your topic. Again, it's a good icebreaker and warm-up and a fun diversion from a long day of presentations. And you can use it to present something exciting or surprising about your topic. "I would like everyone to take out a piece of paper and write down, *in order,* which colors from our new multicolored widget line you think are the most popular. The winner will receive a gift certificate for dinner for two (now you *really* have their attention). After the game, we'll review the new product roll-out and what we plan to do from here." Be careful not to spend too much time or to get the audience's competitive juices—usually present in business situations—flowing too freely, for it can become a distraction.

Remember that there is no one technique that always works. Often, a good opener may use more than one of these tactics. You'll get plenty of chances to practice these ideas. In the meantime, you should pay attention to what other presenters do and what tactics they employ. Above all, keep in mind that the opener is the opener—it isn't the whole pitch. Some presenters get carried away and overdo these openers—resulting in *losing,* not capturing, the audience.

How Long Should the Opener Be?

The length of the opener depends on the situation and the audience—audience familiarity, your credibility, the topic itself, time, importance, and distractions. A good rule of thumb is that the opener and the closer should each consume no more than 10 percent of your allotted presentation time. This follows the businessperson's golden "80/20" rule—that 80 percent of your time or effort should be spent on that which is most important. Thus a "10/80/10" time allotment is a good place to start. For a one-hour presentation, the opener and closer would each be six minutes. For a fifteen-minute presentation, they each would be a minute and a half, and so forth. Again, this is a rule of thumb that can be broken if the situation requires an especially strong opener or closer. But remember that short and crisp is usually best.

Other Opener Tips

The following sections present a few other tips and tidbits handy for constructing good openers.

Don't Self-Deprecate

We've seen it over and over. The presenter takes the podium and *immediately* starts apologizing for his presentation, his lack of preparation, the fact that he just got the job, the fact something's missing from the pitch, the fact he just got in late last night. It's a part of natural human self-consciousness, we suppose—but you shouldn't do it. While it seems like a friendly way to build rapport, it causes audiences to lose faith in you and what you did bring to the party. One possible exception to this rule is that it's sometimes helpful to apologize for being late. But this is situational. It shouldn't be built into your opener.

Be Flexible

It's a good idea, especially early in your speechmaking career, to write out openers. But you should recognize that every situation is different and that you need room to maneuver or adapt to the situation. If your session is running late, don't stand up there and rattle through an entire opening story! Read the audience and let the opener adapt to the signals they send. They will usually tell you—either directly or with body language—if they're looking for more (see Chapter 6 for more on reading the audience). So while writing out an opener may help, it's probably not a good idea to stand there and read it.

Anticipate Interruptions—and Take Care of Them in the Opener

We mentioned the lunch thing before, along with what should happen if you or someone else has to leave at a predetermined time. If you have a guest presenter, introduce them in the opener and set the audience expectations for who they are, what they will do, and when they will do it. Get the "housekeeping" issues out of the way. If there's a handout, either hand it out right away or tell the audience what it is, and when it's coming (more on handouts in Chapter 5).

Stay in Context

If the presenter before you has just laid out an excellent description of the business environment, don't do it again in your pitch. Where possible, take up where others have left off. Sometimes this involves day-of-show adaptation, but it may also pay off to talk to other presenters (preparation!) in advance.

Again, Be Careful with the Analogies

Excessive use of sports or dating analogies—or other clichés—can dull the "golden moment" of audience capture or worse yet, offend some.

Remember: Introduce Your Body

No, we're not advocating nudity here—quite the opposite, in fact. In the body, we made the point to avoid things that don't relate or contribute; in the same vein, we suggest only putting things in the opener that help introduce the body of the presentation. Items in the opener can help the audience, help you, or introduce the body directly—but in some way or other they need to lead the audience to your water and to make them drink.

The Body

In Chapter 3 we explored the content and logical flow of the presentation body in some detail; we won't repeat most of that here. Instead, we'll provide a few tips on managing the presentation of the body in context of the entire presentation, including the use of *transitions* to get yourself and the audience cleanly from one point to the next.

Mind over Body

You've prepared your "magic bullets" and all the supporting material—facts, anecdotes, alternatives, point/counterpoint, and so forth. What's left to think about? If you did a good job constructing the content, the rest is fairly easy. Mainly, you need to "tune" the presentation to make sure points get across smoothly, paying attention to time, pace, emphasis, order, and visuals, and layers of detail. Balance and flow are extremely important. Out-of-balance presentations miss points and are uncomfortable to the audience. Remember two main goals: first, to keep the audience attention you've worked so hard to earn, and second, to ensure the audience indeed "gets" the main points you want to make.

Time

This one's obvious and yet so often forgotten. If you've chosen the "10/80/10" opener-body-close construct, make sure your body indeed fits within 80 percent of your time allotment. So many presentations dwell too long on the first couple of points and fall apart at the end, leaving out what may be your most convincing points. Prepare the points and the script to occupy the time allotted—*no, wait*—less than the time allotted. Time must be made for questions, unanticipated clarifications, or interruptions. The surest way to throw the whole presentation out of balance is to try to present more than time allows

Pace

Closely related to time, pace is important. Don't spend half your time on one point, then the other half on the next four. Things will get left out, and the audience may leave with the wrong impression about what's important

Order

This is a subjective issue. Many presenters present their strongest points at the beginning and end, leaving the weaker or smaller points in the middle. Audiences tend to better remember what's at the beginning or end.

Emphasis

Make sure the points you want to emphasize are emphasized. If there's a point you want the audience to take away, put it in capital letters in a prominent place on a slide, and signal the audience in your delivery that the point is important. In a minute, we'll talk more about the "valuables" and how to make sure the audience gets them.

Layering and Detail

Make sure that the amount of detail is just right for the point, for the topic, and for the audience. We discussed this in Chapter 3, but it bears repeating. The best presentations "layer" the details, with "mainstream" slides, backup slides, and references to other material. If you use this technique, no matter how much you fail to anticipate the audience's need for detail (and you always will), you have the proper coverage and backup, and you won't aggravate the audiences that want to skip it.

Visuals

We'll talk more about visual aids in Chapter 5. In general, people remember what they see more easily than what they hear. The right number of high-impact, easily understood visuals will gain lift with the audience. Too few, and especially too many, will send your pitch into a tailspin.

Identify the Valuables

When building and presenting the body—the content—it is very important to make sure the audience gets the "valuables" or *takeaways*—the key "nuggets," "gems," and "goldpans"—and walks out of the room with them. This requires the right emphasis both in building and delivering the presentation. The first step is to identify the valuables as you build the content. Then, as you build the opener, body, and close of the presentation, find effective ways to highlight them in the presentation and delivery. "Valuables" can include any of the items described in the following sections.

Nuggets

Nuggets are the main points or pieces of information—the major takeaways—in your presentation. A nugget can be a fact, a synthesis of facts, or a conclusion. You want the audience to remember the nuggets, use them, and be able to relay or share them with others. "Sales of multicolored widgets grew 30 percent when we added green to the color assortment" or "The new 'Customersoft' platform in our call center reduced average customer wait times by 25 percent."

Gems

Gems—or "Aha's!"—are nuggets that are positive discoveries or surprises. "When we offered green widgets, customers stopped buying red ones altogether. It turned out it's because they want to use them in their gardens." Figure out what will be surprising or revealing to the audience and highlight it. The emphasis might be a little stronger than that of the nugget, as the audience *expects* the nuggets.

Goldpans

Goldpans are the things you don't know but need to find out. They can be questions or missing information important to build a complete picture of your topic. You don't have the answer, but you've found something that *needs* an answer. There's a nugget or gem in there someplace; you just haven't found it yet. You want the audience to take away your promise to answer the question and an expectation of how you plan to answer it—which, by the way, provides a hook and builds interest in your next presentation. "We found that customers shifted their purchases from red widgets to green widgets. By next week, research will tell us why."

Goldpans are also sometimes used as a "call to action" in the closer. "Individual department expenses appear to be a large part of the reason our profits are down. Please take the time to re-evaluate your department's expenses so we can verify the cause and develop further action."

Nuggets, gems, and goldpans are often highlighted in presentation materials with color or some other visual cue. Some presenters make an entirely separate slide to convey a valuable. Some put them at the bottom of a slide inside a box or some other form of visual call-out. In delivery, there will be obvious emphasis, but also pauses and question-and-answer opportunities built in around the point. Each presenter—and each audience—will find its own preferred way to bring valuables to the surface; it becomes a matter of what is most comfortable and effective.

Transitions

Good presentations—like good conversation—have effective transitions or "road signs" to guide the listener. The objective of transitions is to get the listener from one part of your presentation to another smoothly, comfortably, and without confusion. The listener needs to know when the topic changes and why. They may need a brief review or a rest to "clear the mental palette" before absorbing more material. Think of a transition as a road sign—or a rest area—along the side of the presentation highway. The forms and types of transitions are many and varied; let's explore a few.

Linkages

Linkages are like the road signs you see when crossing state borders: "Leaving Ohio" or "Entering Michigan." You know right away which state you are entering and which you are leaving. The same idea applies to presentations. If you are leaving the market research data and moving on to financials, don't just throw the financial summary up on the wall. At the end of the market research section, tell the audience that you're leaving, and tell them what you're entering. "That concludes our review of customer research. Now let's move on to look at the financials." This way the audience knows exactly what's happening. They won't be lost when all those nice pie charts suddenly turn to columns of dollar figures.

Like those occasionally seen at state borders, the signs don't have to appear right at the boundary. The signs may be a few hundred yards on either side, so as not to make the transition too abrupt. Similar tactics used in presentations are helpful, particularly when the subject matter is complex and requires intense concentration. "Let me make one more point about the market research, then we'll switch to the financials." Abrupt or unexpected changes don't sit well with many audiences.

Summaries

A favored and effective tactic used by many presenters is the short, interim summary. Such a summary serves a dual purpose. The first is to review and "nail down" what has already been said. The second is to provide a smooth transition. These summaries are often used to reinforce the main takeaways. "Now, before we move on to the financials, let's recap what we learned from our market research. Customers prefer green widgets by a two-to-one margin over red ones, and they prefer to buy them locally through their dealer." These transitions not only smooth the flow, but also build (or retain) attention for the next topic.

In fact, this type of transition can also be used to lead into the main points of the next section. "Now as we move on to the financials, you'll see that red widgets are also twice as profitable." What did we do? We "told them what we told them," then we "told them what we're gonna tell them" about the financials. It's sort of a microcosm of the entire presentation, with the transition serving as a minicloser and miniopener between sections of the body.

Pauses

Another favorite transition technique used by presenters, especially professionals, is the pause. "The pause that refreshes" is a good slogan for most speeches. Pauses allow the audience to "catch a break," absorb prior information, and get ready for more. You'd be surprised how effective a pause—even a short one—is in improving the audience's listening capacity. A pause also serves to break the monotony. How many times have you heard a speaker drone on and on—after a while, it becomes like elevator music. The pause—and its silence—provide a useful break and will actually get back audience attention. Audience anticipation builds about what's next. During delivery, pauses are good impromptu tools for re-engaging audience members who are drifting off or causing distractions. Naturally, that kind of pause can't be planned. Remember, of course, that the pauses can't be too frequent or too long. Otherwise, they soon merely feed distractions, becoming a golden opportunity for the audience to whisper to each other about post-meeting refreshments! A pause is a "rest area," not a recreation area.

Question-and-Answer Breaks

The question-and-answer break is another favorite transition tactic. It combines the essentials of summaries and pauses and serves further as a meter of audience interest and comprehension. At the end of a section, simply stop to ask the audience if they have any questions or comments. That forms a nice pause, and the questions and answers can often help summarize or reinforce the topic. Audience members who need to rest can rest, and those who want to question or challenge have the opportunity to do so.

Realize that question-and-answer sessions need to be used and managed carefully. Too many "Q&A" breaks will have the audience thinking the whole thing was a big Q&A session or that you didn't have much to say yourself. If the topic just covered isn't likely by nature to generate questions, or very many questions, the Q&A will lead to awkward silence. Realize also that quite the opposite can happen—a lively Q&A session can throw the whole pace off track and unwillingly turn the presentation initiative over to one or a few audience members. Regaining control and keeping to your time objectives is difficult. So be careful to keep the Q&A sessions timely and not let them take over or dilute the presentation.

Transitions should be smooth and somewhat varied. Don't use the same kind of transition each time—they *do* wear out. Be careful to make them the right length and to have them in the right places in your speech. And remember—what we've talked about here is *planned* transitions. Unlike road signs and rest areas, transitions can be inserted, changed, or taken out during the delivery to achieve the best result. Now that you have a better understanding of the different types of transitions and how they're used, let's move on to the closer.

The Closer

Everything you've done up to now, naturally, leads to the closer. If you've done everything effectively, the closer should occur easily and naturally. But if there is unfinished business in the presentation itself, or if the closer is handled awkwardly, it can be your worst nightmare while on stage—and it can ruin an entire presentation. Closing a presentation leaves a lot of room for creativity, but there are a few guiding principles to share.

What Should the Closer Accomplish?

Closer objectives include the following (and most should be constructed to *accomplish* each of the following):

- **Road sign.** The beginning of the closer tells the audience that you're through with the content. The result is (or should be) a shift from absorbing content back to you and your message.
- **Review.** The closer is an ideal opportunity to repeat the message and key findings and to reinforce them.
- **Request.** Most informative or persuasive presentations make a request—a call for action, a call for commitment, or a call for understanding

- **Relevance.** The closer makes a transition between your presentation and the greater "big picture" world around you. You can tie the importance of your presentation to the success of the company, or you can explain just how what you want to do will bring world peace or mitigate world hunger.

Structure

Recall the "two triangles and a square" presentation structure presented in Figure 4-1 at the beginning of this chapter. The closer is the bottom, right-side-up triangle, occurring just below the body. The shape depicts the structure: the closer starts with a sharp, focused statement, usually a crisp review of your message forming a transition from the body. The beginning of the closer should let the audience know, in no uncertain terms, that the body is "over" and the closer has started. "Now you've all seen the product, the research, and the financials. I believe you'll agree with me that our multicolor widget line has worked well and should be expanded."

From that focused transitional statement, you can move to review the key points in the content and then to review the broader context of the presentation. The best closers start specific and get broad—but may have a very specific call to action at the end.

Tell Them What You Told Them

Remember that one of the reasons you're on stage to begin with is to help the audience. It's the old "win-win" situation. You help the audience absorb, understand, and grasp your message and supporting points. They'll reward you by siding with and supporting your position and call to action. The most effective way to help the audience take away what it needs to take away is to tell them what you told them. A quick, sharp review never hurts. But don't repeat the entire presentation over again, and don't bring in new points never before heard. It's amazing how often that happens!

The "Big Picture"

It's a natural thing to wonder how any message relates to the grander scheme of things. How will it improve the business? The company? Customers? Employees? Individual audience members? It's often good in closing to reinforce benefits and draw links to other things the audience holds as important. Sometimes it's also good to make a prediction or a challenge. "Our new multicolored widgets are not only a hit with customers, they will also build our market share and revitalize our company's brand image and will show once again that our company is a leader of innovation in American industry." A word of caution: Don't get carried away. If your plan doesn't solve world hunger, don't say that it does.

Call to Action

It all boils down to this: What is the audience supposed to do/commit/think/believe/understand or help you with as a result of your presentation. Good presenters carefully craft and deliver a call to action at just the right moment. What's the right moment? It's when the audience is ready, when they have absorbed everything else. Usually—but not always—it's at the end.

Some presenters put the call to action earlier in the close, then repeat or reinforce it at the end. The call to action highlights the audience's "role" in the message—what you want from them. If nothing else, you want the audience to walk out of the room remembering your call to action, and—hopefully—*why* they should do it. There's no "formula" for presenting a call to action. It will vary by the audience and situation. Obviously, a football locker-room halftime audience will hear a different and louder call to action than an audience learning the virtues of buying burial plots. Now here's our call to action for you. Follow the structure and tools presented in this chapter, and build better presentations that knock 'em dead in the business world!

In Short . . .

Audience attention is captured and retained best with a good opener, good transitions, and a good closer built around the presentation body. The trick is to connect with the audience and reduce their burden by guiding them effectively through the material.

Do's	Don'ts
• Build the body first—then the opener and closer. • "Tell them what you're gonna tell them, tell them, and tell them what you told them." • Keep the size of the opener and closer in perspective—10/80/10 is a good rule. • Use the opener to build rapport, put the audience and yourself at ease, set expectations, and tactfully "hook" the audience. • Use the opener to put the audience and yourself at ease. • Mix tactics and techniques in openers. Keep them interesting and surprising. • Clearly identify the "valuables" in your speech. • Keep the audience moving with you—and rest them—with transitions. • Review your message, connect with the big picture, and provide a call to action in the closer.	• Don't spend too much time on the opener and closer—either during preparation or delivery. • Don't apologize or self-deprecate in the opener. • Don't ramble anywhere, particularly in the opener or closer. • Don't overuse analogies or clichés. • Don't use the same type of transition over and over. • Don't leave out the opener or closer.

Figure 4-3. Do's and don'ts of guiding your audience

5 The "Hard" Stuff

The "eyes" must have it, too. Visual aids turn the ordinary into the extraordinary.

Yet another presentation drones on and on. The sermon continues in a dry monotone, punctuated by just a few irrelevant hand gestures. A business storyteller, and not a very good one at that. Like a lawyer relaying parts of a contract: section this, stroke that, dot something else. You pick up a yawn to your left, nervous fidgeting to your right. Your mind drifts off to warm tropical places, and the message and context of the presentation are forever lost. You get up and walk away with nary a reminder nor a record of what was discussed.

What's missing here? True, the subject matter—and the presenter, for that matter—may in fact be dull and boring. Sometimes that just can't be helped. Not every business topic is going to be interesting. But there's something bigger going on here. The human mind is an insatiable consumer of visual images. Visual images are stimulating. Visual images reinforce the other senses, particularly our sense of hearing. For all but the most interesting sound stimuli, the mind always "looks" for something to go with it. Ever notice it? The eyes are always scanning, always peering, always looking for something to focus on. When there's a visual image to go with something picked up with another sense, the combined sense becomes much stronger. People may salivate when they hear about chocolate cookies, but they salivate more when they smell and see them—the cookies become an imminent reality.

Visual Aids—What and Why

Visual aids are the body of physical or visual material prepared to accompany a business presentation. In today's computer age, this most frequently translates to presentation slides, and we'll talk further about this popular but sometimes abused medium. But visual aids appeared on the scene long before the vaunted laptop. Remember flip charts? Blackboards, and their evolved descendants—whiteboards? Transparency projectors? Opaque projectors? And what about examples and samples—physical, touchable manifestations of the product or idea being discussed? All of these techniques and technologies are used toward one common purpose—to give the viewer a visual impression and record of what is being talked about.

In practice, visual aids actually serve two purposes. First, as we've covered, visual aids serve to reinforce the audible message. They not only give the eyes something to do, they also provide a visual snapshot of the topic item. Visual aids help with structure—they give quick sound bytes or images that help the mind grasp and file away information more quickly and effectively. In the parlance of Web page designers, visual "eye candy" helps attract viewers to the important stuff and then helps them remember it. Visual aids, in short, *attract, organize, and reinforce* your message and your talk for your audience. "A picture is worth a thousand words" is true for all communications—don't ever forget that. But in the case of business presentations, even a picture *of the words* can be important in the fast-paced, fast-grasp information-overload world of business.

Beyond their value in attracting, organizing, and reinforcing your presentation for the audience, visual aids also serve other purposes for presentation and the presenter. They help the presenter stay organized. They facilitate transitions. And they can also provide useful rests or breaks for the audience in some circumstances.

Organizing You, the Presenter

Well-constructed visual aids not only help the audience stay on track—they actually help the presenter stay organized and on track, too. Smart slides serve as an outline not only for the audience but also for you, the presenter, to follow. More than an outline, visual aids provide a *set of cues* to help with transitions and topic introductions and to interject enriching stories, anecdotes, and supporting information. Old-fashioned cue cards or a presenter script may, in fact, not be necessary for the presenter with a good set of visual aids. Outline and "bullet" slides, graphs, and tables all serve well to help the presenter govern the flow of the presentation.

Transitions

Presentation materials help the presenter, and the audience, move from one topic or one point to another. When the audience follows a presentation slide and gets to the end, they are prepared for the transition to the next slide—the next point or topic. Visual aids serve as road signs for the presenter and audience alike—"Stop Ahead," "Curve Ahead," or "Exit" signs that help smooth the flow.

Emphasis

Sure, it's possible to verbally emphasize key points and takeaways as you go through them. Good visual aids offer you the power to do it better, more convincingly, more "grippingly." Just as bold or italicized text helps guide the eye—and the attached brain—to the important stuff on a printed page, visuals done right—color, highlights, pictures, boxes, callouts, or explosions—instantly guide the audience to the point. Physical examples—to not only look at but touch, feel, smell, or play with—further expand the impact. Particularly for the more "photographic" minds in your audience, visual highlights etch an unforgettable image in the audience brain available for immediate recall. Nothing works better than visual aids for emphasizing a point.

Rests and Breaks

Just as the movie or filmstrip broke the monotony in your junior-high classes, visual aids can be used for a short pause, a longer break, or simply a laugh or smile. They are often critical to retaining audience rapport and attention. A funny photo or cartoon figure on a slide is a subtle approach. A full, midpresentation break to show an illustrative, or even funny, example related to the topic also works. Are you talking about high-tech or computer support? Show an example of a laptop run over by a car and tell a story about it. Visual aids can be used simultaneously to reinforce a point and offer a break. When talking about property insurance, for example, show a film of a real house fire. You'll be rewarded with oohs, aaahs, and an audience rescued from the jaws of dramatic boredom. Visual aids, in fact, provide an opportunity to exercise creativity, not only in their form but also in their use in the presentation. Visual aids provide the spice, the flavor that makes food not only edible but *interesting* and *memorable.* Just as in cooking, overused or misused visual aids can not only ruin the meal but leave a lasting unfavorable impression. Care must be taken to use the right visual aids in the right way to help you and the audience to get the most out of the presentation. Anything else is a waste of time—and may be worse than that. Always remember that visual aids are there to support your presentation—they are not the presentation itself.

The standard presentation slide in its various forms will be seen most often in the business world—therefore, we'll spend the most time in this chapter examining presentation slides and some of the visual enhancements and impressions they can create. We'll touch on the use of tables, charts, graphs, and animation in addition to ideas and tips for form and structure of presentation slides themselves. You may not become a slide or PowerPoint® expert by reading this chapter, but you'll get a handle on some of the basics that will almost invariably "spiff up" a presentation for the better. Along the way, we'll provide ample guidance for what not to do. There is plenty not to do if you want to avoid trouble. We'll also touch on the use of other media, such as flip charts, boards, and physical visual aids. Last but not least, we'll spend some time on the strategies and tactics for physical "hard copy" handouts that you may want to leave with the audience.

Slip-Sliding Away

True, the advent of the ubiquitous PC may have revolutionized the crafting of presentation materials. What once took hours—days—to get done at a professional graphics studio can be done in minutes with a good software package and an inexpensive inkjet printer. Or if your business environment includes a laptop and an LCD-screen projector, it becomes simpler yet—just a matter of "plug and play." Having said that, we'll be quick to point out that the basic fundamentals of slide presentations have been around long before the PC. The graphics shop had already come into play, and some businesses used expensive layouts and 35mm "Kodak Carousel" slide projectors in the dark ages before the 1980s. More often, people simply wrote out their slides on a piece of clear acetate, or they used the age-old flip chart in much the same way today's PC junkies grind out slides one after another. (Do flip charts and tripods fit in aircraft overhead bins? We're not so sure . . .)

Regardless of the medium and the technology, the effective use of slides comes down to *organization, style, layout, use of images,* and *color.* These terms are somewhat self-explanatory, but they're worth expanding anyway, as follows:

- **Organization** refers to the slides and visuals as a complete body—the number of visuals, the sequence, and the tie-in to the message and logic being conveyed.
- **Style** refers to the use of words and language on the slides.
- **Layout** is the physical graphic design of the slides or visuals.

- **Use of images** means the employment of graphs, charts, tables, grids, pictures, screenshots, and pictorial metaphors to convey information more vividly and precisely.
- **Color** is mix of colors and use of color to highlight important points or messages.

The rest of this section expands on the effective blending of these elements to achieve your desired results. Though we base some of our advice on Microsoft PowerPoint—the most widely used desktop presentation software—this section is not intended to be an in-depth hands-on course on PowerPoint or any other tool. Other resources are available for that. What's important to remember is this: The right use of these slide design elements will be an asset to your presentation, while a misguided use will be a liability and may irrecoverably detract from the quality and effectiveness of your pitch. Create assets—and avoid liabilities.

Slide Rules

From here, let's examine some simple, easy-to-follow guidelines that should lead to high-impact visuals and help you avoid some of the pitfalls of using them.

Get It in Order: Organization

Effective slide presentations have the right number of slides, in the right sequence, with the right amount of information on them for the audience. The number of slides can vary by the topic, audience, and situation—the time allotted, for instance, will naturally govern the number of slides you can present. Here are some rules of thumb:

- **The five-to-ten rule.** Most presentations should contain five to ten slides in the mainstream presentation. The human mind is good at grasping from three to seven things at once—depending on the mind, the interest, and the topic—after that, most everything tends to become noise. Five to ten slides gives you three to seven in the body and allows for a good title slide, opener and closer.

  Obviously, five to ten is not a good rule if you're giving a five-minute speech! Rolling through slides so fast that the audience barely has time to read the first line is deadly—your speed becomes a distraction, and the audience starts to wonder what it *isn't* getting from the material. You should allow at least two to three minutes for every slide you present. Obviously you will need more if the point is complex or critical to the main point of the presentation. And don't forget to allow time for questions and clarifications.

- **Main roads and side roads.** Good presenters learn to organize and sequence their slides so there is a "mainstream" version with simple clear points in logical order as well as a "backup" version with illustrative data, charts, and supporting detail. The "backup" may be feathered in to the mainstream version or it may be kept as a group of separate slides at the end. Regardless, you can see the imperative to keep organized and build your own road map to keep track of "what is where" in your presentation.
- **As brief as possible.** Of course, if your point is straight and simple—forget the organization and backup—a simple 1-2-3 slide "brief" can be most effective. Sometimes the most effective presentations of all consist of only *one* slide. One slide is all that's necessary to reinforce the point, attract and maintain attention, provide something to remember, and keep presenter and "presentees" organized! If you *can* do it, *do it!*
- **Create a storyboard.** For any journey, it's good to have a road map. Before crafting individual slides, we suggest creating a one-page storyboard depicting the slides (or other visual aids) and their sequence. This is how the organization formulated in Chapter 4 (opener, body, closer—and logical argument, such as "what-why-how-who-when-where") is put into visual presentation form. You may have started something like this already to help organize and deliver the message. The resemblance to the storyboards constructed by movie and theater producers is not coincidental. With a storyboard, the sequence and level of detail become clear, and you can decide where to insert special visuals, such as graphs, charts, pictures, and physical examples. Storyboards help achieve balance between summary and detail slides and help in planning transitions. The storyboard is based on your script. It guides the preparation and presentation of visuals.

There are different ways to create storyboards. We usually start with a "blank" storyboard, add slide titles, and sketch in detail as it is decided (pencil and paper is fine). Following are examples of a "blank" storyboard and a more "fleshed-out" version. Again, we suggest a fairly well thought-out storyboard before constructing individual slides or visual aids to minimize rework and achieve good balance and flow. If you used index cards or other similar aids to plan your message and content (Chapters 3 and 4), the storyboard should evolve easily from that exercise.

The presentation in Figure 5-1 makes a "business case" to buy a new "Widgetcruncher." In this pitch, the title slide is used as a background for the opener, which will be delivered verbally. The presentation goes straight to the nitty-gritty of the strategy—the "what" and "why." The "why" is supported by the "how"—points that really support and detail the "why" rationale. At this point, some detail is called for, so there is a sidetrack into the detail—which may or may not be presented depending on the audience—using graphic visual aids. Finally, your "how much" and "when" slides summarize resource requirements and timing, proactively answering major audience questions. All of this comprises the body, which will be followed by a summary slide and closer. Note the use of bullets throughout the mainstream show—simple, crisp, to the point. Anyone walking into the room at any time would be able to "catch up" with the pitch almost instantly. There is little to be confused about. The incorporation of pictures and numbers at key places keeps attention and makes the points more real.

Of course, we realize that not all presentation topics are this straightforward or simple, but the approach is still effective. In fact, the more complex the presentation, the more important the storyboard becomes.

Keep It in Style

We'll now move from looking at the presentation as a complete set of slides to the creation of individual slides or visuals. Style, layout, use of images, and color all play a part in getting and maintaining audience attention and effectively conveying the message.

What do we mean by "style"? Style can be kind of a loosely applied term, and for many it might seem to include elements like layout, color, and use of images. Specifically, here, we refer to the way words and language are used on the slides.

Don't Put Too Much on a Slide

If you put too much on the slide—whether it's words, pictures, or a combination of the two—the result is predictable. One of the following will happen.

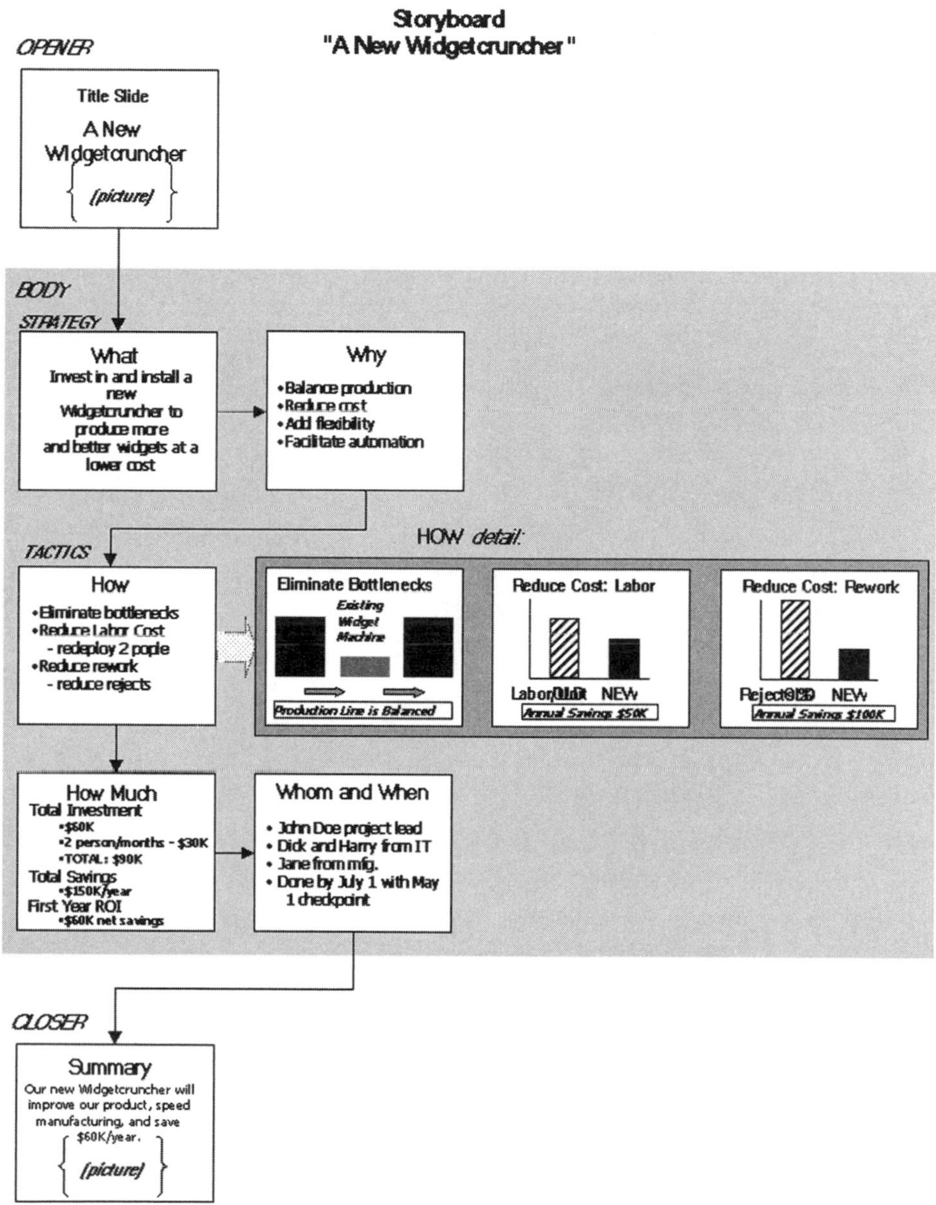

Figure 5-1. Basic presentation storyboard

1. Stuff gets too small to see.
2. People (including you) can't connect the visual with what's being said.
3. You lose your audience altogether as they squint and sift through the vast amount of material.
4. All of the above.

Slides should convey one or a few main points. Words and graphics should be viewable as blocks of information, such as a table, set of bullet points, or small diagram—not a bunch of loose, haphazard words and images. Stay away from paragraph-length text, large spreadsheets, and detailed flow diagrams wherever possible.

When in Doubt—Bulletize!

If there is no more obvious way to convey your message, use standard bullets to make your points. Bullets are short blurbs of text—usually sentence fragments—itemized and sequenced using small graphic icons to highlight each one. "We would like to buy a new Widgetcruncher because it will balance production, reduce cost, add flexibility, and facilitate automation" becomes:

- Buy a new Widgetcruncher to:
  - ✓ Balance production
  - ✓ Reduce cost
  - ✓ Add flexibility
  - ✓ Facilitate automation

Figure 5-2. Example of "bullets"

Note the use of the "checkmark" as a subordinate bullet. Like a numbered outline, this helps the mind organize (and deliver, on your side of the podium) the information. You can also use outline-style numbers and letters directly on your slides.

Note again how the use of bullets works. Bullets are all of the following:

- Easy to read.
- Easy to remember.
- Easy for you, the presenter, to follow.
  - Your speaking outline.
  - Your guide to making good transitions.

Bulletized points can be longer than the short phrases listed above if necessary, sometimes as long as three lines of text. But the writing style should still be brief, crisp, and conversational. Bullets are almost like answers in response to direct questions in a phone conversation or similar situation, where the idea must be conveyed quickly, easily, and without confusion.

Points and Fonts

Physical text styles can vary according to the type of presentation and the style of your organization and audience. Usually, if you've kept your points simple, larger fonts work—the larger the better. Eighteen or twenty points or larger is best. Usually we avoid font sizes smaller than twelve points unless the text is part of a larger "grouped" visual such as a diagram. As far as text style, the sky's the limit. With conventional business presentations, Arial (standard block letters) or Times New Roman (newspaper-styled block letters) are familiar standards. For a slightly less formal or more consumer look, Comic Sans is attractive. We avoid script and overly stylish fonts—they are too hard to read and can be distracting.

Our customers will respond to our new rewards program because . . .

- it is exciting
- they get better service
- it delivers real, tangible dollar value
- it helps them learn more about our products
- it requires little effort on their part

Figure 5-3. Comic Sans font

And who is that little guy clicking his heels in joy at the thought of participating in the new reward program? That is a PowerPoint "screenbean," illustrating the idea of adding images to "spiff up" your slides. We'll have more on screenbeans in a minute.

Highlight the Highlights

No matter what form of communication you're engaged in, it's important to make note of or highlight the really important points—the points you want to be sure the audience remembers. There are a lot of tools and tricks for accomplishing this. One of the more straightforward is to highlight key words, phrases, or sentences in bold, italics, or color. Another way to get the highlights across (remember nuggets, gems, and other takeaways from Chapter 4?) is to give them their own special and prominent position on the slide. By just being there, the audience will become conditioned to interpret them as highlights.

Suppose, in the example just presented in Figure 5-3, a slide preceded the one illustrated that extolled the benefits of the "reward" program for the company. (Set aside for a moment that a customer-conscious presenter would probably do the customer benefits first.) A summary highlight could appear at the bottom of the slide, as shown in Figure 5-4.

Our customers will respond to our new rewards program because . . .

- it is exciting
- they get better service
- it delivers real, tangible dollar value
- it helps them learn more about our products
- it requires little effort on their part

Our rewards program is a win-win proposition.

Figure 5-4. Bullet slide with highlight summary

Layout: The "Art" of Presenting

Like a good photograph, the layout, or composition, of a two-dimensional visual aid (that is, a slide) can be critical. As with the photograph, your eyes should be drawn to the right place or places in the right sequence. Certain items should capture your attention. Items that distract or lead your eyes off of or away from the picture should be avoided. Beyond the analogy of the photograph, since there are many slides in a pitch with much to convey, consistency becomes important. The following sections include a few more pointers.

Center, Left, and Right

What do you look at when you see a picture or slide at first glance? The lower right corner? The top edge? Most likely, your eye goes for a center of interest, usually at or near the center of the picture. Or if there is no center of interest, your trained eye goes for the center, anyhow. Further, as our brains are all creatures of habit, we (in the English-speaking world, anyway) all read from left to right and from top to bottom. It's a good idea to create slide layouts that follow this flow. Don't put the slide title or most important material at the bottom right (unless you want the rest of the slide to build up to it). Set the slide up so the important material is at the center. Each slide has its own miniopener and minicloser. Set these up at the top left and lower right if you can.

As indicated by the very subject matter of this chapter, a picture is worth a thousand words, perhaps more. So now we introduce Figure 5-5, a typical slide layout as an example.

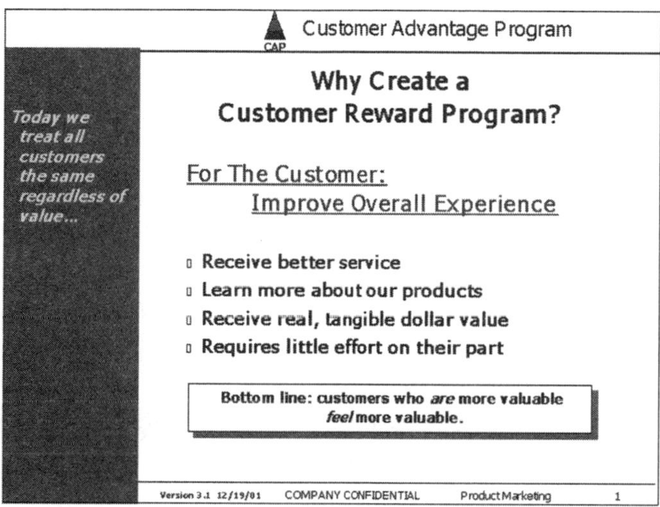

Figure 5-5. Sample slide: customer advantage program

We'll let you digest this example on your own for a minute, then take it apart.

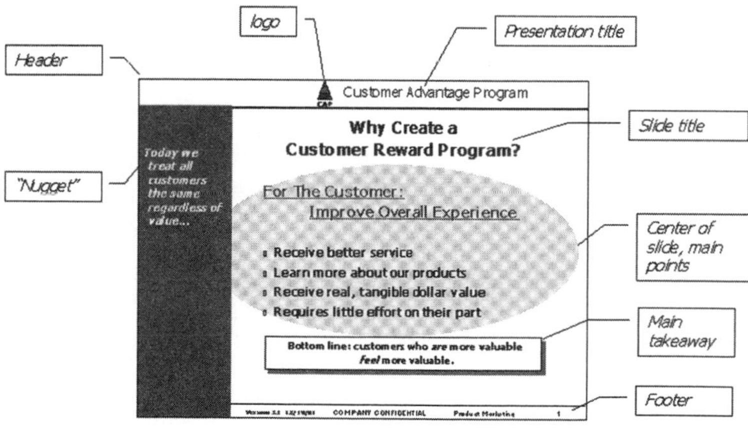

Figure 5-6. Sample slide explanation

You can see the logical use of the center of the slide to make the primary points. The eye probably hits the center first, then goes from the top left to the lower right, picking up the "Aha!" realization in the left-hand box that indeed, today, all customers are treated the same, regardless of value—and here's what we're gonna do about it. These key points are all presented inside a common "wrapper," including a *header* and *footer* identifying the presentation itself and providing a look. The header contains a *logo* representing the project or program itself—again an identifying mark that adds professionalism and helps build your "brand" internally.

Do a Header (and then a Footer)

Somehow, presentation materials of all sorts—whether documents, letters, or Web pages—all look more professional with a header and a footer. Additionally, the header and footer contain key organizing information like the title, date, slide number, slide file, slide status (draft or final), and in the example presented, a logo representing the department or project being presented. If someone finds one of your slides on the floor, they'll know immediately where to take it. If you get lost in the middle of your show (happens all the time), you can figure out where you are without clumsy fumbling or searching. All of these elements not only help organize, they also provide a look, sort of a *uniform,* that makes your show look more official, and yes, more professional.

South of the Borders

Another popular visual tool is the border. Borders add interest, guide the eyes to the right place, add to the "uniform" look, and provide an opportunity to highlight key information or navigational aids. The top and bottom borders in the sample slide segregate header and footer information. The left-hand border/text block gives an opportunity to add a key text point as was done here. As with all your presentation elements—don't get carried away with borders.

Attention, Please

Layouts can be designed to get attention or to keep the audience focused, either through specific images placed at key places, or by dynamic, visually stimulating backgrounds. Many slide packages offer dramatic layout backdrops—but again, overuse is overuse.

A "Trademark" Layout?

Microsoft PowerPoint and many other presentation programs allow you to choose from a palette of "canned" layout masters or to create your own. Prepared layouts are nice. They are consistent from page to page and can create that guy-in-uniform professional look. Create every presentation using the same format, and it becomes your own personal organizational trademark. Layouts can convey messages about you and your organization, project, or idea—subtle, loud, creative, energetic, and so forth. Most of all, they must support your presentation and its message—not detract from it.

In PowerPoint, it isn't so easy to figure out how to set up your own master. You might expect this set of tools to be found under "Format"—instead, it is under "View." Go to "Master," then "Slide Master" to create permanent locations for your header, footer, titles, borders, and other common slide elements. You can also insert images or backgrounds to become part of your master.

There are also "canned" masters (now we go to "Format," "Apply Design"). These masters are very professional but, we think, overdone. Most of them are distracting. If you try to reproduce them as hardcopy handouts, you may have fits with printing time and legibility.

Finally, one of the best—and most politically correct—things to do is to use your company's masters. Many companies have developed their own guidelines and "look" for slide shows—it behooves you to use what's out there. In most companies, using the company uniform or "wrapper" is a good thing. It is usually possible to add your own project logos, department names, headers, and footers to these masters.

Image Imagination

When one thinks of "images," one usually thinks first of photographs or fancy graphics depicting the topic itself. Beyond pictures and illustrations, images include charts (graphs), tables, grids, shapes, icons, logos, metaphors, callouts, connectors, and backgrounds. Although simplicity usually calls for basic bullet slides, good images have their place, especially in the "knock 'em dead" business presentation. Graphs, tables, and grids can be particularly powerful tools for breaking down and explaining a topic as well as for organizing and presenting large amounts of data. We find that tables are a must for the business presenter's repertoire; charts follow closely behind.

In this section we examine some of the more popular visual images. Obviously the range of possibilities is endless. It is influenced by the software or tools you use and the business or corporate environment in which you operate. A complete treatment of graph building, for example, is beyond the scope of this book. Most software programs have learning resources, both "on board" and at Web sites supporting the package. Microsoft "PowerPoint Central" is a good example. In this discussion, we'll stick more to the wisdom and "do's and don'ts" that should help you as you use and learn the details of these media.

Charts

Charts, or graphs, are ingenious devices invented long ago by mathematicians to illustrate concepts and data. Charts come in all forms, shapes, and sizes and can show data in many ways. The basic idea of a chart is to relate data to each other and to "norms" represented by the axes. Most typically we use a standard "X/Y" graph, in which the X axis represents a controlled factor, such as time (called the "independent variable" in math parlance). The Y axis shows the value of whatever you're measuring as it changes with the X variable—time in this case (this is, the "dependent" variable). The Y axis can represent almost anything—numbers, dollars, and percentages—whatever is the most meaningful way to measure and convey the element.

That's enough mathematics, for now. You want to "knock them dead," not be bored to death by math, right? The following list presents some effective uses of charts.

- **When charts should be used.** There is no hard and fast guideline for using a chart. Typically they are used in the body of a presentation to show something important that can be represented by numbers. Charts are a visual substitute for data. They can denote key things about the data—particularly trends and comparisons. You can use this to think backwards. If there *is* a key trend or comparison worth highlighting, then consider using a chart. A good chart, like any other picture, can be worth a thousand words.
- **Don't get carried away.** We see people come in with forty-slide presentations, in which all but the title slide and closer are graph slides. Too much! The mind can absorb only so much, and only so much is important anyway! It doesn't make sense to chart the temperature of the conference room! The three-to-seven rule comes into play here, too.

A good presentation can usually be built around three charts, maybe a few more, maybe only one. It's better to have the *right* points and the *right* charts than to have lots and lots of charts. Having said that, keeping a series of charts as *backup* material is just fine. A very high-impact chart can sometimes be used as an opener. Be careful not to make it too complex or vulnerable to questions and comments, which could throw you off the track right out of the starting blocks.

- **Right type of chart.** Once you've decided to use a chart, it's important to choose the right *type* of chart. Modern software packages include all kinds of variations, combinations, and 3D versions of charts. It's a good idea to experiment with them as you develop your presentation repertoire. Here, we'll stick to the basics:
  - Line charts are the most basic, fundamental type of graph, familiar to all with at least high school math. Line charts are best to show trends, but can also show comparisons or comparisons of trends. (See Figure 5-7.)
  - Normal bar or "column" chart. Bar charts are mainly comparison charts but can also show trends. Bar charts show a vertical bar for each point on the X axis. Comparative bar charts show side-by-side bars for multiple variables—Widget A and Widget B, for example. (See Figure 5-8.)
  - Pie charts. Pie charts are composition charts, showing the breakdown of a variable. Sales by region, total sales, and sales by product all belong in pie chart territory.
  - Stacked bar charts are good for showing composition, totals, and trends. A stacked bar has, in each bar, several variables separated out as separate portions of the bar. The cumulative total is represented by the total height of the stacked bar. You can see trends in the total, and if you look carefully, trends in the composition of each bar.

Again, there are many, many variations and possibilities within the universe of chart types.

Chart Musts

There are a few "must-do" things in charts. These seem simple, but it's amazing how often they are overlooked or done incorrectly. When done correctly, graphs add "knock-em-dead" power—but as you'll see, when important things are done wrong, your presentation is what gets "knocked dead" in a hurry.

Make It BIG Enough

Sometimes it's nice to weave a chart into a slide with bullets and other elements. A chart makes a good picture to illustrate points already being made otherwise, normally a good idea. But frequently the graph is so small that the audience can't make out important details, such as line or axis labels. Sometimes they can't make it out altogether. Do you want to present to a room of squinting, distracted faces? Probably not. Make the chart big enough for everyone to get the point and the key details necessary to understand the point.

Label the Axes

You're just about to make the big point about how sales have hit bottom and, due to your new program, are starting to rise. Suddenly a hand shoots up from the audience. "Does your graph show weeks or months? And what are the sales? Units or dollars? Please clarify." Your shoulders slump. You walk back to the projection screen and point to your graph. "Sorry, this is months, and this is millions of dollars." You step forward—and forget the point you were just about to make. The audience fidgets, and the golden moment is lost. You get the point. Axis labels are one of the most common things omitted or done incorrectly. On the X axis, are you plotting "time"? What are the units of time? Years? Months? Weeks? Days? How about the Y axis? Units? Dollars? Millions of dollars? Percentages? *Make sure the axis labels are BIG ENOUGH to see.*

Scale the Axes Properly

From the audience, you see a straight, horizontal line on the chart in front of you. It looks like market share is flat. But the presenter goes on and on about how the company is gaining market share. Market share looks flat on the slide. What's up? Well, maybe the market share has indeed gone from 21 percent to 26 percent—a healthy gain in most circles. But it looks flat on the graph. Why? Well, the Y axis scale shows percentage—as it should—but the scale goes from zero to 100 percent. It's technically correct, but a five point jump from 21 percent to 26 percent gets kind of lost on that scale, and there's a lot of wasted white space on the chart. Instead of zero to 100 percent, it makes more sense to scale the chart from, say 10 to 40 percent (if you do 20 to 30 percent, some in the audience might think you're overstating your case). Most software programs automatically assign minimums and maximums, but sometimes they don't do it in such a way as to best serve your needs. Avoid too much "white space" on graphs.

Label Your Data

This is almost obvious—but if you're showing and comparing sales trends for Widget A and Widget B, for goodness sake make it clear which line is which!

Keep Graphs up to Date

Incomplete graphs are another momentum-wrecker. You're presenting in April, and your graph shows data through last September. That hand is going to shoot up in the audience again. Either get the data, put a note on the graph that says "data not available" with the reason why, or pull the graph from your pitch.

And How About a Title?

Titles may seem unimportant—especially if your graph is embedded in a larger slide, itself with a title. Still, a good title is important, and a good subtitle can help further explain what's in the graph. Again, the idea is to avoid thought-wrecking questions in the middle of the pitch. It also makes it easier to export your graphs to other media—such as your boss's executive review.

Chart Tips

Here are a few additional tips on constructing charts:

- **Insert text boxes** to highlight or explain key data or changes.
- **Color is great.** But if the chart will be copied on a standard black-and-white copier, colors can blend together. Use patterns or clearly identifiable line point "icons" to keep lines separate. If you can get the idea across in black and white, that's better—color enhancements will only help, but don't depend on them too much. We had to use black and white in this book—so you can, too!
- **Put frames around graphs**—particularly if you have more than one on the page. Otherwise, they blend together, and the eye has trouble separating them.
- **Use spreadsheets as a slide "base."** If the graph is to be presented over and over again, it's usually better to keep and update the data on a spreadsheet, such as Microsoft Excel. Usually the graph can be created right there and exported to the slide program. It's more difficult to keep graphs updated in most presentation programs.

Examples

Let's examine the two chart examples in Figures 5-7 and 5-8. These charts, a line chart and a bar chart, were both created from the same data to show two-year sales trends and fluctuations for two products, "Widget A" and "Widget B." The trend—and in this case, the shape of the line—and the comparison between the two products are important. The line chart shows the trend and fluctuations better, while the bar chart highlights the comparison between two products.

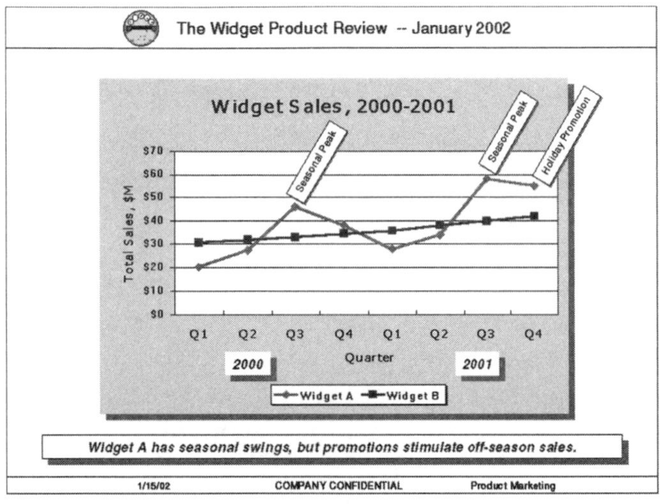

Figure 5-7. Line chart example

Figure 5-7 shows a line chart embedded into a larger standard slide format created for the presentation. Here are a few items and techniques worth noting:

- **Inverse video.** The data field is shown in white against a gray background. This is an effective compositional tool to bring forth chart itself and keep the eyes there. Otherwise, the lines themselves—their beginning and end—are harder to pick up.
- **Axes are labeled.** In addition to the "quarter" labels, "year" labels have been inserted to help "road map" the quarterly labels.
- **Shadows.** Shadows are used on all boxes to give a more professional effect and to help draw the eye to each box. Make sure the shadows are consistent.
- **Callouts.** There are text box callouts explaining key points on the graph, such as the seasonal peak or the effect of a sales promotion. Callouts are good for explaining things, but avoid using too many.

- **Slide format.** Note the header, footer, use of logo or image in the header, and the highlighted "take-away" at the bottom.

Now let's look at Figure 5-8, where the same data is constructed as a bar chart.

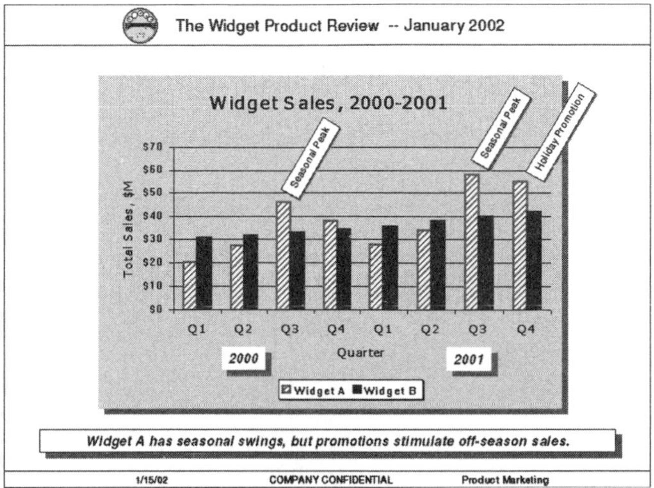

Figure 5-8. Bar chart example

Again, we see the same features as in the line chart. The bars show the trends but, more emphatically, the comparative sales for each quarter. Solid colors were avoided to make the two widgets stand out, even in black and white.

Tables

Tables are extremely powerful tools for conveying, relating, and comparing pieces of information. Rule of thumb: If you can use a table effectively, do it!

Tables are simply row-and-column constructs for listing and comparing data or knowledge. They can be shown with separating grid lines, like a miniature spreadsheet, or they can be formatted as simple rows and columns of words, numbers, or phrases. Here are a few points to keep in mind about tables:

- **Keep them modest in size.** We mean "table," not spreadsheets. Showing bloated spreadsheets will kill presentations. Good tables are five by five—five rows and five columns—or smaller.
- **Use bullet points, phrases, or numbers**—not sentences. Tables are a concise way to show information, so wordy sentences inside the cells defeat that purpose—and are usually too small to see anyway.

- **Clearly identify headings.** If you fail to identify the top and side headings, they will look as if they are part of the table—the data being compared.

There are many ways to use tables—the list of possibilities is almost infinite. Some of the more straightforward and popular uses for tables are the following:

- **Before/after comparisons.** Line up a group of attributes, top to bottom, and show how they behave before and after the change you want to make.
- **Advantages/disadvantages.** For a group of items, show the advantages and disadvantages of each.
- **Is/should be/action.** For a group of items or attributes, show in Column 1 what it is or how it is performing. In Column 2, show what is should be or should have been. In Column 3 (if necessary), show the difference, and in Column 4, the corrective action you are recommending.

Figure 5-9 shows a simple table—one that compares types of charts—embedded into a presentation slide. Note the clear delineation of titles (across the top with shading, along the side with a line), the use of bullet points, and the use of different text styles and centering to further separate headings from the text. Again, tables such as these are powerful tools for conveying lots of information in once place. There are a million ways to prepare and use them.

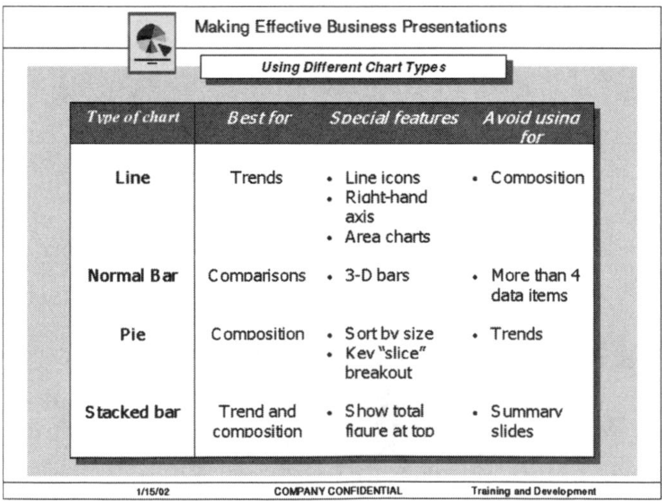
Making Effective Business Presentations
Using Different Chart Types

Type of chart	Best for	Special features	Avoid using for
Line	Trends	• Line icons • Right-hand axis • Area charts	• Composition
Normal Bar	Comparisons	• 3-D bars	• More than 4 data items
Pie	Composition	• Sort by size • Key "slice" breakout	• Trends
Stacked bar	Trend and composition	• Show total figure at top	• Summary slides

1/15/02
COMPANY CONFIDENTIAL
Training and Development

Figure 5-9. Table example

Grids

A grid is basically a hybrid of a table and a graph—a table with scale, so to speak. Grids, particularly the standard quadrant grid, are standard tools of business consultants worldwide. Quadrant grids "position" data or concept elements up into four squares according to the scale on the horizontal and vertical axis. The best way to show this visual aid is, logically, with a visual aid.

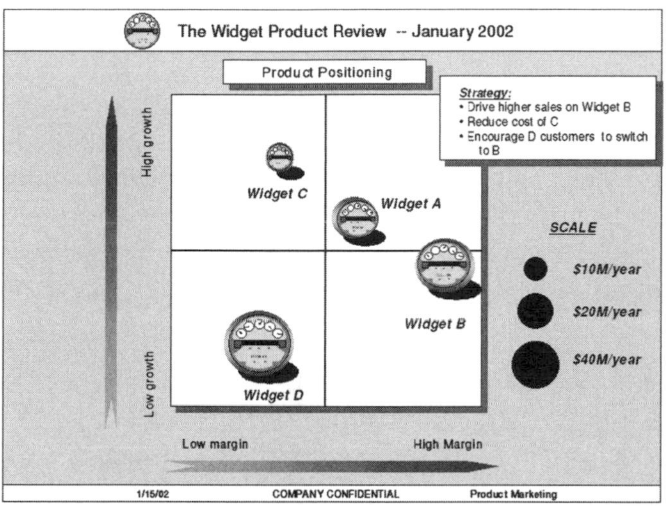

Figure 5-10. Quadrant grid example

A *lot* of things are happening in this high-impact product positioning slide! Admittedly, it gets close to being too much happening—this is where your experience and sound judgment come in! First, we observe the four-quadrant grid. In this example, profit margin is shown on the horizontal axis, with margins increasing as you move to the right. On the vertical axis, growth (sales growth—label this specifically if not obvious to your audience) is shown, with the highest growth at the top. Then the four widgets are placed, using symbols, where they fall on these combined axes. You can use specific numbers or "gut feel" to place the points, in this case, the four widget products.

But that's not all. Note that each widget "icon" is a different size. What does that represent? It's the size of the business represented by that widget, in millions of dollars. A key at the lower right shows the scale. (Again, more detail might be required for an unfamiliar audience—ten, twenty million of *what.*) Finally, a highlighted box shows the marketing strategy for widgets, based on the above chart. You could go even further to show directional movement, with arrows, perhaps from the location at the last review. Note that you could have used a simple table to show the same information.

Product	Growth	Profit Margin	Annual Sales
Widget A	High	High	$20M
Widget B	Medium	Very high	$40M
Widget C	High	Low	$10M
Widget D	Low	Low	$50M

Figure 5-11. Grid information in table format

This table would have done the job, but the key comparisons are more easily retrieved from the grid. It has more impact. This sort of grid can be used for all kinds of comparative presentations—this format is a favorite for showing competitive positioning, for example. And as mentioned above, it is a favorite of professional business consultants, who probably create the most high-impact—and expensive looking—presentations of all.

Shapes

Now we move on to the little stuff. That includes anything from the whole-slide visuals to the little building blocks that can help make a pitch work or spice it up to make it more attention-getting. The discussion of shapes is fairly straightforward: you use squares, circles, or triangles to house data and convey ideas. Loosely described, triangles imply direction or relationships between large (base) and small (top). Squares imply factual information, diamonds imply decisions, and circles imply processes or nodes (stopping points) in a process. Here are a few pointers:

- **Don't use too many shapes.** You don't want your slide to look like the floor of a nursery.
- **Inverse video works.** We don't like to use inverse video on whole slides, but white or light text inside a dark shape is effective. Test to make sure text is visible when projected and printed.
- **Think about connectors.** Especially when documenting a process, shapes should be connected. Use connecting lines and arrows when appropriate (Microsoft PowerPoint offers a particularly useful set of connecting tools under "AutoShapes").
- **Use shadows.** Shapes come to life when shadowed, or put into 3D, or when given a background. Use shadows consistently, but don't overdo it.
- **Use metaphors.** Certain "specialty" shapes convey their own meaning. One of our favorites is the set of puzzle pieces found in most

presentation packages. Each of your slides or points can be assigned a specific puzzle-piece icon. Then, at the end, you illustrate the puzzle pieces fitting together into a useful whole (see Figure 5-12). Again, image helps convey thought.

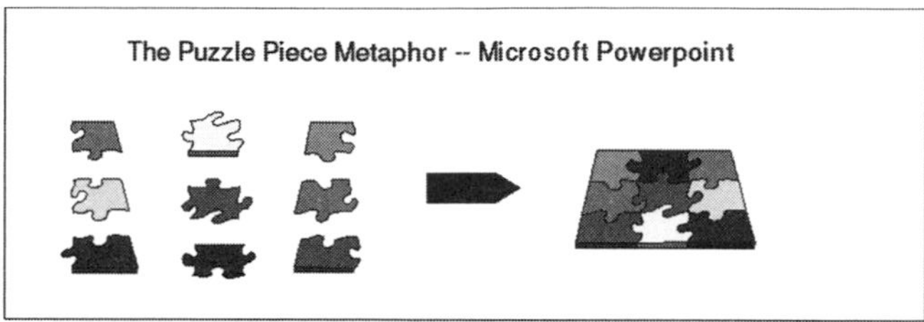

Figure 5-12. Puzzle piece metaphor—Microsoft PowerPoint Icons

The puzzle pieces just introduced under "shapes" are but a minute sample of the drawings, images, and doo-dads available in the form of clip art. Most presentation software contains a standard set of clip art. A trip to the software store yields dozens of inexpensive packages to expand clip art libraries. Some of this clip art can be used to better illustrate or communicate ideas—pictures of computers, phones, documents, vehicles, buildings, and other things you'll see in the business environment. Some convey human actions or feelings, and some are really just for fun.

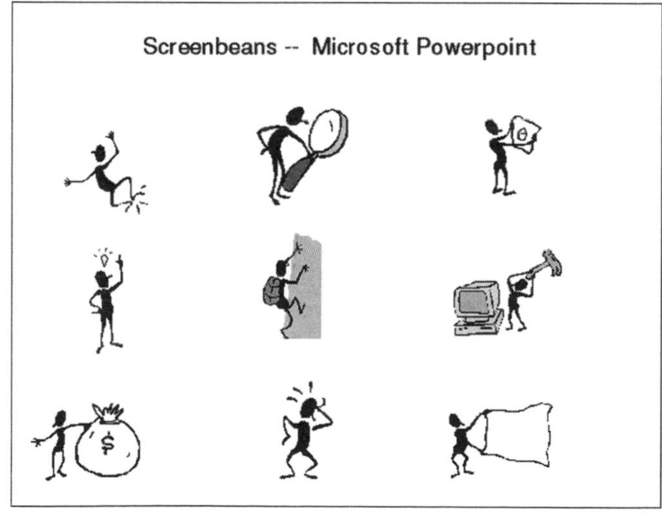

Figure 5-13. Screenbeans—Microsoft PowerPoint

You'll develop your own favorites over time. In Figure 5-3, we introduced a "screenbean"—that little guy kicking up his heels in delight at the thought of a customer rewards program. These screenbeans come from Microsoft PowerPoint clip art. One per slide or per point can work well to convey or reinforce an idea and to establish rapport with the audience. However, if you're presenting your company's misfortunes to a group of angry stockholders or security analysts, they might not be such a good idea. As with all else in the making and presenting of visual aids, don't get carried away.

Logos

As demonstrated in a few places already, we like the use of logos in a presentation, where they are appropriate. These logos can be company logos, and they can be your own. Company logos may be available internally, or you can get them yourself off your computer screen or from the Internet. You can create your own logos for your projects, programs, products (if there isn't already one in the marketplace), or your department. These created logos add impact. They also accomplish an internal branding that can serve you well and give your slides a more professional look. Again, don't get carried away.

Callouts and Connectors

Callouts are useful to highlight or describe an important point in more detail. We used callouts to explain the "sample slide" in Figure 5-5. Most contemporary software program have callouts, or you can draw your own.

Backgrounds

We've also talked about backgrounds. Neutral backgrounds, such as the light solid-fill boxes we used to bring the charts and tables out more clearly in Figures 5-7 through 5-10, work very effectively. We find the more intricate computer-screen backgrounds available in most software packages to be distracting, harder to read, and harder to reproduce in hard copy—so stay away unless you have a clear rationale for using them.

Copying and Linking Images

Modern business desktop software has evolved to the point that word processing, graphics, and spreadsheet programs all work together reasonably well. Microsoft Office and Lotus SmartSuite are two popular examples. Integration affords many benefits, particularly if you give regular or repeated *update* presentations. You can maintain a data table and create a graph in

Microsoft Excel, for example, and place a copy of the graph and/or part of the data table in your presentation slide. Every time you update the Excel worksheet (really, a database), the resulting graph or excerpt in your slide presentation is updated automatically. Likewise, you can maintain a table in Excel or Microsoft Word and have it update *automatically* in your presentation. If you're giving the monthly production review, all you need to do is update your spreadsheet. Your slides will update automatically.

Here's how to do it. Simply highlight the object (chart, table, spreadsheet cells) in the source program or application. "Copy" it, then open your slide presentation, find the spot, and do "Paste Special." Identify the object type (for example, "Microsoft Excel Spreadsheet Object," or "Microsoft Word Document Object"), and then check the "Paste Link" box. The object will be copied, and all updates in the source program will be automatically and instantly carried over into your presentation.

Copying Screens and Web Pages

Simple, powerful tools are available to capture, or "snag," images right off your computer screen. These tools give you immense power to create images, particularly if you're working with material sourced from the Internet. Essentially, these programs allow you to draw a box around whatever is on your screen and create a bitmap or JPEG file to save and copy into your presentation. Those "picture" images, in turn, can be sized and shaped as you wish on your slide. You can snag an entire Web page or anything you want from it, such as a photograph, logo, text blurb, or any other image object, and have it in your presentation in less than a minute.

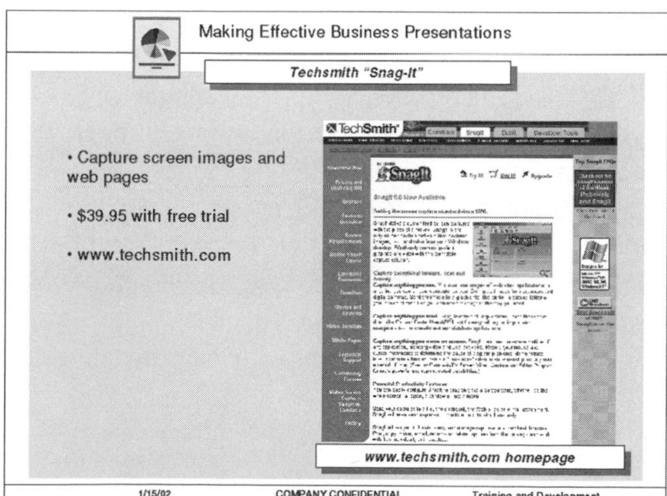

Figure 5-14. Screenshot and logo added to slide

Snagging is a great way to add images to the body of a slide or a simple logo to the header. If you need an example of a Web page for your pitch, this tool is indispensable. (Live Web pages are difficult to manage in presentation settings!)

Several packages are available. We'll recommend Snag-It, actually a software development tool provided by a company called Techsmith (*www.techsmith.com*). A trial download is available for free, and the package can be maintained and updated for a small fee ($39.95). Don't let the fact that the package comes from the software development world fool you—it is extremely easy and straightforward to use.

Animation 101

If your company or business is a laptop-and-projection shop, by now you've probably seen animated presentations. New slides are "uncovered" with a right-to-left "wipe" or emerge as a series of random squares like a Windows screensaver. Bullet points or objects come up one at a time, as the presenter talks. Pretty neat stuff—how do you do that?

Frankly, in a two-dimensional black-and-white paper medium, it's hard to demonstrate the full capability of animation. And we'll warn you right now that it's easy to get carried away with animation. Stuff dancing in from all directions, with explosions or firehouse sound effects—who needs all of those distractions? We suggest using simple right-to-left bullet or object animation, with *dimming* (faint images left on screen) for objects already covered. Each slide starts with a header and footer and blank body. Click the mouse, and your first bullet or object (such as a chart) appears from the left side of the screen. You talk about it and click again. The first object is "dimmed"—faded to a background gray or blue color (your choice). The next object is brought forward in full color. The process is repeated until you reach the end of the slide.

How do you do this? In PowerPoint, this is done through "Slide Show," then "Custom Animation." For each slide, a list of the objects is shown—you highlight the objects you want "animated" and arrange the sequence. Check the "dimming" box. Then save the presentation. Select "Slide Show," "View Show" to run the animation. You should do this several times *before* the show to get comfortable with the effect and the sequence.

Using simple animation accomplishes some worthwhile goals:

- **It provides visual cues** to you and the audience.
- **It helps pace you and the audience.**

- **It prevents audience eyes from wandering** forward to points or topics not yet discussed.
- **It helps make or clarify transitions.**
- **It makes the presentation livelier.**

Again, we caution against the overuse of this tool.

A Few Words About Color

Color can be a powerful tool for making a presentation and its content stand out. Color helps attract the audience to information and is almost expected—to the point that when you see a well-tuned monochrome presentation, such as a black-and-white photograph, that stands out. The main idea of color is to liven up the presentation and to capture attention and create memory. Ask yourself—what would get your attention? What would cause you to remember something?

Color is great, but it shouldn't be too complex or "loud." For practical reasons, such as making copies of your presentation, color choice needs to be simple. It should be possible to get your point without color at all. Color evokes moods and emotions. These can be different for men, women, different people—all kinds of research has gone into that. Symbolism is sometimes useful—green for money or affirmative meaning (go); red for debt, emergency, stop, or excitement; black, blue, or gray for stability. Subtle palettes convey sophistication and richness grays, gray-greens, gray-blues, gray-browns. And naturally, your company colors or color palette should be used when possible. If you work for "Big Blue" (or are doing business with them), then use their grey-blue color where it makes sense. Be careful about using color when you're unable to present in color, and be careful about using color in backgrounds where the color might blend in too much with colors in your highlights (purple on lavender just doesn't work) or when copies or printouts will be made of your pitch.

And About Other Media

So much of this chapter has been spent on slides and the creation of slide presentations that you might think there's no other way to craft or deliver visual aids. While slides are becoming more and more the universal norm in business, other media are still important—if nothing else, they add variety and help in those ticklish situations where the projection system fails to work! We'll talk about flip charts, blackboards, and white boards, and the most "real" visual aid of all—the physical example!

Flip Charts

Flip charts probably had their heyday in the 1950s and 1960s, when people first started to travel to give sales and similar presentations and before the advent of computers and convenient transparency viewing systems. Flip charts can still be a powerful medium. What's nice about flip charts is that they can be used to lead—and record—a discussion (more in Chapter 6). Particularly for more participative presentations—or where capturing feedback is important—flip charts can be an excellent tool. Flip charts are also handy outside the traditional, electricity-supplied conference room. Are you giving a presentation outdoors to a group of contractors or construction workers? If so, you'd better not count on your laptop system.

The rules for constructing flip charts are similar to slides except that greater simplicity and focus on legibility (size and neatness) is required. You don't need a header and footer, and the less you have to repeat from one page to the next, the better. For obvious reasons, images need to be kept simple. The larger the audience, the simpler and the larger the lettering that is required. You can do a little more if you're constructing your pages with a computer and large printer or plotter, and still more if there's a physical handout to go with your flip charts. Be aware that most flip chart setups don't allow you to easily resequence once the sequence is set.

Flip charts can be a handy diversion from the traditional slide-based norm. If you're working with an audience that will have already seen six hours of back-to-back slide shows, the change to flip charts can be welcome relief.

Black (and White) Boards

The use of blackboards—and their evolved descendants, the dry-erase "white" board—can also be quite effective. Many of the principles discussed with flip charts also apply. White boards are the best tools for interactive presentations, where audience comments or feedback are to be captured. White boards also allow the presenter to control the presentation flow in a way similar to slide animation—writing one point on the board at a time and talking about it. White boards work well for unprepared or "impromptu" situations. They also are the best medium when a substantial amount of detail needs to be in view all at once, such as a complex system design. For this type of presentation, it's a good idea to show up long before your presentation and carefully draw your pitch on the board. The audience will be yours from the minute they walk into the room. Watch out for the common white board "gotcha"—using permanent markers on a white board instead of the intended dry-erase variety. You'll get a laugh from the audience but a mess to deal with later.

Physical Examples

There can be no example like a good physical example. Physical examples appeal most strongly to the senses and thus to the memory as well. If you can pass around the "Widgetcruncher" under discussion so that people can see it, feel it, touch it, smell it, and so forth, you've done the most to deliver an indelible image. Real things are the best examples—if you're talking about a chocolate chip cookie recipe, pass some cookies out to the audience. You'll hit all five human senses broadside, they'll remember it, and it will do wonders for your rapport (cookies are sometimes a good idea even if they aren't the topic of your presentation). With physical examples, recognize that they can be distracting—if your audience is passing something while you're talking, eyes will wander toward the object and away from you. Often it's better just to hold it up in front of the audience. Examples kept behind wraps—behind a curtain or under a sheet for revelation at the end of your speech—can build anticipation and excitement and help hold attention to the end.

Handouts

Handouts are important backup, support, and memory tools for the presenter. They increase audience comprehension and retention. They also encourage your audience to take notes—a good way to increase retention of what you say around your slides. Handouts can also be used as a transition or break between different parts of your presentation, should you decide to give them out in installments. For most presentations, you should be prepared to give a copy of your slide set, or at least an excerpt, to your audience. These are usually printed with multiple slides on a page ("Print/Handouts" in Microsoft PowerPoint). Color is nice, but black-and-white printouts are usually sufficient.

Particularly when using handouts, a good cover slide is in order so the recipient can readily identify your pitch later. It's also important to always include your identifying contact information on the handout. If the handout is used later to review your material, audience members may well wish to contact you. And much like a business card, it serves to further reinforce your professional stature and your name as a "brand."

When do you give handouts? Different presenters handle this issue differently. If handouts are passed out at the beginning, people tend to leaf through them right away, distracting them from your pitch. Having said that, the value of handouts as a medium for your audience to capture notes or thoughts from your talk shouldn't be ignored. And the installment approach, while partly solving that problem, comes with its own downside: the pass-out process can be distracting and time consuming. It really depends on the nature of your pitch and what you're trying to accomplish—and your audience. We'll explore the use of handouts and workbooks in greater depth in Chapters 6 and 8.

Handling Complex Presentations

Almost inevitably, particularly if you're an internal speaker—internal to the organization as opposed to an external invitee—you'll be faced with describing a complex process, business strategy, business change, a system design, and a complex set of financials at your presentation. The success or failure of such a presentation depends to a large degree on your ability to organize your presentation and to create clear, well-organized visuals.

When approaching such a presentation, there are a number of things to keep in mind. The following sections describe some of these important elements.

Think "Abridged"

For both individual slides and the pitch as a whole, think of ways to simplify. You live and breathe the stuff every day—whatever it is—but remember, the audience has only so much cognitive bandwidth to devote to your message, particularly the details. In most situations, your audience simply doesn't need—or want—to know as much about your topic as you do. Where they don't need to know detail, keep it to yourself and make it available on demand. There must be a way to condense that twenty-step flowchart into three, four, or five larger blocks, each of which summarizes the numerous details inside.

Think "Mainlines" and "Sidelines"

The "Mainline" is the main pitch that will appeal to the broadest segment of the audience. These slides contain the broadest, most important information required to convey your message. "Sideline" pitches contain more detail—the "explosion" of detail. Have the sidelines ready, and know when to use them.

If it seems important to satisfy an audience need at the time, grab the sideline. Otherwise, refer the audience member to the handout or offer to confer in a "parking lot" conversation later on. This, of course, depends on who the audience member is (your boss's boss?), the amount of time you have, and the nature of the question.

These last few comments are delivery issues only—and we'll talk more about delivering complex presentations in the next few chapters. The main thing to remember as you prepare your talk is to have the sidelines available and clearly organized. When the audience sees that they are available, they often rest assured that you *have* the supporting information, that you've *done your homework,* and the need to see them will actually diminish!

Think "Callouts and Color"

Complex presentations with detailed slides usually benefit from the effective use of callouts and color to highlight the truly important facts or numbers. Presenting financial statements is a good example. First, they should be abridged—no complete financial statement will fit on a slide. Then, the most important "bottom line" should be highlighted—in color, using bold or italicized fonts, and so forth. Key numbers requiring explanation can be dealt with using highlights. Don't get carried away—any presentation of more than five to seven highlighted facts or figures usually gets confusing.

Think "Variety"

Repeating the same type of slide or visual over and over again adds to audience boredom and anxiety. If you're presenting ten bullet slides in a row, or ten graphs in a row, you can run into trouble. Mix the styles of your visuals. A bullet slide followed by two graphic slides or a graph and a table provides variety and avoids unnecessary "wear and tear" on the audience.

Think "Rest"

Again, the main enemies of the complex presentation are boredom and fatigue. The human mind can absorb only so much before it takes off for a warm, sunny beach. It's a good idea to provide small rest breaks and transitions to help audience minds "catch up" and stay fresh. Good "road sign" slides help signal the transition and get the audience to focus on the next item will help. Pauses during delivery also work. A little humor—a cartoon or quote—inserted somewhere in the flow also help to relieve the burden.

A Few Final Thoughts on Visuals

Visuals are an increasingly important and expected component of professional business communication. Once you could just stand at a podium (or on the rear of a railroad car) and simply talk and wave your hands. Now most audiences, who are ever more pressed for time and bandwidth, expect good visuals to go with your talk. Aided by modern technology, the visual part of a presentation has grown to match the importance of the actual delivery. It takes an exceptional delivery to overcome poor visuals, just as a poor delivery will negate good visuals. Could it have come full circle, as some of our colleagues suggest—where doing the "perfect" pitch *without* visuals is more memorable for its novelty? Perhaps. But don't go there until you sharpen your presentation skills and learn to use visuals effectively.

When developing slide-based visuals, you want to develop a consistent style that works for both you and your audience. Creative, colorful slides with well-chosen, quality images are effective, but there's a sharp difference between "done" and "overdone." If the audience is getting lost in your slides or distracted by your creativity (or omissions), your presentation—and your ability to deliver it—will go downhill in a hurry. The rule of thumb is simple: Stay within yourself, do what the audience needs, and don't overdo your slides.

In Short . . .

Visual aids serve to capture and retain attention, emphasize key elements of your message, and structure the delivery (for both you and the audience). Further, they work to provide a consistent "wrapper" around your work. When used effectively, they can build your professional image, stature, and personal "brand" within the organization. Creativity can make—and break—your visuals. Do—but don't overdo. Always fine-tune and evolve your visual "style" as you build your presentation skills and experience.

Do's	Don'ts
• Build and use storyboards. • Use images wisely and to support your point. • Create a simple, identifying layout and design that "brands" you. • Use company (or customer) layouts, images, and themes when available. • Think composition, flow, and message delivery for each visual. • Use headers and footers—with titles—on all slides. • Make everything big enough to see. • When in doubt, use bullets. • Use tables when you can. • Use callouts and color to emphasize key points or numbers. • Create backup or "sideline" slides for "on demand" details. • Use variety—not too many graphs, and not too many bullet slides. • Remember to use slides as your own organizing aid during delivery. • Make handouts available when appropriate.	• Don't use too many slides, particularly in "mainline" presentation; five to ten is best. • Don't put too much on a single slide. • Don't try to be fancy. Don't use visuals or images for their own sake—make sure they contribute somehow to the message and your presentation. • Don't present complete spreadsheets or flowcharts. • Don't forget to label graphs clearly. • Don't present out-of-date graphs or images. • Don't overdo animation. • Don't forget about media other than slides—flipcharts, physical examples.

Figure 5-15. Do's and don'ts of using visual aids

6 They Really Like Me, and What I Have to Say

The right pitch—given the wrong way—will still fail. Plan your delivery as you planned your speech.

It's time for a transition. We've provided two introductory chapters, then three more (Chapters 3, 4, and 5) that explored the development and construction of a good business presentation. We've covered developing the message, doing the research, structuring the content, and building the visual aids. Everything, by now, should look good on paper, index cards, acetates, PowerPoint, or whatever you decide to use as tangible worldly evidence of your craft and your pitch. In a business sense, you've assessed the market and designed the perfect product to meet its needs. To continue the analogy, it's now time to go to market.

What we're talking about is delivery. Specifically, that means delivering your presentation in such a way as to make the most—get the most attention, make the most impact, and achieve success. You want to sell your product, sell your idea, achieve learning, change an opinion, or build an internal "brand" for yourself or your department. What you do *with* the presentation you've created *on the day of the show* has everything to do with how successful you will be.

Now it's time for the transition. In Chapters 6, 7, and 8, we switch gears and focus on how to effectively *deliver* your pitch. In this chapter we talk about how to customize your delivery strategy—your format and conversational style—to enrich your content and best meet audience needs, and your own needs, on that day and in that place. We'll explore how to achieve special goals, such as getting audience feedback, ensuring learning, or making a sale. We'll explore how make the most of audience interaction and how to plan your actual "talk" for greatest effect.

Chapter 7 goes deeper into the final preparations. In Chapter 7, you learn how to "scope out" and manage the presentation venue ("the stage") to best meet your delivery strategy and plan. Then we'll do the "dress rehearsal"—the *practice, practice, and more practice* to fine-tune your pitch—both the structure and the delivery—to ensure you get what you want. Finally, Chapter 8 talks about what most of us dread the most—what to do, how to handle yourself, and how to handle the audience while you're on stage and actually standing at the podium. This includes what to say, how to say it, how to stay relaxed, how to avoid and deal with problems, and how to make the "golden moments" come though.

Special Delivery

Your goal with any business presentation is to share your ideas or points of view and sway others to your way of seeing. This chapter is about enriching the message you've started to develop. It's about making the message more accessible to your audience. It's about making *you* more accessible to the audience and making the collective wisdom of the audience more accessible to *you*. The result will be a more memorable, and therefore more effective, presentation or session.

One of your first tasks in this process is to customize your presentation to your specific audience. Customizing your work requires a little attentive research, but it is a worthwhile means of achieving the goals of the day. Because you appear to know your audience as a group, and because you have taken the time to understand the professional world they inhabit, your message becomes more relevant and your credibility immediately soars. Recognizing the audience, recognizing your goals, and recognizing the moment will lead you toward creating a presentation format that works.

Customization applies in two ways: delivery format and conversational style. Your delivery format governs the amount and type of audience interaction—how much of your presentation involves you talking to them versus them talking to you or each other. The second aspect of customization, conversational style, concerns the adaptation of your words, tone, and manner in such a way that expands your audience rapport. Done right, customization helps you get your point across and smoothes the flow of the session. Do it incorrectly, and you'll be fighting an uphill battle all the way.

A One-Way Street?

What do we mean by "delivery format"? In a word, it's how you structure the session and how you use your time. Depending on the audience, the time allotted, and your objective, the delivery of your presentation will take on different forms. The question is—how should you structure your delivery? How much audience participation or interaction are you looking for? How much should you expect? Is your presentation best served—and are your objectives best served—by making the presentation "one way" (you speak, with no response or minimal response from the audience), "two way" (audience participation encouraged or required), or a combination of the two?

The best way to explain this is by offering examples. Delivery formats can include the following:

- **Straight speech.** You take the podium and "straight-line" your presentation, beginning to end, with a pause or two for questions at the end. You may advise the audience to hold questions for the end or hold them for the "parking lot"—separate time for one-on-one dialog outside the meeting forum. This format may be either by choice or necessity, for instance, if there is a severe time constraint.
- **Speech and Q&A.** Like the straight speech, this format includes more time set aside, typically 25 percent or more of your time, for questions and answers. Questions can be encouraged throughout the presentation, at specific intervals, or at the end.
- **Speech and participation.** You give the presentation but allow frequent breaks for audience questions and dialog. You encourage and facilitate that dialog. You may offer a few tips on what you're looking for. You may also try to steer the participation toward your end and toward reinforcing the message, increasing the learning, or meeting some other audience need.
- **Speech and discussion.** You give your talk, and then allot substantial time after your talk or at a prescheduled interval for the audience to engage in a discussion. There may be separate "breakout" discussion groups. Discussion time may exceed presentation time. You provide the topic and an expectation for what you want, and you may have a predefined strategy for splitting the audience and assigning leadership to get the best possible collaboration and results from the discussion.
- **Speech and workshop.** Similar to speech and discussion, this format has more focus on execution and results of the workshop. This format is suited only for large blocks of time—a day or more—in which groups can assemble, interact, and work together to address a large topic or issue. The speech may only introduce the topic, "kick off" the workshop, or bring the groups back together to review the achieved result.

- **Training.** Training presentations are usually long (a day or more) and have segments combining the above formats. In fact, with a training presentation, it is usually a good idea to mix formats to avoid boredom and repetition. The human brain is like the human body—sitting in one position for too long will yield adverse results.
- **Sales presentation.** A sales presentation will usually follow a "speech and participation" format, but there are specific techniques to guide what you say and how you say it. We'll give a short summary of what makes a good sales presentation in a minute.

Several variables drive your choice among the preceding formats, including the following:

- **Intentions and needs.** Clearly, your intentions and needs play a big part in defining the presentation format. If audience participation feedback is important to achieving your desired result—whether it means providing information that you need or want or confirming audience understanding—then by all means, encourage and provide mechanisms for audience feedback. You may want to capture what the audience thinks about your topic or how they feel about your angle or "pitch" on it. You may want to use their feedback directly in your work, or you may want to see where the issues and concerns are that you need to address for the next time. The more you need or want from the audience, the more time and structure you should allot for collecting it.
- **Time.** Another major driver contributing to your format selection is time—or the lack thereof. Sure, some of you would like to stand up there all day discussing your topic. You and your message are the center of attention, so why not? Well, the realities are twofold. First, time in business is a precious commodity, and second, not everyone in the audience is as interested in your topic as you are (surprise!).
- **Audience needs.** And what about the "customer"—the audience? Audience familiarity and motives also play a role in format selection. If the audience is totally unfamiliar with your topic, chances are there will be less need for discussion but more need for Q&A throughout to grasp what you're talking about. And some audiences simply feel left out if they don't get a chance to participate. Questions provide a useful—and necessary—safety valve to clear up audience misunderstandings, anxiety, or simply the need to be heard. You can use this to your advantage. The more that audience members are actively engaged in your program, the

	Description	Percentage of Total Time	When Used
Straight Speech	Short pauses, a few simple questions only.	90	Tight time constraints. Audience already familiar with topic.
Speech and Q&A	Time allotted for questions at breaks or at end.	75	Time constrained, you want to answer audience questions only.
Speech and Participation	More time allotted, participation encouraged.	60	When audience feedback is desired.
Speech and Discussion	Time block allocated for discussion (fifteen minutes to two hours).	50	When audience input is valuable to other audience members. When audience needs to be part of decision or conclusion.
Speech and Workshop	Large time block set aside (two hours to the whole day).	40 or less	When audience must reach its own conclusions or recommendations or learn on its own. Where complex issues need to be discussed and concluded on.
Training	Long: four hours to multiple days. Varied formats used.	Varies	Audience learning is the primary objective.
Sales Presentation	Varied formats, participation in certain phases.	Varies	Building a business relationship. Where audience input may influence the ultimate delivery.

Figure 6-1. Audience Participation

more they take ownership of it, and the more they feel ownership for the program, the more they will get out of it and support you, the presenter.

The Audience Plays a Role, Too

Unlike a movie or stage play, the audience can, and perhaps should, play a role in your presentation. Whether that is acknowledgment and applause, a supporting role, a clear part, or even leadership of the presentation is up to you. You decide what you feel best serves your objectives. The best situation is where the audience plays a role that *you* define and want and that participates constructively in your presentation. The worst role the audience can take, of course, is the one where they turn against you and start beating you up for something you did—or didn't do—or because you misread their issues or expectations. Without careful consideration, the audience "role" can easily turn into the latter and destroy even the best-prepared presentation. Audience participation occurs at five levels. You want to decide before you start which of the following levels you want to encourage:

- **Listening.** This is the "straight" speech. Even though the audience doesn't say anything, they play an active role by listening attentively. Even in this case, you as presenter are responsible for making sure they play this "role" adequately.
- **Questioning.** The audience listens quietly to what you have to say, then asks questions at appropriate intervals to clarify your points or introduce new ideas or points of view.
- **Interacting.** The questioning becomes more prevalent, and questions beget other questions. Small "what if" discussions start to break out. People in the audience will speak up, not only with questions but with clarifying comments to support your point.
- **Applying.** At this point, the questions evolve into more of a discussion, such as how to apply or improve on what you're talking about or a detailed understanding of how the topic impacts them and the business.
- **Leading.** Now the participation shifts over to audience leadership. The audience, in a word, takes over. Key members and leaders in the audience ask the questions—of you and sometimes each other—and lead the discussion. When key audience members (like your boss or the company vice president) are leading in a helpful way, this is a good sign

of congruence with your thoughts. You can encourage this kind of leadership, particularly when time allots. When they take over because you've "blown it," watch out. Your goal is to try—without ruffling feathers—to regain control. Be careful about letting the audience lead—make sure it is healthy, constructive, and controllable.

There's a Hand up in the Back

The right amount—and the right kind—of questions and audience participation can build rapport, confirm your expertise, and greatly enrich the outcome of the presentation. But how do you make audience participation happen, and how do you deal effectively with the result?

Constructive questioning isn't always easy to achieve. It seems like when you want the audience to ask questions, they all sit there in stone-cold silence observing the second hands on their wristwatches. Other times, as you race against a time constraint to get your point across or to get through a complex point, hands shoot up and voices ring out everywhere. How do you manage this to your benefit? The following sections describe a few keys to making questions and audience participation constructive.

Set Time Aside

This one is obvious but often forgotten. If you anticipate—or desire—questions, make sure you leave ample time to make it happen. You don't want questions to consume the valuable time you need to make points, and you don't want your closer to happen in a last-minute rush or to be left out completely. And you don't want to skip or gloss over audience questions. That can frustrate the audience. Worse yet, it can damage your credibility, and it can leave important observations and "gems" from the audience undiscovered. A good rule of thumb is to make at least 25 percent of your allotted time available for questions and participation. More is better. (Obviously it doesn't make sense, in a half-hour pitch, to talk for five minutes and throw the whole thing open for questions.) Your judgment is required, and it's best to err on the high side.

At The End, or Along the Way?

How best to handle audience questions is a topic of ongoing conversation with all presenters and public speakers, and opinion is pretty evenly divided.

On the one hand, many experts think all questions should be held until the end of the presentation. They feel questions ruin your rhythm and throw you off track and are a distraction for most of the audience, too. This approach is inarguably the cleanest and easiest way to handle questions.

On the other hand, there are almost as many experts who feel that you achieve greater audience participation if you allow questions during the body of your presentation. They feel audience questions increase attention and generate a more active involvement with the subject matter, helping people absorb more of your message. Both approaches work; both approaches are acceptable. The approach you should take is affected to a degree by certain factors—your purpose, time allotted, the topic, and the audience itself. If the topic is complex, questions held to the end might be confusing. They are better dealt with at the "golden moment," which means you should set time aside during the body.

Set Expectations

Let the audience know up front, under no uncertain terms, that questions are possible or even encouraged. If you are going to ask the audience questions during your talk, let them know that, too. If you plan question breaks or wish to have questions held to the end, let the audience know in your opener that's what you'd like to do. When people know what's coming, they can adjust their actions accordingly. But remember to be flexible. If there are strong indications up front that the audience wants to participate more than you thought, do what you can to try to accommodate that. Remember who the customer is.

Think Possible Questions Through Beforehand

As you might suspect, it isn't such a great idea to solicit questions, then not be able to answer them! In Chapter 8, we explore the mechanics of how to best handle questions "on stage." The point here is that if you encourage or expect questions, you should be prepared to answer them. Know your stuff, *anticipate* what the audience might want to know, and prepare backup materials as slides or handouts to support your answer, particularly if it's complex. And be prepared if the question is off-topic or if it involves detail not of general interest to the audience to deflect the question to another time or venue, such as a post-meeting phone call or "parking lot" discussion.

Some presenters have very effectively used the technique of anticipating questions and preparing materials that show the question with its answer. This is the well-known "frequently asked questions" or "FAQ" session. Audience questions get answered, and you get a chance to show the audience your level of preparation and understanding of their needs. Further, you avoid unnecessary interruptions and can dedicate valuable Q&A time to the new material.

Remember, You Can Ask Questions, Too

You can also ask for audience comments on your subject matter. This will get people to share their knowledge and give them the opportunity to participate. The result is that the participant has ownership in the success of the program. You could try an approach like, "We were talking about the challenges of regaining lost clients due to poor customer service. I'd be interested in hearing personal experiences we may have had in this area." When some people are too nervous to ask a question, they may feel more comfortable talking about things they have done. If you can give them a focus that enhances your presentation, everyone wins.

Audience "Plant"

You can also arrange for someone in the audience to ask a provocative question. This is where the time you spent introducing yourself or networking with influential audience members can pay off. It can be a way to get "experts" in the audience to help you at critical points in your presentation. If in your discussions with these people they raise an interesting point, you can suggest they raise it again during the meeting. "Petra, that is such an interesting issue. Perhaps you could raise it at the session. Let's touch base beforehand." Not only does this aid the presentation and its outcome, it can also provide the "safety valve" that a particular audience member needs.

To conclude, we'll reiterate that both the audience's and your professional needs can be well served if you encourage and effectively manage audience participation and questions. Audience participation helps further everyone's understanding of the topic. It provides variety and helps the audience stay focused on the topic. It helps the audience "get things off its chest," and it helps you gain knowledge and insight on your subject and where the audience has issues with it. Done well, questions and participation can really help, and they should be built into your delivery where possible. Done poorly, questions and participation can throw even the best presentation off track. (And if the *presentation* is done poorly, we *guarantee* the questions will throw you off!) It's all about how you design participation into your presentation delivery and how you deal with it while "on stage." (We'll talk more about that in Chapter 8.) Any questions?

OK, Let's Discuss This

In smaller groups, and when you have more time flexibility, discussion groups provide a powerful learning experience. They enable participants to get absorbed in your topic by talking about it themselves. They are especially valuable in identifying problems and solutions and in skill development. Discussions are normally planned, but they can also be created on the fly or "impromptu" if audience needs dictate and time allows it.

It isn't necessary to be on stage all the time to become a successful business presenter. Your primary goal is for people to learn from the experience. If they gain from interaction with their peers, you still win from having facilitated the process; you are seen not only as a speaker but as a leader and team builder.

Discussion groups are only practical with smaller audiences. Even a ten-minute discussion group takes at least twenty minutes to administer, and there is diminished impact if the important points made in each group are not shared with the audience as a whole. That means you also need to bring the smaller discussion groups back into the whole and then take the time to hear their findings. As a rule of thumb, a productive discussion group takes at least thirty minutes of your presentation time, and at that it is only when run with a firm hand.

Discussions are designed and executed in a variety of ways. You can have an open discussion with an entire audience, or you can break out into groups and reconvene with answers. The size and design of the breakout group has a lot to do with the results that come out of it.

If you want a discussion or breakout to succeed, you must manage it carefully and with a firm hand. You must clarify the objectives and, as much as possible, describe the technique and format. You must clearly specify the end result. If you want one person in the discussion group to present their findings to the rest of the group, say so up front. You may want to provide helpful guidance, such as, "If I were you, I'd list out all of the alternatives and discuss the advantages and disadvantages of each, then come to a recommendation as a team by weighing each alternative and making the best choice." The more guidance you can provide, the less "wheel spinning" will go on in the group while group members attempt to get traction with each other, the topic, and what you're looking for.

A few specific tips for running group discussions are presented in the following sections.

Plan the Group Composition

Know how many you have in mind for each group. If there are specific names you want in each group, plan that in advance. (And make a slide—audiences like the preparation and seeing their names in print—and will feel more important.) Remember that composing groups on the fly can consume time and create confusion.

Get the Right Group Diversity

Group people who can not only work together but who also represent different interests or perspectives that can enrich the outcome. Put a marketing guy, a production gal, and a finance manager together. Think about (or learn, if you're an outside presenter) the breakdown of job titles beforehand. You may want different job titles in the same group to increase understanding of each other's viewpoints. Very often you want people with a common bond to work together. For example, in a "Hiring the Best Employee" selection seminar, we want managers who hire similar types of people to work together. In the discussion, group members will be working with peers facing similar challenges and with common interests. There is also a second purpose—we want them to experience working together in the presentation setting to increase the likelihood they will work together beyond the presentation.

Think Small

Generally, the smaller the discussion group, the faster and often the more effectively it works together. But you sacrifice some of the diversity you might get, relating to the preceding point.

Be Clear on Activity and Purpose

Explain the time frame, suggest (or appoint) a group leader, and explain the roles of each participant. Explain the desired outcome and how you want it brought back to the team. For example, you might say, "You have just twenty minutes for the first part of this discussion. I want you to talk about the professional behaviors that make someone ideally suited to become successful sales, customer service, technical, or financial professionals within your company. I will let you know when you've reached the five-minute mark. By then you should be in full discussion. I will announce the fifteen-minute mark, and that is your signal to start reviewing your findings and reaching agreement on them. I'll give you a two-minute warning to wrap things up, and twenty minutes from now we will once again be one big group and ready for the self-appointed leader from each group to share your findings. Let's begin, and remember, you have just twenty minutes."

Get the Right Environment

If the group needs white boards or flip charts to facilitate their discussion and report back to the larger team, make sure those resources are available. Also try to identify locations in the room or building (or outside, if it works) where the group can convene without bothering other groups—or other employees who may be working nearby. Make sure there are chairs, tables, lights, writing utensils, and so forth. A clock is also a good idea so groups can manage their time.

Manage by Wandering Around

As the discussion groups convene, it's a good idea to walk around and keep tabs on each group. Know what they are doing. Be available for questions or advice, and let them sound ideas on you. Help them stay on topic and keep track of time. You'll be surprised what you'll learn as you listen in to these very real-time discussions of your topic by real and involved people.

Actively Manage Large Groups

When discussion groups are large or consist of the entire audience, you'll have to play a greater role as a facilitator. With the entire audience, you may also have to or want to lead. Doing so will ensure objectives are achieved and tangents are avoided. In large groups, it is important to make sure all voices are heard—not just the loudest. As leader/facilitator you bear responsibility for making that happen.

Take a Break

Before, and maybe after, a discussion, it's a good idea to take a break. People look at the transition and the change of location as an opportunity to go to the restroom, get refreshments, check voicemail, and the like. Rather than missing important input or doing a round-up during or after the allotted time, you'll be better off getting it all out of the way beforehand. The key to discussions is making sure they involve the audience and achieve the desired outcome. Discussions that result in little more than repetition of the points you've already made serve as little more than time-consuming breaks. Give the audience the help and direction they need, and respect and include all points regardless of their origin. Pay close attention to reports from the discussion groups, and make sure to summarize and document the important discussion takeaways for yourself and the audience.

Get Your Act Together

You'll find over time that audience participation cannot only be useful and required but that it can also be fun. Good, experienced presenters—particularly professional trainers—have found special group exercises and role-plays to be great tools. Do you want to teach an audience how to handle a "problem"? How to handle a diverse group of customers, or highly unknowledgeable or unskilled customers? Create a small stage play. Have a member of the audience play the seventy-five-year-old lady who thinks that the computer mouse should be used like a sewing machine foot pedal. Have other members play the technical phone support or salesperson, trying to give the customer a clue what a computer is all about. Let them have a few minutes to develop a script, then let 'er rip. Not only will there be ample chuckles and guffaws, but the group will learn something. Learning can (and should) be fun!

Such role-plays can be used effectively to play out more complex interactions between people or between people and products. It's amazing what things bubble up that you and most of your audience never thought of. But watch to make sure that things don't get out of hand and that heavy-handed humor doesn't obliterate the learning. Watch for the natural "hams" in your audience—make sure they don't replace the task objective with a personal agenda to entertain everyone.

The Effective Sales Pitch

Most of you, somewhere along your career path, will have to do a sales pitch. For many of you, it may be a full-time job. For others, you may be selling yourself. In many day-to-day business presentations, you're selling an idea or concept, which is largely a standard sales presentation—but you're doing it to a familiar audience or setting. But we thought it would be a good idea to talk about the art of selling and how it relates to traditional business presentation skills.

Good sales presentations draw from all skills presented in previous and upcoming chapters, but they focus on accomplishing a specific purpose: making a sale. They require both specialized content and delivery. The right content with the wrong delivery won't make the sale. The right delivery with the wrong content will likewise put you back out on the pavement.

Time and space allotted us in this book don't allow a thorough exploration of sales and sales techniques. Many, many books have been written to address all aspects of the sales process. But we thought we'd share a brief structure and delivery strategy used in a corporate training program from Wilson Learning, Inc. The approach breaks up the sales presentation into four stages.

Relate

In the introductory phase, the goal is to relate to the customer and the customer's needs and to break down relationship tension between you and the customer. You establish rapport by identifying yourself, your company, and your purpose. You say a few things about the customer and the customer's company that you might know about. You tell a few stories, share experiences, and lay out the premise for your pitch ("tell 'em what you're gonna tell them"). Basically, you *connect;* you establish a healthy communication channel. This phase might take 10 to 20 percent of your time, depending on how well you know the customer/client and what their needs are.

Discover

Once the "opener" is done and your presentation is on track—once, in other words, you've established rapport and earned attention—the next phase begins. You talk about the customer's business and try to assess needs. Better yet, you confirm needs you may already know about. You establish *task needs* (customer business issues and problems that need to be solved) and *personal needs* (what the buyer him/herself wants to accomplish, what personal preferences they have). You confirm your credibility with the customer. You solicit active audience (in other words, customer) participation and feedback all along the way. You summarize the customer's problems and needs and ask for agreement. This stage is a fact-finding and confirmation phase that allows you to move forward with the pitch itself. This part might be 30 to 50 percent of your pitch, depending on how familiar you are with the customer and their needs.

Advocate

Now we get to the actual sale. This section is divided into task appeals and personal appeals that relate to task and personal needs. Here you present the benefit path—the solution, the advantage, and the benefit for the customer. Along the way, you ask checking questions. (Here, too, audience interaction and participation is important.) You may have picked up new information during the discovery phase, in which case in this phase you may want to redirect or change emphasis on some of your points. "On the fly" adjustments may be required. If you've prepared well, they should be easy to achieve. You close this portion with a final appeal to buy the product. This phase is also 30 to 50 percent of your pitch.

Support

You've delivered your "thunder." In the support phase, you openly discuss with the client their fears, risks, and objections. This is very interactive—you let the audience get their thoughts and feelings off their chests. Gently, you try to alleviate these objections and bring the client to your position. You do whatever you can to close the gap between your offering and what the client needs, either in business terms or personally. Gradually turning the audience from listener to active participant and advocate is the whole idea. Careful adherence to this phased approach won't yield a sale every time, but you can see how a carefully planned combination of design and delivery can work together to persuade and achieve a desired result.

	Purpose	Type of Interaction
Relate	Establish rapport, reduce tension	Friendly dialog
Discover	Establish task and personal needs	Active participation, request input
Advocate	Make task and emotional appeals	Ask checking questions
Support	Overcome objections	Discussion

Figure 6-2. Sales presentation format

Speaking the Right Language

Your company has just reported its first loss ever. It caught everyone by surprise. Your company's stock hits the news. It is the most actively traded issue, down three points to $15 a share. A severe round of belt tightening is sure to come. Your chief financial officer walks into the room, smiling and laughing. He grabs a few slides, but before turning on the projector, he starts on one of those horrible three-nuns-in-a-convent jokes. He turns on the projector, and the first slide shows a picture of the beach on the Kailua-Kona coast of Hawaii. "Yep, we didn't make it," he exalts. Do you get the feeling he's just unloaded a boatload of shares and booked his sun-drenched vacation, while you all sit there watching your assets depreciate and waiting for the ax to fall? What a way to establish rapport. What's wrong with this picture?

The fine art of presenting goes beyond just what you say. It goes deeper, into how you say it. Like acting: it isn't just the lines themselves, but the emphasis, the image, the relevance, the timing, how well it connects with the audience, audience expectations, and audience *mood.* In short, *situation counts.* How well you adapt to the situation or conform to it counts even more.

Before taking the stage, you should carefully consider the situation, the audience, and the context. That's because you want to set the right tone, use the right stage "image," and use the right words. If you do that, you establish rapport and build a reliable connection and communication channel with the audience. As we'll explore further in Chapter 8, it isn't *just* the words, tone, and manner that count—it is all the other behaviors and mannerisms you exhibit while on stage. But while your "stagecraft" is mainly an issue on the day of the show, the tone and manner part of your delivery is something you can plan for in advance, hence its inclusion in this chapter.

They Really Do Like Me . . .

Rapport counts. If your audience takes exception to you—guess what? They will probably take exception to your message. We say "probably" because sometimes the "position power" of the presenter or sheer strength of a presenter's position will overcome blown rapport. And sometimes the presenter will be able to "course correct" to get things back on track. If the CFO in the example above brings the pitch quickly down to earth, offers the right assurances, and convinces everyone of his integrity later in his speech, it will still come out all right. But if he had done it right in the first place, how much easier would it have been?

We all like to work with upbeat people. We all like to work with people who show an interest in others and who listen rather than just wait for their turn to talk. We find people energizing who have a passion for what they do because their passion is contagious. The behaviors that draw you to others and that draw them to you are the behaviors you need to develop and learn to amplify for larger and larger groups. Many people are terrified of speaking in public. They are in awe of those who can carry off a relaxed conversation with 500 as if it were happening around their own backyard barbecue.

Yet there is no real secret to it. Good presenters are just people who have learned to take their rapport-building skills from a one-on-one application to larger audiences. They developed these skills at work, using coworkers, managers, one-on-one meetings, and group meetings of all sizes and natures to hone and polish their rapport-building skills. You can and should do the same. Fortunately, you don't have to be a smooth-talking politician or evangelist to sway others to your point of view. (Although studying speakers like that certainly could give you some interesting insights into personalized mass communication.) What you need to become aware of, practice, and amplify are those habits you have already developed to get along with others as part of your standard professional communications tool kit.

The establishment of rapport starts out of necessity in the opener, and it must be nourished throughout the presentation. We examined key elements of a good opener in Chapter 4. Here we'll share some specific skills and techniques for establishing rapport.

Be One with the Group

Audiences tend to favor or side with people who make some attempt to spend time with them, to get to know them, and to get to know their issues. The CFO who spends time in the crowd before giving his bad-news talk on financials at least looks as if he's trying to relate to people. Audience members who observe this give him points in his favor—even if he or she didn't talk to them personally. Mingle before your meeting by phone or in the room, and keep mingling at breaks. You may get something from those you mingle with that helps you, too.

Show Empathy

Audiences relate to speakers who *really* understand their situation, their problems, their work issues and the challenges of their job. Your job as speaker is to focus on them and their needs and to assuage their fears. You can do this by showing how your experience has been similar to theirs. A little humility goes a long way, particularly if you're a top muck-de-muck addressing a group of subordinates or lower-level contributors. You probably should try to recognize some of their issues and express gratitude for their efforts to deal with them. Try an approach like this: "Boy, you guys really had to hustle to get those holiday shipments out." Or you can try: "I'm really grateful you and your team could take time away from your duties to come listen to me today—and give my thanks to those who staffed the phones in your place." Remember—focus on *their* needs—not yours.

Bring out the Positive

Say good things about their company, their department, organization, or location. It never hurts to identify the positive. If the team you're addressing has some positive achievements, a little recognition conveys a lot of understanding and makes everyone feel good. For our CFO friend delivering the bad news, a quick word about how your department did its part to control costs goes a long way.

Share Something That Helps Them Know You

If you're an outsider—your audience doesn't know you or know you well—it helps to tell a little about yourself. Share an experience, a story either in business context or something purely personal, so they know something about you or your experiences. Sometimes it works to share a story about an experience with one of their products or services or a similar one with a competitor's. Or you can tell about a time when you had a job similar to theirs.

Act as if You Know Them

A good general principle is to act as if you know your audience, as though you are one with them, and as if you are part of the team and culture. Friendliness on stage leads to good conversation on stage. Of course, this can be carried too far. Don't put on a fake Texas accent when speaking to a group of Texans—you'll be sniffed out as an imposter upon utterance of your first word!

Show Enthusiasm

"Bees are attracted to honey," goes the saying. If you're enthusiastic about what you're doing and about what *they* are doing, chances are the audience will follow suit. People naturally turn on to enthusiasm and turn away from boredom and negativity. The situation is delicate when the audience is negative and you are presenting something to reinforce their view, but you can still be positive and enthusiastic about what you plan to do about it!

Do It as if One-on-One

Think about how you would try to relate to someone in a one-on-one situation. You would probably share a little about yourself, find out a little about them, use a positive tone, and exhibit empathy, understanding, and a desire to find the common ground. Share your emotions. If you're glad, sad, nervous, or fearful, don't be afraid to share that. Our CFO, if worried about his future in that job, will only make the audience feel more comfortable if he shares *that* feeling.

A Little Humor or Irony Goes a Long Way

A good bit of self-deprecating humor about yourself, your business, your work, or your group can help ease tension, reduce fear, and increase comfort. Humor lowers barriers between you and the audiences. It sends a signal that you're human, just like they are. Jokes are okay, but it is imperative to make sure they are appropriate for the situation. As we said, a little goes a long way—good, subtle, personal humor establishes rapport more effectively than a stupid joke. Too much humor is risky both for audience rapport and for keeping your presentation on track.

Before moving on, we have one final comment. Don't confuse rapport with credibility. Although they often go hand in hand, just because you have audience credibility doesn't mean you have rapport. You may know your stuff, and the audience believes you know your stuff, but you haven't given them the reason to listen to you. You may be telling them something they have to—but don't want to—know. Until they develop an interest in you, and connect with you, your words and message will go right out the window. Likewise, if you have rapport but no credibility, everyone will like you and listen to you, but won't be persuaded in the slightest to do what you want them to do. Establishing credibility helps to establish rapport, but it is by no means a done deal.

. . . But They Ain't Gonna Li

You've developed your pitch, and you're in process of design
But now you're concerned that the audience may not accept y
they will disagree, maintain a different point of view, or just b
uninterested—in short, that they will be hostile. In the business
us tell you, this is common. Business is far from an absolute science. There are few absolutely right answers. Organizational dynamics, interpersonal and inter-organizational competition, contention, conflicting ideas and themes, history, management, and human personality all turn the business setting into a thick soup of potential problems for the presenter. We're not talking just about distractions, interruptions, or nonresponsiveness—we're talking about how to connect with and be respected by an audience who may not be exactly on your wavelength. Audiences may not be against you—they may just be against your point of view. Or they may indeed be against you or your department. Adapting your presentation to these situations is an important element of customization, and they should be thought through in advance. Here are a few words of advice:

- *Understand the context.* You have a feeling—or you know—why your audience opposes you. Why? Try to reason with them, as if you were one of them. It may be something far beyond what you said or asked for. It may be conflicting imperatives they're received from another source. It may be a bad experience that you don't know about. Your support call center won't adopt your program? Perhaps they had a horrible experience with the last program someone tried to ram down their throats….
- *Research.* You're not sure—so find out. Know where your objections—and objectors—come from, in advance. Do a little "wandering around"—in person or by phone—before the meeting. Ask a manager, ask an audience leader, or ask "rank and file" audience members at random. Try to pick apart the reasons. Make peace offerings. Make sure they know you are willing to listen to and address their concerns so that they come forth with the clear picture.
- *Try to put major issues or fears to bed.* If you know the source of the audience's angst, try to deal with it head-on and early in your pitch. "I know you had a bad experience with the last call center program implementation. You can rest assured that I'm aware of the reasons for the failure and the grief that it caused. I've thought long and hard about

how to avoid that sort of problem in the future, and I'm committed to making sure it doesn't happen that way again . . ."

- *Recognize their point of view, and share their concerns.* Similar to the preceding, try to perceive things the way they would, both in your mainline presentation and in the conversation around it. Focus on audience *benefit.* "This new program, once implemented, will be well worth the trouble. It will make your jobs and your lives easier, and I guarantee you won't experience the problems you did last time . . ."
- *Recognize the positive; compliment if you can.* If there are things that your audience has done well and that they hold dear, make sure to recognize them. "I know you're under a lot of pressure, and you may feel that yet another marketing program is hardly what you need right now. But remember, you won an award for being the best customer support call center in the industry last year, and this is the perfect kind of program to expand that industry leadership . . ."
- *Be willing to compromise; be flexible.* People like to buy; they don't like to be sold. And they don't like to have things rammed down their throat. They want a two-way street. They will be more flexible if they perceive that *you* are more flexible. Offer options and choices where you can, and, if possible, lighten up on some of their other burdens and fears. "I know implementing this new program will be a lot of work and that there are some risks. Recognizing that, I think we can drop the bar just a bit on our calls-per-hour objective, or we can go for a staged implementation to reduce the burden."
- *Don't try to do too much.* When people perceive that things are being rammed down their throats, stress levels—and resistance—begin to rise. Make time, prepare to go slow, and give people an outlet by giving them time to raise issues, objections, and questions. Allow time for discussion. Otherwise, resistance will grow to the point where people stop listening. The hostility will pick up right where it left off (or will grow) for the next presentation. If you've ever sat in on a well-crafted presentation announcing a layoff or workforce restructuring, you'll see firsthand the difference between the too-fast version and the slow, discussion-oriented version. If you ever want to see anxiety personified, observe the behaviors of the folks in the "too-fast" version!
- *Don't argue.* One of the worst things you can do in any presentation is to argue. Typically, the argument evolves between you and just one or two

audience participants. It throws your pitch off track, makes else uncomfortable, and we have yet to see where a major disa was resolved "on stage." The best advice when you see an argum brewing during your presentation is to take it out into the "parking lot"—into a side discussion away from the main venue. If you anticipate the disagreement prior to the pitch, make sure you sit down with the likely opponents beforehand. Not only will you avoid the uncomfortable situation, but you might actually get agreement—or better yet, a new *supporter*—before your presentation even begins.

- *Be willing to admit that you might be wrong.* This goes almost without saying. While some presenters are insecure and constantly wondering whether they're doing okay and speaking well, others are so arrogant that they simply refuse to admit that their facts are wrong. Confidence is one thing—it is important to exude confidence before, during, and after the presentation. But confidence and candor suggest it's a "must" to be able to admit that you're wrong. Admitting mistakes confirms your objectivity and your humanity. It will usually get the audience more on your side unless there are too many of them in the wrong place. Whatever you do, don't try to cover up or lie your way out of it. One way or another, it just doesn't pay in the long run.
- *Try to make your presentation interesting and fun.* If audience hostility is because they just plain don't want to be there (ever have to sit through one of those compulsory all-day workspace ergonomics sessions?) your best preparation is to go out of your way to make it interesting and fun. Substitute role-plays and hands-on activities for a dry lecture. Add a few cartoons or funny stories or real-life experiences. Make it shorter—let everyone leave early if possible. Play some good introduction games (see Chapter 8). Have a funny or interesting guest speaker come in (face it, we business presenters aren't *all* fun and interesting to listen to).

The bottom line here is really to anticipate the problems you might have and, through adequate preparation, to do something constructive about them. Audiences like it when you appear to have gone out of your way to adapt something to their needs or address their specific issues. The whole point of any presentation is to get the audience "on your side" and to absorb your information. You can't do that if you aren't willing to bend a little. Recognizing that not all of these issues can be dealt with in preparation, we'll come back to handling problem situations "on stage" in Chapter 8.

and Other Seasonings

ation phase of your presentation, there are a few d work through. (Actually, in our estimation, preparation—it starts with the initial assignment minute the spotlight shines your way on stage— g as you assess the results of your presentation and fore advancing to the stage-testing phase, there are ion in store. First, it's a good idea to *name* your presentation (sounds pretty basic, but often done poorly or omitted altogether). Then, it's important to build out the opener so that you can rehearse and internalize it for the day of the show. In many situations, you will be introduced to the audience, and you have an opportunity to control that introduction to your favor. Finally, it's a good idea to do a final check on language and humor used in the presentation. These issues may seem to be minor, but the right preparation can avoid awkward moments on stage.

What's in a Name?

We know we aren't talking about your firstborn child—only about your presentation. Never thought a name could be important, eh? Thought you could just walk up there, rattle off your opener, establish rapport, and get on with it, right? Not so fast. If you're part of a long agenda, whoever is planning the meeting will want to know what you're presentation is called. "Peter's Pitch" in all likelihood just won't do it. But beyond "indexing" your pitch into a program, names or titles serve well to gain audience interest and attention. They may also serve well to help the audience remember what you said. Finding a good title is probably more important in an external presentation with an unfamiliar audience, but titles can also help focus your efforts for internal, familiar audiences as well.

If the presentation is likely to be given over and over, in different situations, you can retitle each one to fit the themes of each new meeting. Developing a custom title will also give you the focus to customize other aspects of your presentation to your specific audience. When you take the time to customize a presentation, even one you may have given all over the world, it will sound as if you had prepared the whole thing with this specific group in mind.

The first place you should start looking for presentation titles is with other people's ideas. Start collecting and saving meeting agendas for the session titles. Go online and check out the meeting agendas of upcoming association meetings. You can also use any of the following:

- **Use the old reliables,** such as:
  - The ABC's of_____
  - The Nuts and Bolts of_____
  - The Myth(s) of___
  - The Magic of_____
  - _______101
  - Back to Basics____
  - Beyond____
  - The Secrets of_____
  - Do-It-Yourself_____
  - _______Doing It by the Numbers
  - The Commandments of______
  - Excellence in______
- **Adapt popular book, song, and movie titles.** There have been countless presentations on hundreds of topics that cannibalize best-selling business books like the Pursuit of Excellence, One-Minute Manager books, or songs or movie titles, like "Close Encounters with Your Customer Base."
- **Use an action verb,** such as:
  - Win____
  - Keep____
  - Beat_____
  - Succeed____
  - Defeat_____
- **Use a problem that your presentation sets out to solve,** such as
  - "The Challenge of_____"
- **Use numbers,** such as:
  - The Six Rules of____
  - Eight Paths to Success with___
  - Ten Commandments for___
- **Take a question everyone in the audience has asked themselves at some point.** For example, take "How do I make quota and still have a personal life?" and adapt it into your title as How to Make Quota and Still Have a Personal Life.

- **Be challenging and ask a question,** such as:
  - Are you Good Enough with/for/at______?
  - Can You________?
  - How Will You________?

Regardless of how creative—or how straightforward—you choose to be with your title, it's important to think it through. A presentation title is like a book title. It will get the reader (your audience) to pick up a book they might not have otherwise selected, while a bad title won't usually cause them to set aside a book they were planning to read anyway. And it's often a good place to show some creativity and have a little fun.

Getting the Opener Right

Building out your opener comes last in preparing your presentation. This is the only practical way to do it. Your opener is the headline and the teaser for your entire performance. Until the rest of the presentation is written, you won't know exactly what it is you have to introduce. As we've already shown in Chapter 4, the opener sets the audience's expectations for your session. It's the part where you "tell 'em what you're going to tell 'em." The audience comes with questions about the session. They are wondering what it is about, what they can expect to gain by paying attention, and how long it will last. And one of the most pressing questions, particularly if you're an outsider, is "who is this person?" The meeting leader or "MC" usually addresses this using the introduction you prepared. If, however, you end up introducing yourself, and it can happen, you need to give that prepared introduction yourself at the very beginning of your session. In a moment, we'll discuss the introduction in more depth.

Particularly if you're an inexperienced speaker, we recommend writing out your opener, or at least the key points and "lines." The opener should then be rehearsed and modified to get proper length and timing. By the day of the show, you should be able to deliver most of the opener without the manuscript. Openers you deliver with your head buried in notes don't come through as genuine and are less likely to capture attention. They also send a warning flag that the presenter is unprepared. So write the script, practice it, internalize it, and make it as natural as possible. The following are some of the elements of the opener.

- **Acknowledgements.** The neophyte speaker sometimes suffers from the temptation to treat the first few moments as an Oscar acceptance speech, thanking all the people who got them there. Don't give in to this temptation. Acknowledgements should usually be dealt with shortly and swiftly right after you stand up to speak. Some speakers prefer to do them after the main body of the opener, when they will have already captured audience interest. Some will leave them to the very end. A single line will often do: "Thank you. First of all, I think we should all recognize the hard work of _____ and _____, without whom we wouldn't have gathered here today."
- **Rapport.** Spend the right time building rapport. We form opinions about others very quickly. We do it based on appearance, on body language, and on initial interactions with us. Thc audience will react to you on the same criteria. One of the best ways to establish rapport is to be open and friendly and to let your audience know that you are happy and honored to be with them. We discussed some of the elements of rapport-building earlier in this chapter.
- **House rules.** Set the protocol and rules of engagement. Here you will talk about the length of the presentation, if there will be breaks, and how you will handle questions.

  "Our session will run for two hours, so we'll take a ten-minute break at the halfway point [never get too specific]. If you have questions as we go along, please feel free to ask. I will handle your questions in one of three ways.

  - When I can, I will answer your question then and there.
  - You might ask a question about a topic that is coming up in the presentation in a few minutes. If so, I'll ask you to hold the question till we get to that point.
  - You might ask a great question, which for one reason or another doesn't fit into the agenda and time constraints of the day. When that happens, I'll tell you and offer to address it at the end of the session when we know that we have covered everything we have to.

If you are not going to handle questions in the flow of your presentation, the foregoing would end as follows: "Our session will run for two hours, so we'll take a ten-minute break at the halfway point [never get too specific]. If you have questions, we'll have a Q&A period at the end of the session. If you'd prefer, you can write your question down."

Context and Content

Your presentation needs to be put in context. Your introduction outlines the topic of your presentation and the role it plays in the professional lives of your audience. Putting your presentation in context gives the attendees an immediate frame of reference. Let the audience know that in addition to knowing your topic, you have gotten to know them by speaking to a number of them as you were preparing your presentation. This tells them that you have made an extra effort to make your presentation relevant to their needs. You will want to cover the following issues:

- That you are honored to be with them.
- That you know something about them as a group.
- Why your topic is relevant.
- How you will be addressing it and why.
- What the audience can expect to gain.

It always works well if you can relax the audience by making them laugh. That's why you see so many speakers opening their presentations with jokes and funny stories. Sometimes you laugh in response and sometimes you don't, because not every speaker is also a stand-up comedian/comedienne. You would do well to bear this in mind. You already know whether you can crack people up at the drop of a hat, so if comedy isn't your thing, don't try it. It isn't necessary and you aren't obligated. As a rule of thumb your opener shouldn't take up more than about five minutes of your presentation time.

How to Control Your Introduction

The right introduction will increase your confidence and prepare the audience to accept you and your message. The wrong introduction will destroy your concentration, throw you off track, and may make the audience wonder why they came.

Leaving your introduction up to the MC may sound logical. The organizers invited you. Presumably, they know all about you. Right? Wrong. Your name will be mispronounced, they'll name an employer you haven't worked for in years, forget your credentials, and get the title and topic of your speech wrong. In two short minutes, a well-intentioned but ill-informed meeting leader or MC could set you up for disaster. How do you deal with this? It all depends on whether you're an internal or external speaker, how familiar the audience is with you, and how familiar they are with the topic.

If you're an outside speaker, it may or may not be helpful to send a resume. Resumes probably give too much for the harried meeting leader/MC to digest. There's a risk that the highlights won't come through—your professional credentials might be overlooked, while your job twenty years ago working at the local drive-in might come through. The remedy is to write your own introduction—a short, sweet paragraph with exactly what you would have them say. Highlight your position, your *relevant* credentials (including outside credentials, memberships, and so forth; key relevant facts about your work experience; and maybe a reference to your education). Then add a brief "commercial" or teaser about the talk you're planning to give and why you're honored to give it. The opener may or may not be read the way you prepare it, but it will help guide the introduction in your direction, and it will score points with the meeting leader for your willingness to help.

Remember that your introduction shouldn't take longer than two minutes to read, and it should focus on those aspects of your background that are most relevant to your presentation. It isn't necessary or desirable to have the MC read your life history. What the audience wants is a brief teaser about the content of the program and your credentials for giving it. You should write your introduction as you want it read. Remember as you prepare your introduction that the spoken word has a different rhythm and cadence than the written sentence. It is less formal and more direct.

Here are a few more tips especially relevant to the outside speaker:

- **If necessary, help the MC pronounce your name.** "Our next speaker is Martin Yate (pronounced as in "late for a very important date, there is no 's' on Yate"). If you want to add pronunciation guidelines, put an asterisk by your name, and then add the pronunciation guidelines at the bottom of the page. Is pronunciation of your name that important? Of course it is. You are engaged in this entire process as a tool to increase your professional credibility and visibility, and you want people to get your name right.
- **Highlight your credentials.** Make sure the audience is well aware of your credentials. Proud as you may be of the achievement, your introduction probably doesn't need to include your Sunday school scripture prize. Credentials can be specific ("CPA, Ph.D.") positional ("V.P. Marketing") or more generally related to real-world experience: "Peter has spent the last twenty years doing graphic presentations with a world leader in graphic media, Hewlett-Packard." Third-party endorsements, previous speaking engagements, awards or citations,

degrees and licenses, and appearances in publications all help build your "platform." Keep it brief and focused on those credentials that apply to your upcoming presentation. "Josh has worked in his community's Big Brother mentor program for many years, and was recently recognized in the professional community for his ongoing involvement with the ethics committee of the National Association of _________."

- **Give the title and topic of your presentation.** Write into your introduction the exact title of your presentation, what you will be talking about, and the benefit the audience can expect to reap. "The title of the presentation is 'Stand Up, Be Seen, Be Heard.' As professionals in your field, you all know that making presentations is part of your life. It can be terrifying, and when you do it poorly it can damage your reputation. Our speakers today will remove the fear of preparing and delivering effective business presentations, and give you all the tools to knock 'em dead next time you get up on stage. You will learn how to ______, _______, and _______."
- **Finale.** If you want, give the speaker the words that will bring you on stage: "Ladies and gentlemen, let's give a warm welcome to our speaker Jane Smith, with her entirely unique workshop, a presentation that has received raves from businesswomen all around the country." This may be helpful for some MCs.

Obviously, if you're an internal speaker familiar to the audience, and you're speaking on familiar topics, this can be simpler and less formal. A sentence or two will do to usher you on stage and clue the audience in to what you will talk about. It still may be helpful to remind the meeting leader what you will talk about, how long it will take, and what some of your most recent relevant experiences are. You may have already provided this information when originally asked to speak—it's your call on whether this is important. Your experience with certain managers or meeting leaders inside your organization will shape the amount of effort you decide to put into openers.

Here are a few more tips:

- **Contact the MC.** Make sure you establish contact with the MC or meeting leader. Offer to prepare an introduction—or whatever would help make their job easier.
- **Make the MC or meeting leader an ally.** That will help get things off on the right foot and create flexibility to do things your way, should that be needed.

- **Take extra copies of your intro/bio with you.** The MC/leader may misplace theirs, or they may want one to help build the presentation packet the audience may receive during or after the show.
- **Remember that bad things happen.** Even with all your careful preparation, the MC can still screw things up for you by leaving out the most important part of your introduction, getting your name wrong, or, as has happened more than once, introducing you as someone else giving a totally different presentation. Such nightmares happen very rarely, but being aware of Murphy's Law will enable you to be prepared for any eventuality. You can usually set things straight when you start talking—but don't focus on trivia (remember, the audience probably cares less than you do) and don't—whatever you do—appear to be raising conflicts or arguing with the MC/leader. "Thank you, Jim. I'd like to add _____" will usually suffice.

The Right—and the Wrong—Words

Certainly every business professional has a good idea of which words are and aren't appropriate to use in a professional or business setting. Unless the use is specific and relevant—directly related to the point or emphasis of the point—swear words, slang words, and so forth just aren't cut out for business settings. This is particularly true where diverse audiences and varying levels of familiarity are present. The rule of thumb is simple: When in doubt, don't go there.

A slightly more subtle twist, borne out of experience, where we believe you can get into trouble is in overusing of buzzwords. "We can evolve our business model to build world-class capability in delivering seamless, integrated, customer-focused solutions by leveraging our core competencies, creating more mindshare, and driving expanded visibility in the marketplace." Wow. What was all of that? If you dig in, word by word, it all may make sense. But it's too much. Yeah, using all of those two-dollar words may make you look smart and "with it," but too much is too much. People will tune it out—or worse yet, make fun of you. In most business situations, reward is given to the person who says the most in the simplest, easy-to-grasp manner.

Our recommendation: A few buzzwords and catch phrases is probably okay, but it's a good idea to review your materials and make sure you and your slides talk in plain English.

The Art of Being Funny

Humor can be an important ingredient to "spice up" an otherwise dull or impersonal presentation. We've already talked about humor in a couple of places. Suffice it to say that humor can help in many ways—and it can also hurt. How can we use humor? Some of the following ways are appropriate:

- **Build rapport.** Humor gets attention. The right kind of humor, in the form of a funny or even self-deprecating personal anecdote, helps to blend you with the audience and make you one with it. The right kind of humor gets your audience on your side, looking for more, while the wrong kind can alienate you forever. Humor makes people like you. We think dry, subtle, natural humor works better than planned, forced jokes. The more it is in context with the presentation topic, the better. We're not trying to convert you all into stand-up comics.
- **Relieve tension.** Humor can provide necessary relief when things are tense or ominous. "Laughter is the best medicine" is the appropriate expression. But be careful not to laugh at the audience's expense.
- **Liven a dry pitch.** Some presentations are, by nature, inherently dull. A little live humor—an anecdote or two, a funny experience, a droll expression or acronym can help bring a lost audience back.

The tools of humor are many and varied—irony, quotes, funny predictions, funny stories or anecdotes, self-deprecating comments, tongue-in-cheek "deprecations" of certain (hopefully friendly) audience members or departments—can all serve the purpose. If you spend more than 5 percent of your preparation time poking around joke books or Web sites, however, you're getting carried away. Remember: be subtle and natural—*be yourself* as much as possible. And when you get the laugh you want—move on—don't dwell on it or reach deeper for more laughs.

A Few Final Thoughts on "Going to Market"

We're almost at the "day of the show." You've now done most of your homework and have a credible, well-prepared talk to give. You've thought about the audience from the very beginning—its needs and wants, its issues and agendas. You've adapted your material to the needs of this particular audience on this particular day. All systems should be pretty much on "go" now—if the meeting leader called you frantically to say, "Today's speaker was delayed by a snowstorm—could you possibly come talk to us in an hour?"—you'd be pretty much ready to do it. That's a good test of whether you're ready. If you could stand up and do it at an unexpected moment's notice, you're probably there.

We'll leave this chapter with a few tips and final thoughts on final preparation.

Keep Your Eyes and Ears to the Ground

Before the presentation, watch the audience. Mingle with them at breaks if you can. Even before that, call a few audience members to get a better idea what they are looking for. Note all of the cues, no matter how small, to get a grasp on where the audience is "at." Know the situation—who presents before you, who presents after you, what breaking news audience members, your boss, and so on may have become aware of just before your talk. If the guy before you just got beat up for going over time, shorten your pitch a little to avoid the risk, and, better yet, to please the audience. Learn to read your audience and the situation well.

Work Closely with the Meeting Planner

Whoever is hosting the meeting, whether an internal manager or meeting leader or a meeting planner from an external organization, make sure you know her agenda. Talk to her openly about what she is looking for and what you plan to do. Make sure you're clear on things like the following:

- The theme of the meeting.
- Meeting purpose and how the audience/company/organization hopes to benefit.
- Who will be there, and from what organizations.
- How your pitch fits into the overall agenda.
- Who is presenting before and after you.
- Other meetings, before and after.
- Desired tone: formal, informal, serious or light.
- Audience knowledge, expertise and interest, and size
- Your time allotted (be as specific as possible) and time of day.

Remember—the more you know, the more prepared you are. And the more prepared you are, the better your presentation will work, and the easier it will be to deliver.

Work with Audience Leader or Key Audience Member

All audiences have leaders. Some are "position" leaders—as in the highest-ranking manager in the room. Some are "task" leaders—experts in the field or on the subject. And some are "informal" leaders—usually more outspoken people that others simply look to for leadership and advice. As part of the preparation process, you should make sure to identify who these folks are, then make some attempt to find out what their expectations and issues are. By doing so, you may turn a negative, question-riddled presentation into an absolute lovefest, where the audience leader practically gives the presentation for you. Believe us—nothing is easier than when the audience leader *leads for you* and your cause. And nothing can be worse than when the audience leader *takes over* because you're blowing it. The difference between these two scenarios is often a result of the preparation you do.

The Buck Doesn't Stop When Your Speech Stops

Good marketers follow their product into the marketplace after its introduction to make sure things are right, to correct errors, and to decide what enhancements might make for an even better product. Good presenters do the same. When your speech is over, don't simply throw it in the can and start thinking about beaches—think through what you did and how well it worked. Ask the audience or key audience members for feedback. Is this part of preparation? Even though it's *after* the show? You bet. You are preparing for the *next* show.

In Short . . .

You've built your presentation—now it's time to prepare the delivery. You must customize it to fit the situation, the audience, and time allotted. You must decide how much audience interaction you need, and how to go about getting it. You must think about the situation and context and about possible audience difficulties—and how to adapt your presentation to make the most of the situation. A few finishing touches and you're ready to go to the next stage—the stage.

Do's	Don'ts
• Remember, think of the audience as your "customer." • Plan audience interactions. • Allow appropriate time for audience interaction. • Lead the audience toward the kind of interaction you want. • Be clear on expectations for interaction. • Work with audiences, meeting planners, and audience leaders beforehand—and after the presentation. • Make sure you build rapport in a manner appropriate to the situation. • Reinforce the audience, remove negativity, and work to reduce audience fears and tension. • Be flexible and willing to discuss your points. • Foresee "problem" audiences and develop a plan to deal with them. • Write out an introduction for the meeting leader, and write a script for your opener.	• Don't go over time limits. • If at all possible, don't stifle interactions. • Don't force a discussion if there's nothing to discuss. • Don't forget to ask questions of the audience. • Don't argue with the audience. • Don't overuse or force humor. • Don't use too many buzzwords.

Figure 6-3. Do's and don'ts of audience interaction

7 'Twas the Night Before Presenting

All dressed up with someplace to go—never stop preparing for your speech.

You've worked hard—for days—designing and building your show. Or, if you procrastinate like most of us, maybe you just did it all in a couple of intense hours earlier this afternoon. Regardless, tomorrow morning is "showtime." As such, there are still important items to think about as you finalize your preparation.

But you thought you were done! Nice slides, all the right facts, a good message and "spin," an audience assessed. What more could there be? Well, unless you're an impromptu on-camera genius, any stage performance will benefit from a good stage setup and practice. We're not saying you have to memorize a speech to perfection and build a Broadway-quality performance. Nope—here's the real issue: confidence. For most of us, the real issue with presenting is nervousness or stage fright. Where does stage fright come from? For a few of us, there may be a phobia or two in background. But for most of us, it's a natural thing, and it's inversely proportional to the amount of preparation we do for whatever we perform. If you set the stage—the environment—to your advantage and practice your script effectively, nothing will be a surprise or distraction the day of the show. Everything will go the way you want it to!

But it takes a little further investment—*a little more preparation*—to pull it off. In this chapter, we'll first cover stage setup—learning and modifying the physical presentation setting to your advantage. Next, we'll share a few insights on setting *yourself* up—what to wear, how best to fit in and avoid distractions. Then we cover some ideas on scripting and what to bring with you and finally how (and how much) to rehearse the pitch itself. By the end of this chapter you should be ready to walk into that room and confidently deliver a winner.

Environmentally Friendly

If you present often, we're sure it's happened before. You walk into the room, set down your laptop and look for a plug. You see nothing on the table, nothing on the floor. Uh-oh –it's in the wall in the back of the podium. Not what you had in mind—you're a "pacer" and like to move back and forth as you speak. The vision of broken computer parts all over the floor and anticipated embarrassment of tripping over the cord runs through your mind. You start to get nervous. But you plug it in anyway. You turn on the laptop, boot it up, and then grope for a port to connect your video cable to the projection system. Finally you find it. You connect, and all you get is a gray screen sporting the logo of the projector maker. Your laptop is displaying everything just fine, but nothing in the projector or on the screen. A lady in the back of the audience steps forward, does a few things in your "Control Panel" display settings, and *Voila!* Thank goodness she was there, but by now you've almost forgotten what you were going to say.

You put the first slide up onto the wall. Hands shoot up everywhere and shouts emanate from the back of the room. "Can't see a thing!" The sun is shining brightly through the window, and the lights glare brilliantly from the ceiling. It's about 110 degrees in the room as a result of the sunshine and the packed audience (really, it's only 95, but it *feels like* 110!). You, of course, are wearing a three-piece wool suit. You take the jacket off—but there's nowhere to put it! There is no place to hang the flip charts you brought, and, because of the seating arrangement, no way to break the audience up into three distinct groups to do the workshop you were planning. You glance wildly around the room searching for a light switch, and see it in the back of the room. Not sure you can get there without falling over half of the audience (and such close contact may not be such a good thing anyway as you feel the sweat trickle down your ribcage), you walk out of the room to try to get to the rear door. As you leave, the impulse to keep right on going and head for the parking lot is almost overwhelming, but you get it under control.

It isn't usually *this* bad. We admit that, but we've made our point. Look out—there will be a time or two, whether you're an occasional speaker or a seasoned professional—where Murphy's Law takes over. It can get really ugly. Distractions work on your brain and on audience attention. If you look like a fool, you probably are, in their estimation. We think that Mr. Murphy is always there somewhere in the background, lurking and waiting for his chance. But whether he's able to lurch forward and do his thing or not depends on how well you understand and prepare the speaking environment that you will ultimately use.

Know Thy Venue

The trick is—if at all possible—to get to know the presentation venue beforehand. Maybe not as well as your own living room, but you should "scope it out" for key essentials and become familiar enough so that you feel comfortable when you present. And if you can't "check it out" in person, talk to the meeting planner, another presenter, or audience member who may be familiar with it. If you arrive at the hotel the night before, go take a peek at the room before heading out for dinner. Or if you're presenting in a corporate facility, get there early—maybe before breakfast—and ask someone to show you the room. Remember that comfort begets confidence. And confidence is the key to overcoming nervousness and delivering an effective presentation.

Two things bear consideration when examining a room or venue: the *facility itself*—how big it is, where things are, how you *control* the environment—and the setup or *arrangement* of that facility (seating, visual aids) to best serve your purpose. Here's what to look for and what to do.

Getting the Room Under Control

It may seem a little bit pedantic to suggest you go the night before and look the room over. After all, do doctors check out the operating room before routine surgery? Do lawyers go peek at the courtroom? Do airline pilots take a gander at the cockpit? In general, they probably do not. Why would it be different for presenters? Because presenting is a staged performance that takes place in front of an audience, that's why. The surgeon who can't find the light switch simply adjusts his time course, walks around, and finds it before making the first cut. The patient can wait (is *that* why they're called "patients"?). The airline pilot knows the cockpit because all 737s she flies are just like it. Can you count on those things as presenter? Yes, but keep in mind that you, as presenter, have an audience.

What you do in front of that audience counts for a lot, and you don't want to waste their time. You want to appear in control. You want to be in control. And in the presenting world, every cockpit is different. Every seating arrangement, every audio-visual system, every microphone is different. Every room has its own set of sirens outside and steam pipes thumping away in the wall. Presentations riddled with distractions die the death of a thousand cuts, and you don't want this to happen to you. If you're not convinced by now, you will be after having some of the experiences illustrated in our chapter opener.

Following are a few of the things to think about, both before and during your pitch. You should attempt to do all of them before the show. The day or evening before the show is best, but it also works to do your scouting before the show starts. One of our favorites for all-day meetings, if the day or evening before isn't available, is to check things out before breakfast. If you arrive to do a short pitch as a part of a show already in progress, give yourself enough time to scout with your eyes while an earlier presenter is on. Check out the lighting, the location of switches, audio-visual equipment, and so forth. Don't be afraid to ask the meeting planner or even another presenter for insights during a break. Things to check include considerations covered in the following sections.

Room Size

Room size can have a lot to do with how you plan your presentation delivery—and how you may use visual aids. Large rooms (and large audiences) produce special problems with visual aids in that the visuals might be hard to see. If in doubt, you should make arrangements to test your visual aids "offline" to make sure people in back can see. It may involve changing the position or location of the projector (something you definitely don't want to do in the middle of your show), and it may also mean leaving out certain visual aids altogether. You will, of course, have to speak louder and more clearly so folks in back can hear. And you will also have to put more care into handling questions so that the whole audience hears both the question and the answer. You may want to rely more on handouts or copies of key slides.

Finally, you'll run into the situation where you have a small audience but a large room (because that's what was available). You'll want to develop the seating configuration to keep people together and to keep from having to shout just so that guy in back can hear.

Presenting in excessively small rooms presents other problems. An audience in a jammed room is challenged for comfort. People get fidgety if not fully engaged, which generates more heat and makes it more difficult for you to move about as you please. You'll want to adjust to this, and shorten your presentation if at all possible. With many organized meetings, jamming as many people as possible into a given space is always a consideration for the planners. Flexibility to arrange the room as you please may be limited.

Room Temperature

Large groups of people kick off a voluminous amount of hot air (and that's just when they are sitting quietly, not speaking). A room that seems comfortable before the meeting fills up will get toasty within twenty minutes. Look back on your experiences of sitting toasty-warm buried amongst 1,500 peers with a speck of a speaker droning on behind a podium in the distance. You get drowsy and your mind wanders. It is very difficult to keep the energy upbeat when there are snores and snuffles emanating from the back rows.

Before the meeting starts, you need to learn from the resident staff where the heat controls are and who controls them. Opinion on ideal heat for a meeting room varies, depending on whether you are sitting listening, or moving around speaking. If it is warm for the audience, they get drowsy while you get sweaty. If it is comfortable for you, many people might be cool.

From a speaker's point of view, about 65 degrees is ideal; you won't overheat, but it won't be ideal dozing temperature. Now you may get comments from the ultrasensitive, in which case you can raise the temperature just a couple of degrees. Is such a subterfuge acceptable; we hear readers muttering? Yes, if you look at why you are speaking in the first instance. You are speaking because some organization has spent a lot of money or has a lot on the line and is holding a meeting to share valuable information with a large group of people. That primary goal cannot be met with a sleeping audience in the mix.

Frequently you won't be able to control the temperature yourself. But, particularly if you're giving a long program—a training or workshop, it's a good idea to learn in advance who the people are who control these things and how to contact them

Lighting

Lighting is another factor that affects attention spans. Harness that nice dim lighting demanded by computer-generated graphics, combine it with a temperature of 75 degrees, and 50 percent of your audience is off in the Land of Oz with the rest of them fighting a hopeless rear-guard action. Bright lighting helps note taking, and it keeps people alert. But it makes visual aids hard to see. Your job—best accomplished beforehand—is to test the lighting so that you get sufficient lighting in the audience—and hopefully, on you—while providing a dim enough aura to see your projected visual aids, if you have them. This won't in most cases be done by professional stage lighting technicians, so you'll have to make do.

Figure out the lighting that optimizes—or causes the fewest problems—and learn how to manage the room light switches to achieve that balance. If there is simply no way other than "binary" (off/on) to control the lights, keep them on if at all possible. Failing this possibility, be prepared to turn them off at key intervals as you present your slides. Bribe someone in the audience to run the lights for you (you don't want to make constant, repeated trips to the switch) and make sure to give the audience a moment after switching lights off or on to allow their eyes to adjust.

Layout

We've alluded to it, now we'll say it—you should attempt to get the room layout set up to best meet your needs. Now, this doesn't mean calling in professional movers to uproot everything before and after your talk, and your flexibility will be necessarily limited if you're one of many presenters. But still, if audience interaction is part of your plan—especially if you want them to interact with each other—the standard classroom pattern of horizontal rows may be less effective. Many times, a "U" or "V" (or chevron) shape helps provide an environment more friendly and conducive to interaction. Audience members can see each other and talk to each other more freely—without talking to the back of each other's heads. Naturally, if you want to discourage audience interaction, the standard horizontal rows may be best (which is probably why they are standard in elementary school classrooms!). See the illustrations in Figure 7-1.

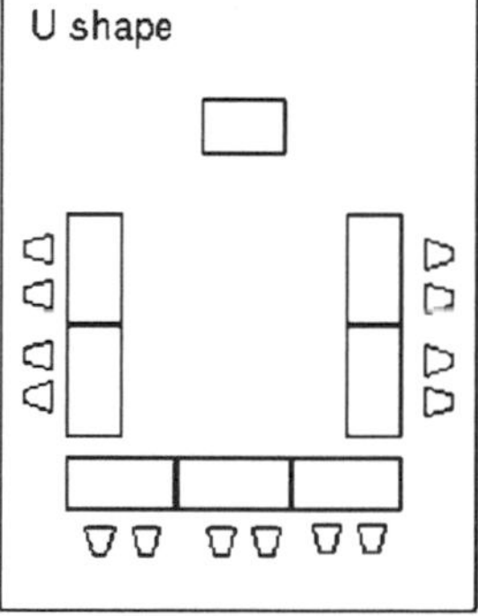

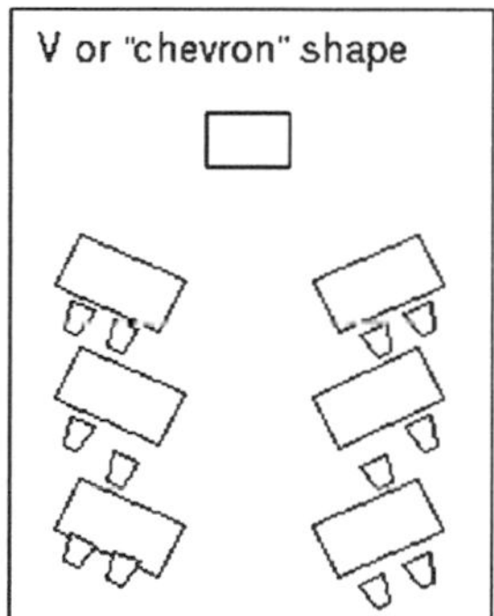

Figure 7-1. Alternative room layouts

Podium Arrangement

This is really part of the room layout, but you'll want to get familiar with the speaker's "end" of the room—the podium and tables allowed. Get an idea in advance how much space is offered. If you're a pacer, get familiar with pacing territory. Also get familiar with the podium or "lectern" (a small tabletop version of the podium) in advance. Get a feel for what and how much you can put on it (before things slide off), what storage it may have inside or underneath, and what controls it might have for microphones, audio-visual equipment, and so forth. A good preacher knows his or her pulpit.

Audio-Visual Equipment

More presentations have been interrupted or compromised because of failed audio-visual execution than almost any other "distraction" we can think of. Slides you can't see, screens you can't lower, projectors you can't turn on or focus, computers that won't work, and microphones that don't work or don't work right are real speech-killers.

Screens

If you're going to show slides—as we assume most of you are—you should try to get a sneak preview of how they look on whatever projection medium is available. If you're presenting blue-background slides on a pale yellow wall, chances are you won't like the puke green color that results (another reason to shy away from colored slide backgrounds). More often, there will be a projection screen. In the more "high-end" venues, there will be a drop-down projection screen. Locate the switch and learn how to raise and lower the screen (we swear each one of these things is different even though they're probably made by the same company), and be prepared to get the right distance between the projector and screen for your presentation.

Transparency Projectors

As goes the screen, so goes the projector. In this case we're speaking of the individual transparency projector (more on laptop projection in a minute). Know how to turn it on, and learn how to focus it. Get an idea of the right distancing between it and the screen to achieve the ideal visual result (size and clarity) for your audience. Check to make sure it turns on and that the bulb works. If you're really preparing, check to see if there is a spare bulb inside—these things always seem to burn out when it's time for your presentation. Learn where the electrical outlet is and where the cord runs so you can avoid tripping over it.

Computer and Computer Projection

It's the twenty-first century, and in this day and age, laptops and VGA projection systems are starting to become the norm in business presenting environments. Yet the complexity and standard evolution of these systems can pose problems for the unwary presenter. Equipment compatibility is the main stumbling block you'll run into. If you are presenting anywhere other than in your own department, it is possible that you'll turn on but not be able to tune in—the VGA settings on your laptop don't go with the type of projector available. Feel like downloading a driver and rebooting for your presentation opener? Probably not. How do you avoid this? Here are a few tips.

- Check in advance what kind of projector will be available. If unfamiliar, get more details.
- A must if possible: Try it out yourself.
- Always—*always*—bring copies of your presentation on one or more floppy disks and/or CD-ROMs. This accomplishes three things:
  1. Projector compatibility problems can be solved simply by using another presenter's laptop.
  2. Other computer problems, such as battery failure or Windows amnesia, are avoided.
  3. You can leave an electronic copy of your materials with your meeting leader or MC (handy for meeting minutes or summary packages later on).
- Just in case—if *at all* in doubt—bring a set of transparencies.

So, here are a few rules of thumb on "high tech" presentations:

1. The more technology you employ in your presentation, the more things can go wrong.
2. That which can go wrong, will go wrong,
3. The more advance preparation or testing the better.

Aids to Visual Aids

Sounds kind of strange and redundant—what do we mean by "aids to visual aids"? Well, it *is* small stuff, but it's still a good idea to check in advance whether flip charts will be available and whether the white board pens are really there and they really work. (We *swear* from experience that those marking pens are always around except when we need to use them—and when they do happen to be available they are as dry as a sheet of aluminum foil in the Mojave Desert!) Check to make sure pens are available and that they are the right pens for the medium (and that they don't leak!). And if you're planning to hang up flip charts or any other presentation or discussion aid, make sure there is *some* sort of system for doing so (thumb tacks, hangars, or tape). Again, don't make mistakes, and be in control.

Microphones

You may or may not run into microphones—depending on the venue and size of the audience. Most conference room business presentations don't involve microphones, but for larger public venues they are often involved, as they also are for larger "in-house" venues such as "coffee klatches" and presentations to large groups of, say, production workers, on the floor. Many people simply freeze when they hold a microphone in their hand—it's the combined notion of additional stage fright (gee, my nervousness and mistakes will be *louder*) and the umpteen million things that can go wrong—too loud, too soft, scratchy, electronic feedback, and so forth. Again, *darn it all,* no two microphones or PA systems are the same! Your best bet is to get a chance to test the microphone and PA beforehand, with no one else (or maybe a colleague) in the room. Get the bugs out, and get a feel for how it sounds and how it projects your voice across the room. If you can't do this in advance, observe speakers on stage before you. And if at all possible, when you "take the stand," try a few sample words or an informal comment or two as you slide behind the podium, just to get the feel. Woodstock-like "testing, testing, testing 1-2-3—number nine, number nine" sequences are probably out of place.

More About Microphones

Unless your audience is smaller than a dozen people and you are in a small conference room, you probably need a microphone. They are easy to get used to and should not be intimidating. If you try to do without a microphone, thinking you can project well enough to be heard, you might well be. But keep in mind—you may be heard as a sergeant major addressing troops on a parade ground.

The microphone is the instrument that gets your message heard while you still get to speak in a normal tone of voice, one that will be able to reflect all the subtle nuances of speech. With a microphone a roar is magnified, a *sotto voce* whisper is more dramatic, and you can use the amplified sound to increase the impact of your message. Without a microphone you have just one voice: full blast, which grates on your audience within minutes; with a microphone your voice is an orchestra.

There are different types of microphones.

- **Podium-based.** This is the standard. All you'll have to do is check how to turn it on and off and then do a sound level check to see that it is at a volume that will reach a packed room. The resident audio-visual professional will have a good handle on sound levels, but do learn how to increase or decrease the volume yourself. The disadvantage to a podium-based mike is that it ties you to the podium. You become a visually boring, static, talking head.

- **Microphone on stand.** Make sure you can raise and lower the mike, know how to turn it on and off, and raise or lower the volume. With a stand mike you are not quite so tied to one place, as you can detach it from the stand and move around. With a handheld microphone, however, one hand is completely occupied and you have to keep it within six inches of your mouth at all times, or the sound will drop off. And not too close, either—you will sound too loud and "pop your Ps" to the audience's annoyance or distraction. Practice raising and lowering the mike, as almost every stand manufacturer seems to have a different mechanism for this process.
- **Lavaliere.** A lavaliere, or lapel mike, is by far the best choice. Inconspicuous and versatile, you can roam the room at will and have both hands free for gesturing, handouts, and pointing at graphics or audience members.

  Lavalieres come in two varieties: wired and radio. A wired lavaliere has the same long, thick power cable as a stand mike, so you have to watch where you are walking and be careful not to get tangled up. However, if you do get tangled up it is always a bit of light relief for the audience and nothing to get worried about.

  The weapon of choice for the professional speaker is unquestionably the radio lavaliere. It pins on your tie, blouse, or jacket and has a short wire to a beeper-sized box that can clip on your belt or go in a packet. With it you have complete freedom and mobility. The only drawback with a radio lavaliere arises in a large auditorium with chandeliers. Sometimes the chandelier surfaces bounce and disrupt the radio signal. If you find yourself in such a venue you will certainly have a resident audio-visual professional on staff who will address the problem for you and if necessary supply you with a wired lavaliere.

Using a Microphone

Your mouth should typically be four to six inches away from the mike, and you should speak in a completely normal voice. You don't want to be too close to the mike or too far. If you haven't worked with a mike before, there is yet another reason to arrange for a dress rehearsal for yourself and your presentation. Do it miked, and use your audio-visual tools. By the time you're through, you'll be more comfortable with the graphics and you'll have ceased to notice the microphone. Test your microphone by talking into it—never ever tap it—and use part of your script. Practice turning it on and off, and make a mental note to turn it off whenever you leave the stage for a break, especially if it's a lavaliere, and you're heading to the bathroom.

Faulty Sound

If the microphone starts to cut out, or if it develops a buzz or a squeal, chances are it will continue and probably get worse. At the first sign of trouble, pause in your presentation and ask for someone to contact the audio-visual expert about the problem. These things happen, so don't be embarrassed: It is not your fault. Continue with your presentation unless things deteriorate beyond acceptability. At that point, see if you can project for a few minutes without the mike. If that is not practical, you might want to consider calling a two-minute stretch break. Two minutes always stretches into five or seven, which is why you don't tell your audience the break is longer.

At the risk of repeating, remember that what happens on stage is a reflection on you. If you fumble with computers or projection controls, you will look unprepared—and that image will spill over into the presentation itself. The audience will get the notion that—maybe—the *rest of* your preparation is weak, too. On the flip side, if you appear to be "in charge"—firmly in control of the presentation tools and venue, this will work to leave the audience with a more positive impression of your speech, your message, and you as a professional.

It Isn't Just a Building

Well-prepared presenters familiarize themselves with the venue building itself and the key services provided. Knowing what services are provided and what things are where will help you avoid midpitch problems and, again, make you look prepared and in charge. And it goes without saying that comfortable audiences are more attentive and more likely to be on your side. It is particularly important to establish this familiarity when presenting at offsite locations—locations that are unfamiliar for you, the audience, or both. A few considerations to keep in mind are the following.

- **Snacks, coffee, and so forth.** Perhaps the meeting planner has already considered this and announced where the coffee and snacks are—if so, good job. But particularly if you are the main presenter for the day—if it's your day—you may want to remind the audience where these goodies are, or when they are coming if they're to be delivered. Audiences always want to know about food and refreshments—never met one that didn't. You have the choice of being their "hero" (and getting attention as compensation) or losing them for half an hour at the first break. If there are no snacks provided, consider bringing your own—subject of course to cost, size of audience, and possible distractions. The way to an audience's mind can be through its stomach—but remember that most business audiences won't be bribed to accept a bad story because you brought good donuts!
- **Restrooms.** All that coffee has to go somewhere! Be prepared to tell your audience where the restrooms are (the more specific the directions, the better—otherwise you'll lose them). Seems kind of obvious, but poor preparation has bad consequences—including when your own biological alarm goes off!
- **Meeting areas for workshops or discussions.** If your presentation involves workshops or discussions—as we mentioned before—it's good to have in mind where these discussions can happen without having groups stumble over each other. Check for available rooms near the main venue, and check to see that they really will be available at the time and for the time needed! Work with your meeting planner to figure out what's right. A small break or conference area or hallway that seems empty the night before could be surrounded by nearby coworkers the next workday—remember to consider their needs for a quiet, productive work environment.

Dress for Success

The moment we set eyes on someone, our minds make evaluations and judgments with lightning speed. In the public forum of a business presentation, a poorly or inappropriately dressed presenter will have an audience muttering to its collective self that, "If he can't put himself together in a professional manner, why should I believe he has anything I can use in my professional life?"

Like it or not, your message, your confidence level, and your overall delivery are all affected by the image you present to your audience, whether that to be one person at a job interview, or one thousand at a convention general session. There are many who say that the respect you receive from the audience on starting your presentation is in direct proportion to the respect your visual image earns for you before you have a chance to say a word. If you dress casually in clothes associated with leisure activities, you may be telling your audience that you do not take them or the occasion seriously.

There is an unspoken dictum in the professional world that a professional look is mandatory to climb the ladder of success, and that you climb only as high as your clothes will allow you. It's not that your outward appearance helps you up the ladder but rather that the lack of a "put together" look will hold you back. Your onstage persona is a microcosm of your entire professional approach to your image and the role it plays in the overall strategy of your career management plans.

Our appearance tells people how we feel about ourselves as professionals, the respect we have for that profession, the respect we have for the occasion, and for each individual member of the audience. In fact, your overall appearance may leave as powerful an impression as your words, as memory is rooted most strongly in pictures and impressions. At the very least you can expect your audience to be strongly influenced by the way your present yourself.

At the same time, the act of putting together that perfect professional image will add to your own self-esteem and self-confidence, which is perhaps the greatest benefit of all. Presenters speak of the time when they are putting their outfits together and getting dressed for the presentation as important meditative and focusing periods, in the same way that a soldier gets psyched before battle by quietly cleaning his weapon. In a very real sense, putting together the right image is the same as polishing a very powerful weapon in your professional arsenal, both for your presentations and in your day-to-day professional life.

But what if everyone is dressed for the golf course or the pool, and the stated dress code is informal? Opinions differ on this one. Some authorities suggest that mirroring the dress of your audience helps ally you with them as "one of the guys." Others believe differently. They say that you are working as a key player at a business event, and formal dress for the presentation shows a respect for your audience. On a personal basis, Martin, from the East Coast, believes in dressing in a professionally conservative manner for any business presentation. Peter, on the other hand, from the West Coast school, believes in dressing for the occasion and for comfort—both physical comfort and audience comfort. Generally, Peter dresses as he thinks the audience would—or just a little bit better. If everyone is in jeans, Peter is in khakis (or in just plain jeans if it's a familiar internal audience). If everyone is in "business casual," Peter may wear "better" business casual or a tie with khakis. If everyone wears a tie, Peter wears a suit or suit trousers on a warm day. And it stops there. If the audience or the more important members of the audience are wearing suits, Peter leaves the tuxedo at the tux rental place—a suit is just fine.

Having said all of this, the safest look is traditional and conservative. Your goal, after all, is to create an image of reliability and steadiness (so that people will have faith in your message as reliable). Additionally, you want your appearance not to make a statement but rather to cause as little offense as possible to the greatest majority of people. This actually makes life easier for you as the accepted professional look is far more limited and less prone to change. You want to avoid distractions; suede jeans outfits or even high-fashion Italian suits, while quite expensive and fashionable, if deployed in a room full of conservative people, may only serve to distract. Likewise, recovering audience confidence and *your own* confidence when you're visibly underdressed is quite difficult—although not impossible if you're good enough to keep people focused on the message.

A Fashion Statement

While men's fashions are experiencing a metamorphosis, a man can still make a fine appearance in a three-year-old Brooks Brothers suit. For women the situation is more challenging. While men can be seen as overly trendy for following fashion, a businesswoman is expected to be current in her dress if she expects to be taken seriously. This is just another interesting anomaly of the business world.

For either sex, this means that you need to give your professional wardrobe a once-over. If a new suit, shirt/blouse, or shoes are required, you need to invest in them. Remember that this whole exercise is about increasing your professional visibility and credibility. Your presentations will always be events when your professional community is focused exclusively on yours truly.

When you know you look right, you can stop worrying about the impression your clothes are making and can concentrate on communicating your message, safe in the knowledge that your appearance is re-enforcing your words, rather than sabotaging them.

Accessorize!

The right accessories can enhance anyone's professional image. The wrong ones can help destroy it.

For Men

The guiding principle is that less is more. Here are some tips.

- **Avoid flashy, religious, or political insignia in the form of rings, ties, or pins.** You may be proud of a particular affiliation, but your entire goal is to promote the professional you—not to be a crusader for your personal beliefs. No matter how worthy or heartfelt, perfectly decent people who could be your allies could be put off your message.
- **Watch your watch.** Your watch should be simple and plain. It's best to avoid Mickey Mouse, oversized, and trendy Swatch watches. Fun as many of them are, they are simply not appropriate to the occasion, and with some people they will detract from the message you are trying to convey.
- **Care for your briefs.** A good leather briefcase or professional satchel adds to anyone's status.
- **Don't forget the handkerchief.** A cotton handkerchief is a smart thing to put in your pocket. This is partly because you will be nervous and might get sweaty palms, but it's also because in shaking hands with many people in your prepresentation meet-and-greet you are sure to come across your fair share of sweaty palms. Do not put it in your breastpocket.
- **Jewelry.** A wedding band is acceptable as are a subdued pair of cufflinks (if you are wearing French cuffs, of course). Anything more is dangerous. It is good sense to stay away from bracelets, neck chains, medallions. Earrings on men are too fashion-forward for most businesspeople.
- **Pocket change.** Seems a little pedantic to talk about loose change in your pockets as an element of building a "knock 'em dead" presentation, but think about it—a pocket full of loose change will shake, rattle, and roll as you move about the stage. Additionally, nervous hands will find their way into your pockets—and guess what? Unbeknownst to you, they jingle away. Distracting to say the least—and at worst, guess what audio frequency microphones tend to pick up the most? Guessed right—just about that frequency that emanates from rattling, loose change.

For Women

Much off the foregoing applies, but women have some other special considerations, as follows:

- **Hosiery.** You must take extra pairs. Laddered hose may not affect what you have to say, but most everyone in the audience will spend at least part of your presentation looking at your legs rather than listening to your message.
- **Jewelry.** Again, keep jewelry to a minimum and keep it sensible. Chains, bracelets, bands, and necklaces will not detract from your image, although a hat with feathers and plumes will. While the more cultured reader will know that Minnie Pearl is long gone, you do still see the occasional woman wearing a hat to make presentations, and it is such an anomaly in the modern business world that it sidetracks everyone's attention. Excessive jewelry will distract with excessive sparkles and rattles when you make hand gestures. People listen to the noises instead of you. Men and women should shine their shoes. We all have scuffed heels from driving, and such a small thing can make anyone look unkempt.

Avoiding Disasters on the Fly

Here are a few more preparation and maintenance tips for getting the clothing and appearance thing right.

Be Comfortable and Look Comfortable

Make sure your presentation outfit is comfortable, and be especially aware of wearing a too-tight anything. Not only can this be too revealing and make some audience members feel uncomfortable and threatened, it can also make you sweat. There is one globally famous speaker of the eighties on the circuit today who is pretty much a laughing stock because while he still has a good message, he's put on thirty pounds but has not bought any new suits.

Don't Carry Office Supplies

Avoid putting pencils, pens, and markers in your shirt and suit pockets, as they convey a nerdy impression. They will leak or clatter or fall out of your pocket at their first opportunity.

Dress for the Climate

You will be warmer than everyone else because of the energy you are expending on stage. Dress appropriately so you don't sweat. For the same reason, you should avoid clothes made of synthetic fibers. They will not wick the sweat and heat away from your body, making you feel and look the worse for it.

Press for Success

The night before, the day of—*whenever*—make sure there is an iron available to get those wrinkles out. Dress early, so your body has a chance to further form your clothes to your athletic contours. When checking into a hotel the night before, get the clothes out and hang them. Get in touch with housekeeping to get an iron or have one delivered the next morning (riskier, but sometimes all they will accommodate).

Zip, Button, Stitch

Yes, it happens. A half-hour monologue, and you later notice your pants (blouse?) were unzipped! Horrible! Absolute panic. Did they notice—and did they listen to *anything* I had to say? How am I to stand in front of them—or even talk to them again? (If this *does* happen, sometimes it helps to confide with an audience member to see if it really was visible—you can save a lot of panic anxiety if it wasn't.) Of course, the best remedy is to make sure it never happens in the first place. Check all of your buttons and do your mending the night before. Get all the details right, and well before you're on stage.

Know Your Stuff

We're in the home stretch. Most of the planning phase is behind you. Now you need to ready yourself for the moment.

Being ready means being "really" ready. Being ready means being thoroughly familiar with your material so that you can almost do it in your sleep. Being ready means being so familiar with your material that the slightest deviation or distraction can be handled with coolness and comfort. When you prepare in this way, you can deal with the problems. You conquer stage fright and nervousness simply by knowing—at all times—what you're doing. And that confidence rubs off—if your audience perceives that you know what you're doing while on stage, they will also think you know what you're doing *off* stage.

What does it take to get your brain completely wrapped around your material and to prepare for those low-hanging branches? Well, in a word, practice. But beyond practice, it's important to thoroughly review the material. As you're doing this, think of your presentation as an outsider would—what would they see? Then use this thought process to think about and anticipate what they might wonder about or ask about, so that you're prepared to deal with those contingencies. Finally, for some it works to have some good notes and backup material, just in case.

Become One with Your Material

Well, this seems obvious, doesn't it? But we're surprised ourselves at how often people present as if seeing their own presentation for the first time. They read the slides. They forget what they were going to say to accompany the visual. They get the wrong visual on the board. They forget to give you a clear statement of message or a clear closer with a call to action. They may even forget the *title* of the darned thing.

Don't just finish your PowerPoint slides, save, and close. Print out a review copy for "handouts," or print the individual slides. Go through it a few times. Whisper what you might say or what the main point of each slide is. Put it down, and then pick it up again sometime later. (Most of our minds supplement conscious learning with subconscious processing.)

We like to do a couple of exercises or "tests" when going through this familiarizing phase. One test is the "fifty-two-pick-up test." Drop all the slides on the floor, and see how quickly you can reorder them. Do it quick, and that means you're pretty familiar. But if this takes a long time, you're not that cozy with the material. A simpler version is to take a few slides out at random and see how long it takes to get them back into sequence. If you're not using slides but index cards or other aids instead, you can do the same. Another test is the "sing in the shower" test—see if you can identify and talk through each of your slides while standing in the shower (or driving, or flying, or whatever)—to do it without looking. These exercises are analogous to what many stage actors might do—for much the same reason.

Think Outside the Pitch

Good actors—and good speakers—learn to manage contingencies. They develop reflex reactions to deal with anything that might happen. The worse thing that can happen when the unexpected question or distraction arises is for you to get off your program, get off your rhythm, forget what you were doing, and have to stop and think about it—or backtrack. You lose the flow, and you may lose audience confidence. The way to avoid this situation is to think about what might happen and think through strategies and actions to deal with it. If you do this well ahead of time, your response becomes a simple matter of reflex—bend your knees, duck low in the saddle, shift right, let the branch pass, lean forward, and then upright. Don't stop the horse, don't get stiff, and don't lean the wrong way.

Some "low branches" include the following:

- **Audience questions.** Invariably, someone will ask a question you didn't plan for. Sometimes these are deliberate attempts to throw you off—or to see how you respond on your feet. Audiences like to test business presenters for a variety or reasons—for competence, for sincerity, for completeness of thought—or sometimes, just for fun! We'll talk more about the mechanics of dealing with questions in Chapter 8, but for this step of preparation, the thing to do is to think about, with everything you plan to say or show, what questions *might* be asked.
- **Program changes.** Because of time, changing business needs, issues brought up in previous sessions, or all of the above you might have to adapt your program. Time crunches, usually caused by others going overtime, are the most frequent adjustment. The order of presenters may be adjusted. Rooms can change, audio-visual equipment can fail, and so forth. Again, it's good to anticipate these changes. If you had to give your pitch in half the time, what would you do?
- **Management imperatives.** You'll be happily presenting your business plan and all of its key strategies and tactics. Your boss's hand shoots up in the air: "What about the financials?" Three days ago, you had agreed with your boss that the financials weren't important at this stage. But now you're caught with your proverbial trousers down in front of not only your boss, but also your colleagues, and your boss's boss!

  What do you do? Well, you might be able to steer the discussion into the "parking lot" if you're lucky, but a better tactic would be to prepare that "just in case" speech. More often, these curve balls will be thrown by the boss's boss, who wasn't there during the planning discussion, or by an outside party. Customers will do this too. They may or may not really want the information—they are just "probing" to see if you know your stuff and to see how well you've thought things through. The best remedy is to think things through and indeed, be ready for the unexpected. Ask yourself: "If I were the audience, what would I want to ask?"

- **External distractions.** We can't control the weather, availability of power, the sirens outside, the last-minute "boot" from the conference room. But we can be prepared to take up "in stride," right where we left off.

Being prepared and thinking through the contingencies allows you to do what you *planned* to do well—and it also is key to handling the unplanned things that come from nowhere.

Get Your Notes in Gear

We mentioned in Chapter 6 that you would probably want to script your opener. By doing so, you get all the elements in order and create a basis for practicing the opener. By the time you're ready to talk, the more you're able to "get off the book," as actors say. The sooner you can do it without aids, the better. Many speakers use notes and use them well, but the more you can do without, the more natural and normal your "conversation on stage" will become. Especially when using presentation slides, it's good to use those slides as your framework, not have both slides and notes running parallel in the background.

Having said all of that, it is still a good idea for most presenters—especially inexperienced presenters—to have a script, notes, or "cheat sheet" at least in background. And we mean really in background—somewhere, as in on a lectern or podium—where the audience can't see them. Notes certainly serve to help you remember key facts and especially complex facts, quotes, or numbers. Your script can also include audio-visual cues ("SHOW FLIP CHART #5"). Questions for the audience can be scripted in. And probably should be. This is an easy-to-forget item, as often while on stage your brain focuses on *you* and the audience *perception of you.* You tend to forget what you wanted to fire in the other direction. If you happen to lose your way somewhere along the way, notes will help to get back on track. Finally, take a pencil or pen with you, as an insight or insightful question from the audience can be recorded right in your notes.

Keep in mind that eyes darting back and forth between the audience and notes are eyes that aren't fully engaged with the audience, and when the audience perceives too much reliance on notes, again, your credibility can suffer.

There's no right or wrong format for notes—just do what works best for you. Notes contain the information you *need.* You must write clearly and big enough that you can grab what you need quickly while "on stage" and without fumbling through stacks of paper or cards. Some folks like index cards—they fit in your pocket and are easy to carry in front of the audience, and they can be arranged easily to include or eliminate certain items. They may evolve directly from your initial research and speech design (Chapter 3). But be careful not to drop them! And index card formats are incompatible with most computer output devices (except perhaps labels), so if you're using a computer to collect facts and design visuals, you'll have to transcribe everything onto cards by hand. Don't cram too much information on cards, use only one side, and make your writing big enough that you can glance at the card then talk to the audience.

Paper scripts can be used in the place of cards and are much easier to build and maintain with a computer. You can get more on a paper script. The downside to paper scripts is that while you can take index cards with you and away from the podium, paper scripts are awkward for this. To use a paper script, you need to stay close to the podium or lectern, which isn't easy for some people. Again, with paper scripts, you need to keep the content simple, well spaced, and large enough to read quickly. And if the audience perceives that you're reading your speech from a paper script, again, credibility can disappear.

Scripts are a good idea to structure, rehearse, use occasionally during your pitch, and record amendments to your speech. Relying on them too much can cause problems. Not having a script at all can cause problems for all but the most practiced and polished presenter. You'll have to decide what form of script works best for you and evolve it over time. The better approach is to learn to use your visual aids as a script. Building your skills so that you need less and less script as your presentation experience grows is a good goal.

Practice, Practice, Practice

It isn't a question of should you rehearse but *how* you should rehearse. Once you have a script that includes stage directions, such as audio-visual cues and handouts and questions *for* the audience, it's time to start rehearsal in earnest. The only way to rehearse a business presentation is to do it for real, just as you would on the day. That means speaking out loud and standing up to do it.

The spoken word sounds very different from the written word, as you'll discover. You'll try reading your script and find it doesn't sound right. That's okay. In fact, it is par for the course. You are just moving from the development stage of the process into and through the refinement stage. Now you'll take those complete sentences you wrote and replace them with the essence of what you want to say. You'll take out the personal pronouns and other extraneous words, and turn theses complete sentences into bullet points.

As you rehearse your presentation out loud, again and again, you will be able to reduce that full paragraph down to two sentences, then down to just two bullet points or one line. Start by rehearsing the entire presentation. You'll notice that some parts of it go more smoothly that others. When this happens, as it will, change pace and focus on the weakest areas. The concentration will likely lead you to make further changes to your script and perhaps even moving whole sections of it around to improve the flow. Once your presentation has a uniform and balanced feel, go back to rehearsing the entire thing out loud.

The best rehearsals take place in the actual venue of the pitch—for obvious reasons. You gain more familiarity with that venue and how you sound there. You get a chance to see how well your visuals work. Practicing on stage—on the *real* stage—is best. But if that's not available, the hotel-room mirror—or the shower—will do.

In rehearsal, you're looking to accomplish four things:

1. **"Get off the book."** Internalize the material as much as you can so you can deliver it naturally and conversationally instead of being prompted or governed by script. Practice makes perfect—but it also makes *natural.*
2. **Fine-tune the visuals.** Rehearsal is the only way to know if your visuals really do work. Are they visible? Are they timely, and do they support the message effectively? Are they too complex, too basic, or just right? Are they too hard for you to follow and deliver from effectively? How about the details? Should the color of that graph line be changed or axis labeling be enlarged? Should a particular slide be saved for the handout? As you rehearse the visuals, you learn to use them most effectively—or to prune them out (or occasionally, to add some) to perfect the accompaniment to your pitch.
3. **Be "on time."** Almost all business presentations have some sort of time goal or target. Rehearsal is the only way to really know whether you can get it done on time, and as we've said earlier, the penalties for going overtime can be severe.
4. **Fine-tune the talk.** Finally, rehearsal is the only way to perfect the "talk"—the things you say (and do) around the visuals, the message, and the main points of your talk. Here, very simply, script and slides are converted into communication. As a good actor strives to do, you'll get the *timing* right for the most impact. You'll figure out how to build up to the main points, and you'll lead the audience in the direction you want to go. You'll practice the close and call to action, and with enough practice, you'll get the emotion and sincerity just right.

Should you have an "audience" for your rehearsal? Different speakers feel differently about this one. Naturally, a friend or colleague in the back of the venue or in your hotel room can give pointers and feedback. But it's hard to use this single friend as a valid proxy for a real audience. A real audience in a real situation feels different and acts different, and your adrenalin is doing different things when you're in front of them. Personal preference and experience are the guiding light.

With all of Chapter 6 and 7 said and done, you're now ready to roll.

Do's	Don'ts
• Prepare, prepare, prepare. • Become familiar with presenting environment—inside and out. Learn to control it. • Arrange room layout to accomplish objectives. • Become thoroughly familiar with audio-visual equipment. Test it if you can. • Bring backups if using laptop projection. • Make your clothing fit the situation. Keep it professional. • Dress comfortably and be comfortable. • Become one with your material. Commit as much as possible to memory. Test yourself. • Think outside your speech. Anticipate what might happen. • Practice, practice, practice.	• Don't party the night before—unless preparations are done. • Don't force uncomfortable audiences to hear your whole pitch. • Don't project slides that cannot be seen because of improper screen or lighting. • Don't be afraid of microphones. • Don't dress too casually, but also don't overdress or dress in unconventional attire. • Avoid distracting accessories or items on your person or on stage. • Don't become too dependent on stage notes.

Figure 7-2. Do's and don'ts for presentation preparations

8 Showtime

Lights, camera, action—what to do when the spotlight's on you.

The time has come. It is the day of the show. All that you've prepared is about to be shown to the world for its benefit and review. If all goes well, your audience will "get it" and be ready to come back for more. You and your department will "get the nod" to proceed with your plan. You will be invited back to speak again or perhaps to speak to your European counterparts in the south of France. Not only will you feel great about it, you will have laid another brick in the delicate wall of your career.

But you still have to get from here to there, that is, from an upcoming agenda item to the "happy hour" mingling at the end of the day and then to the airport, to settle back for that three-hour flight, to catch up on the newest John Grisham novel. That's a matter of just a few hours, right? But in reality, it might as well be days. Butterflies fly freely in your stomach, and your hands are moist with what feels like warm morning dew. Then there's that little tickle in the back of your throat, too.

Nervous? Yeah, a little. You're just not sure how it's going to turn out. You think you're prepared and able to anticipate what might happen. You think the audience will go your way. You are pretty sure they will like you and what you have to say. But you're not completely sure. Is this out of the ordinary? Hardly. All speakers, no matter how experienced or polished, go through this experience. Our bodies have been wired since the dawn of time to preserve themselves from harm, and they have developed very sophisticated systems for signaling when a situation is fraught with danger. Your body knows that this particular situation is not a normal, and therefore not a safe, situation. The result is a chemical reaction in your body to set off the alarm signals to alert you to possible danger.

Some Perspective on Nerves

Standing up in front of people is certainly not the smartest thing to do for a quiet and uneventful life, but then a quiet and uneventful life will probably not deliver your dreams. You want to make your mark. You have determined that increasing your exposure is one of the ways that will bring you that much closer to your goals.

You are going to get nervous when a presentation looms; everyone does. We have never met a good speaker who doesn't experience some form of stage fright. For some it starts with sleepless nights. For others it might be sweating or the feeling they are traveling a million miles an hour, while others experience an overwhelming lethargy. Of course there are also those who experience all of these feelings simultaneously.

The manifestations of stage fright are endless, but they all involve muscle tension, mental preoccupation, and physical stimulation from the adrenaline rush, and they all combine to disconnect your mouth from your brain. "The human brain is a wonderful thing. It operates from the moment you are born until the first time you get up to make a speech," said speaker Howard Grossman. You can watch the news on any given night and you will even see news anchors, celebrities, and politicians, all people used to being in the limelight, all making their fair share of mistakes. However, these people have learned to put things in perspective. They realize that they are held in awe as a result of being in the public eye and that their mistakes only serve to make them human. A flub, blooper, or misspoken word is simply no big deal. The same applies to you.

You may not experience the same degree of celebrity, but when you are on stage you are the center of attention and a celebrity to your audience. So you might as well learn to handle stage fright the way everyone does who finds themselves in the same situation. When you wake up in the night wishing that you had a few more days to prepare, remember that you can't change the past. You don't have a few more days to prepare, and there isn't time to do more research. If you have a few days, you'll feel that a week is required. You will worry, because everyone worries, and you will not completely get over it, because, again, no one ever does. But you can learn to control it, and to channel it. The nervous energy that every performer experiences can give your presentation the edge that makes you stand out. *Use it!* Channel those butterflies and make them fly in formation!

It's (Just) Conversation on Stage

We've always found it handy to think of a presentation as no more than a conversation. The only difference is that in this conversation, you're on a stage, and you're conversing with not just one or two people but an entire audience.

Most of us are good at conversing in normal, comfortable one-on-one situations. (Some of us are *too* good!) If you can extrapolate the comfort, smoothness, and clarity of a normal conversation to your stage presentation, you're bound to succeed—as long as your material and content are properly prepared. The more natural you are—the more you maintain a conversational style—the more comfortable the audience is. More comfortable audiences are more receptive and responsive audiences. And more comfortable audiences make *you, the speaker,* more comfortable as well.

Marshall the Facts in Your Favor

Human insecurity is a strange phenomenon. We naturally assume the worst anytime we approach a situation the least bit uncomfortable. Public presentations are probably the foremost example. You're sure it's going to fail, and that the audience doesn't support you. They are there only to laugh and criticize, right? Wrong. This is one of the most common misperceptions.

You have an army of supporters. You know what? The entire audience really wants you to *succeed. The audience is really on your side.* They are there to improve and to learn something new. They are hoping to gain some small grain of wisdom, some small technique, some new glimmer of understanding that will increase their chances at professional success. They want to help the business or organization succeed. They want to have a good experience. They want you to succeed, because if you succeed they will benefit, and any tensions or discomfort *they* perceive will go away.

No one expects you to reveal a whole new universe of information in your presentation. In fact, the vast majority of meeting attendees is more than happy if they come away with one single useful idea that they can take back to the office and put to work for their personal benefit.

What If I Don't Have All the Answers?

If you were chosen to speak, you must already have a reputation as someone competent in the area of your presentation. *Remember—you know more about the topic than they do—that's why they chose you in the first place.* You know more than the meeting organizer, the managers, and the rest of the audience. You don't have to set yourself up as the sole source of knowledge on your topic. All you have to be is a professional colleague who has developed an area of knowledge, experience, and interest, and has some interesting news, ideas, or lessons to share. You know more than they do. When you don't know, you can still offer a qualified opinion and go find out for sure, later. Don't ever take the stage thinking, "They know more about this than I do." (If that *is* the case, perhaps you haven't prepared adequately.) Later in the chapter we'll show you how to handle questions where you don't have the answer.

And one other thing of importance—real importance: your audience has no idea that you are feeling nervous. To them you are an honored and respected member of the professional community who probably has something worthwhile to say on a subject important to their professional success. Your nervous thoughts and behaviors—while often at the forefront in your own brain—are barely perceptible to most audiences, most of the time. Avoid the downhill spiral—getting nervous, wondering if others see it, getting *more* nervous, and so on. The reality is, they probably don't see it at all. They don't see what's going on inside. Moreover, the audience is likely to be nervous or focused on *their own* image and behavior instead of yours. Know this, and use it to your advantage.

Remember Thy Objective

Getting from nervous to "conversation on stage" often requires some mental and physical exercise. You want to "pump yourself up" as implied above, remembering that you know more than the audience, that they want to see you and hear what you have to say, and they want you to succeed. Sometimes it helps to take it a step further and remind yourself of your objectives. Talk to yourself (not out loud, as that would raise all sorts of undesirable perceptions). You need to reinforce your purpose and objectives. This is perfectly normal. You might ask the questions presented in Figure 8-1, and dig up confirming answers.

Get Yourself in Shape!

Believe it or not, a short "workout" is a favorite "day-of-show" activity for many presenters. Warming up your body serves to warm up your brain. You get the "bad stuff" out of your system. It can also help relieve some of the physical discomfort that stress causes and that is experienced by many presenters. The stress you feel prior to going on stage may be emotional, but it also manifests

Ask Yourself	And You'll Hear
Why did I want to make this presentation in the first place?	Because I have something to say that the audience needs to hear. I am respected by my peers, and it's a sensible part of my career management program to grow professionally.
How many people in my profession or organization do what I'm doing?	I don't know, but the number is miniscule.
What's the worst that can happen?	I can screw up, learn from the experience, and do it better next time.
What kind of people never screw up?	The ones who never try or do anything new.

Figure 8-1. Reinforcing questions that speakers ask themselves

itself in physical ways, most especially in your back, neck, shoulders, and facial muscles. The "workout" can also help get your lungs ready. After all, like singing, speaking requires lungs that are ready, able, and willing to support your enunciation, your enthusiasm, and your emphasis. There are physical exercises you can do to reduce this stress and relieve the accompanying muscle tension.

Any physical exercise you can get in the days coming up to your presentation will help immensely. A good workout loosens up the muscles and gives you an outlet for the tension that is building. Because you exercise, you will sleep better and be less tense when you awake, and in consequence you will handle the stress of the day more productively. You should plan to work out on the day of your presentation if you possibly can. Carve some time out in the morning, or even at lunch or at the break if your presentation is late in the day. Try some of the following exercises:

- **Crunches and push-ups.** Stretch your back and exercise your chest cavity. A few sets morning and night will give any speaker better posture and more confidence. One of the great additional benefits about doing sets of exercises like crunches and push-ups is the immediate gratification of achievement and sense of being in control that you gain.

- **Arm lifts.** Start with both hands by your side and slowly lift them until they are pointing at the sky above your head. Hold for a few seconds and repeat a number of times. We know of one speaker who puts his presentation on a cheap music stand and recites his presentation as he slowly flaps his arms in this exercise, like some giant seagull in slow-motion flight.
- **Head rolls.** Lower your head onto your left shoulder and rotate it in an arc over your chest, right shoulder, back between your shoulders, and back to your left shoulder again. Repeat this a number of times, and then reverse the process, starting with your head resting on your right shoulder.
- **Jaw stretches.** Open your mouth wide and rotate your lower jaw in as big a circle as you can manage. Repeat a number of times with your jaw moving clockwise, and then reverse and do the same exercise again going in a counterclockwise direction.
- **Touch your toes.** Just like you did in school. Didn't think you'd see *this* one in a professional presentation guide, did you! Start upright, slowly bend to touch your toes, and then return to a full upright position standing with good posture. Repeat a number of times.

As you do these exercises, tell yourself that you have prepared as best you can and that every speaker who ever was and who ever will be feels just like you do now. Tell yourself that every other presenter speaking today feels just the same way, and they too are probably going through this same ritual to control and channel their nerves. And by the way, these physical exercises to reduce tension should generally be completed before you shower and don your battle dress. You don't want to be a sweaty, disheveled mess when you are introduced!

Arrive Early

At this point, you're prepared mentally and physically. Your body is ready, your mind is ready, and your slides are ready. Here are just a few more pieces of advice. First, *arrive early.* Your presentation really starts when you leave your desk, home, or the hotel room for the event location. Check that you have directions, contact names, and telephone numbers (cell phone numbers, in this day and age). And of course, make sure you have all of your notes and visuals with you, including copies you want to hand out or leave. Arriving early doesn't avoid Mr. Murphy, but it may help you defeat or get around him. You don't want that last-minute traffic jam, thunderstorm, or phone call to cause you to arrive late. And "on time" arrivals are, in reality, *late* arrivals, because you won't have time to shift focus and energy to the presentation. You'll look rushed. You'll forget things, or you'll drop your slides and stumble over people trying to rush to the stage when called. And you won't get a chance to observe the audience or previous speakers to get the flavor of how things are going.

Entry, Stage Left

Finally, the moment you've been waiting for. Speech in hand, *speech in brain,* you open the door and walk into the room. Quietly, of course. You don't want to create a disturbance for the previous speaker. In fact, we often wait outside the door deliberately for a few minutes to listen in to what is going on and get a feel for audience enthusiasm and response, and to get early clues as to whether the program is on track or not. This is a good time to go to the restroom, straighten windblown hair, get a drink of water, check voicemail and those stock quotes one more time, and so on.

When you do enter, you want to remain inconspicuous. But remember—your speech has begun in earnest, even though you haven't been introduced, and the previous speaker is only on Slide 3. If you look nervous, distracted, or disorganized that may well carry over right into your talk. Try not to drop your slides on the floor, and try to be organized enough so that you can simply reach into your briefcase or satchel just once, and pull everything out together. Look attentive—and be attentive—to the presenter still talking. Audiences like people who blend in.

If the program hasn't started yet, and you have nothing to do, don't fidget and pace nervously like a caged tiger. It's a good opportunity to recheck the room, refresh on where things are, and maybe even do a final check on a slide or two. Better yet, it's a good time to "work" the room—to meet audience members, find out what's on their minds, and begin establishing rapport. You will look more professional, and you'll get useful tidbits of information and audience interest that just *might* help guide the "talk" portion of your pitch.

It's usually not a good idea to make wholesale changes to your presentation based on this input, for although PowerPoint is quick and easy to use, you won't be sufficiently familiar with the result. You might adjust to present *less* than planned if someone from the audience tips you off that "we want to get out early" or "we're way behind from yesterday" or "we saw your memo from last week and completely understand where you're coming from." Or you could receive impetus to present *more* details: "I like your program—but could you make sure to tell us more about the financials?" Last-minute shifts are dangerous, but if you have to do them, this is the time.

When you walk in, someone may introduce you. Should you sit in the audience, where you'll often be offered a seat in the front of the room, while the room quiets down and the introduction gets under way? If you aren't the kind if person who gets nervous before a performance, that seat in the front row might be just the place for you. The audience gets a chance to check you out, and you can establish a little rapport through eye contact, particularly if you're along the side of the room up front or at a table next to the speaker's table (as in a panel). Some speakers prefer to remain and stand at the back of the room, where they are out of sight and can move around without looking like a nervous Nellie to the entire audience. They can also observe the behavior of the audience and figure out who the leaders are. Further, they can sample the audio and visuals to see if everything can be seen and heard. This positioning has another advantage: You get to make a real entrance down the length of the room, and the physical movement and the few seconds it takes gives your body time to adjust to the adrenaline rush it is experiencing.

"Presenting . . . Me"

Here goes. Stand up carefully and gather all of your stuff (actually, having it in hand already is good idea). Walk slowly, at a comfortable, natural pace. Whatever you do, don't climb over people in a rush to get there—"pardon" your way to the front slowly and carefully in a crowded room. When you get to the front of the room, don't be in a rush to talk. The audience wants to get a good look at you. Take the time to turn on your mike, straighten your papers, and take a deep breath. Force yourself to move slowly and methodically. It helps calm your nerves and demonstrates to the audience that you are in command of the situation, even though you may not feel that way.

Now you are *on stage*. Be yourself, that is who got you here, and that is who will get you through the presentation in the best style. Use your normal speaking voice, and as best you can, just relax. Be conversational. With the supporting tools you have developed, not much can really go wrong. This is your moment in the spotlight. Enjoy it.

Your insecurities will already be looking for distractions and excuses, like "the room is too cold, the microphone stand won't go up." Sweep them aside and focus. Concentrate on the central idea of your presentation, the important core of your message, and its relevance to the lives of your audience. Don't worry about the perfect phrasing or a stutter or stammer. If you worry about forgetting your words, chances increase that you will forget them. If you worry about tripping on your way to the stage, yes, you increase your chances of stumbling. Just focus on this: "More than anything right now I want everyone here to see my sincerity, and hear my message."

Speak Out

Be assured; be positive. You are as prepared as you are ever going to be for this particular presentation. Now is the time to relax enough to trust yourself. The skills that got you onto the stage will serve you well and get you off again when you are done. Some neophyte speakers feel they have to adopt a dust-dry seriousness to appear professional, but they are completely wrongheaded in this. No one came to the meeting to see a boring old-style amateur newsreader. They came to learn, to improve, to be more successful, and to become energized. You are there to help them achieve their goals.

You will best achieve this by expressing the natural *enthusiasm* that came with developing your idea. Let your audience know that you are happy and honored to be there with them. Let them know what an exciting day this is for you. You have the opportunity and honor to stand up and talk with your peers about issues that are dear to all your hearts and minds.

In the first few minutes, you concentrate on capturing the attention of your audience with the excitement of your message. You can help yourself achieve this by making every effort to make *eye contact* with people in each of the different quadrants of your audience as you speak. Look at both sexes and at people of all organizational levels equally, and speak to them equally.

But What Do I Say?

By now, with all of that preparation and rehearsal, you should have a pretty good idea of most of what you want to say and how you want to say it. But the first words can be a little tricky. You have to make a transition from the opening to your talk. Sometimes it's okay to just start with your talk, particularly if your opening line is a high-impact attention-getter. If that's the case, a pause or silence before uttering these first golden words can work wonders for getting the audience settled and building anticipation for what you're about to say. But don't wait too long—attention spans are short!

The more common "start" consists of giving a round of thanks to the person who introduced you or who sponsored you. If you're representing colleagues who helped along the way, this is the time to send an acknowledgement in their direction. A "glad to be here" statement helps further smooth the transition, and finally, your talk. "Thank you, Mr. Gallan, for taking the time to put together today's meeting. And thank you, everyone in the audience, for taking the time to come today. I'd first like to acknowledge my Order Processing team for busting their tails to implement the program we're going to talk about today. Without their help, I wouldn't be making this presentation today. Suffice it to say, it means a lot to be here. Today, we're going to review the results of the new order fulfillment program implemented over the course of the last six months . . . "

If there are housekeeping items, such as the time of the show, timing of breaks, format for discussion, rules of engagement, or the location of restrooms, this is a good time. If it's a long day, sometimes it's good to ask the audience how *they* are doing. This builds rapport (shows you're thinking about them) and helps to relax you a bit.

Turn on the projector, hit the first visual, and you're on your way.

Carrying on the Conversation

Speaking is a natural thing. It is simply conversation on stage. The only difference between speaking and an ordinary conversation is that the audience is many, not one. The audience has diverse thoughts, interests, and behaviors. In most presentations, *you* do most of the talking, because it is you they came for. But in most cases, the more *conversational* you can be, the better. Conversation—and most communication, for that matter—is a coordinated set of verbal and nonverbal activities. The verbal portion is what you say and how you say it—voice, inflection, emotion, speed, timing, and so forth. Your nonverbal communications—which are extremely important in a stage situation where the audience is basically staring at you—can make all the difference. Your communications will either relax the audience and support what you are saying or they will be wildly distracting and convey a message you never intended to. Your stage manner is very important. Let's start with that.

Stage Manners

Stage manner consists of body language, facial expressions, eye contact, gestures, and movement. While you shouldn't substitute style for substance, don't forget the performance aspects of your presentation: *Image and body language.* As professionals, we are all aware of the importance of a polished professional look. Here we are going to address an application of the winning nonverbal techniques of the job interview (where we use nonverbal tools to establish the right image and to support our verbal statements) and apply them in the larger context of a business presentation. This body language is what makes the neighborhood dog friendly with one pooch and eager to tear the ears off another; it is what makes you take a second glance at that stranger across the room. Your appearance, gestures, posture, and general demeanor either support your message and make it more powerful or detract from it. Given the choice between going blind and going deaf, nine out of ten people would choose to go deaf, perhaps because of the vast amount of information we are able to gather visually. Speech is a comparatively recent development, but as humans we have been sending and receiving nonverbal signals since the dawn of time.

We all have a set of signals that we employ unconsciously that describe our mood and demeanor. If we learn to control the negative signals and instead employ more positive ones, we have learned a self-management technique that will positively impact not only our business presentations but every other aspect of our professional lives as well. When our bodies complement our words, that message is reinforced. When our body language in some way contradicts our speech, it is human nature to go with body language as a more reliable indicator off the truth

The Face

Your face speaks volumes without you ever having to utter a syllable. Our language is full of expressions testifying to the powerful influence of facial signals. To modify an ancient expression, the face *and* eyes are windows to the soul. When we say that someone is shifty-eyed, or wide-eyed, or tight-lipped, or staring into space, we are speaking in a kind of shorthand, using a set of cultural stereotypes that enable us to make judgments about that person's qualities and intentions.

Tension in the facial muscles, darting eyes, and little eye contact obviously speak of feeling uncomfortable and possibly feeling awkward about something. Pursed lips are often interpreted as someone not wishing to be completely open;

frowning, looking over your glasses, and looking sideways get interpreted as signals of haughtiness and arrogance. It's hardly the way to win friends and influence people.

Smile

The most powerful positive message your face can send is the smile. Many nervous professionals standing up in front of an audience feel they must be serious in tone, formal in posture, and somber in demeanor and in the meat of the message. The result is that they come off as boring and stodgy, and no one hears what they have to say. They don't sway people to their point of view, and they don't increase their personal credibility and visibility. Had they employed a smile, things could have gone very differently.

A smile is the universal signal for friendship that says, "I like you and am happy to be in your presence." Smile at audience members when you meet them individually. Smile as you introduce yourself and speak to them as a group, and smile to emphasize that a particular point was humorous. Let people know that their presence makes you happy. Smile at someone, and most of the time they will smile back; they will have a friendly disposition toward you and your message. Upbeat, happy people (given, of course, a solid core of professional competency) tend to be more influential and go further in life. They are credible, and this upbeat attitude is one that helps draw others to them and thus increases credibility. We are not talking about acting like a grinning monkey, but we are drawing your attention to the conscious use of body language and appearance to influence others. It is a skill you can practice every day, with the added benefit that you will probably have a better day as a result.

Eyes and Eye Contact

Look at someone, and you show interest in that person. Showing interest in another makes her feel good about herself and about you. Remember that each of us is our own personal favorite subject. Making eye contact tells someone that you are interested in his or her interest, or in *his or her* favorite topic.

When you make eye contact (and of course give a little wrinkle-of-the-eye smile) the stranger sees you as having friendly intentions. The barriers go down a little, and the mind opens up, ready to receive your message. Your smile prepares your audience members to accept and adopt your viewpoint.

As you talk to the audience, don't look over their heads. Look at them as individuals. Many good speakers divide their room into quadrants to help them ensure that they are making contact with the entire audience. They'll be sure to make eye contact, smile, address a point, or ask a question of someone in quadrant one, then move on to quadrant two, continually recycling their attention throughout all the rows within that quadrant as the presentation goes on.

They feel that this way the have made at least eye contact with almost every single person in the audience. Such speakers are usually well received because each audience member has the impression that they existed as an important individual and that the speaker was speaking directly to them. This technique is especially useful in ensuring that you make contact with the people in the rear of the room, who otherwise can easily be forgotten and ignored.

This is an important point. Your presentation is only as powerful as your ability to personalize it for individual audience members. Your eyes can help you make personal contact simultaneously with the delivery of the group message. Rotate the object of your eye contact continuously throughout the presentation, and everyone will feel you were speaking with them personally and directly. Remember to work on this awareness in the daily rounds of your professional life, and when you step into the spotlight, you can use this powerful tool unconsciously as you make your presentation.

Body and Hands

Your body's posture and your gestures also affect the reception of your message. With a little awareness, they can be used to increase rather than detract from its impact. How you stand and how you hold yourself speaks volumes about your self-image. Like it or not, we live in a image-conscious world, and in standing up to speak, you become a public person. As the public person you become when you chose to speak in public, you are going to be judged by the same standards as all other public figures—namely, a higher standard. Slouching shoulders, sunken chins, curved backs, and saggy bellies all detract from your image, your message, and your credibility.

Stand straight with your shoulders back and head high. Practice walking well every day and when you stand, stand straight in the same way, and with your legs slightly apart to give you balance and avoid swaying like a sapling in wind. Practice good posture at work every day, and it will be second nature when you step on stage.

Hands, Arms, and Gestures

Hands and arms become a problem when we are nervous. They seem to grow to enormous size and take over our entire consciousness, and there comes an overwhelming urge to do something with them, no matter what. Unfortunately, all too often, the things you choose to do unconsciously take away from the impression you are trying to make. This is because your body is reacting in an elemental way to fear and uncertainty. Here are some things to look out for:

- Try not to fold your arms or cross your hands in front of your crotch. It first says that you are being defensive and that you are feeling naked and vulnerable.
- Hands behind the back can either make you look professorial and remote (not a good idea) or handcuffed and about to be led off to jail for some undisclosed crime.
- One hand in a pocket occasionally is okay for a casual attitude, but don't park it there for long periods, as half the audience will wonder what you're up to down there. Also, be careful not to jingle change or other objects in your pocket. Two hands in pockets is usually a no-no unless your situation is fairly casual. While it conveys a relaxed image, it can also give the appearance of arrogance and encourage you to slouch and jingle loose change. You probably won't notice it, but everyone else will.
- Keep your gestures normal and natural. Arms waving all over the place will distract an audience, while complete absence of movement will make your audience anxious to get on with the trip to the cemetery. Good arm movements convey friendship and draw the audience in.

Stage Movement

It's generally a good idea to move around the stage. Stage movement serves the dual purpose of creating variety for the audience and providing an outlet for your energy. Movement keeps the audience alert; minds and eyes tend to drift if they have to look at the same setting—you at the podium and slides on the wall—for hours. Movements should be natural, graceful, and purposeful. Movements to the screen to point out key points on projected visuals are effective. Side-to-side movements help refresh the audience and avoid the fatigue of keeping their heads in the same position. In many situations, you can move through the audience or walk down the center aisle. This establishes greater rapport, openness, and "oneness" with the audience. The audience feels a greater sense of collaboration and "we're in this together." Don't move too fast, and for goodness sakes, don't pace back and forth like a cheetah in an open-air zoo. Like everything else on stage, you should move to your advantage but not to excess. Always be in control.

	Do's	Don'ts
General	Polished, professional, in control	Overactive, distracting
Face	Relax, smile, be friendly	Frown or purse lips
Eyes	Good eye contact, random, talk to individuals	Don't dart around room or use same contact sequence over and over
Hands, gestures	Relaxed, natural, open gestures	Don't use distracting, "arm waving" gestures, be careful about hands in pockets. Don't use defensive gestures
Movement	Move around the stage naturally, comfortably. Move through the audience occasionally to connect and build rapport. If projecting slides, move to them to highlight points.	Don't race about the stage or pace back and forth nervously.

Figure 8-2. Body language do's and don'ts

Talking the Talk

Now we get to the "speech" part of the speech. We've covered the structure of what you say, the physical context, and the setting in which you say it. Now we get to the specifics of talk. Like most everything else in speaking, there is no one single way that works. That's probably more the case in this arena than anywhere else. Individual personalities will (and should) come through in any presentation.

The prevailing rule is to *be yourself as much as possible.* Remember, this is conversation on stage. If you talk slow normally, talk slow when presenting (within reason). If you talk fast normally, talk briskly and clearly when you present—but not too fast. If you have a naturally dry wit or use a lot of homespun expressions to convey things, chances are you're best off doing so—again in moderation—on stage. If you're delivering the "unfortunately, due to business conditions, we're forced to downsize" presentation, you want to adopt a more serious persona, and leave the petulant sarcasm at the door. So our "go forward" recommendation is "be yourself" as much as possible. After all, it's easier to be yourself than anyone else, isn't it?

Having said all of that, we have a few pointers to keep in mind, mostly in the direction of controlling the feel, tempo, and the "flow of words" to achieve maximum effect.

Be Enthusiastic

We said earlier that flies (and people) are attracted to sweet things. The most charismatic people are enthusiastic about the things in which they believe. Enthusiasm is contagious. We get caught up in it ourselves, and when we do, it sweeps others along with us. Excitement, energy, and emphasis should be sprinkled throughout your speech, and you should "put on a happy face" to go with it. Be in a good mood—or at least act like you're in a good mood. But keep in mind that your enthusiasm must be genuine. Otherwise, it will be suspected and ultimately rejected by the audience. If you don't really agree with or support what you are talking about, it will get picked up in a nanosecond. Think of the enthusiasm you would convey if your were describing something new and exciting to your family or friends in your personal life, and carry that same enthusiasm with you to the stage.

Focus on Others

No one likes an egomaniac. As a speaker, you're the focus of everyone's attention anyway, so you don't need to turn people off with endless prattle about "I" and "me." There's a standard speaker's rule that for every "I" or "me" in the presentation, there should be three times as many "you," "yours," or "we's." As Michael Jordan says, there's no "I" in team. You can incorporate this technique at the very beginning of your presentation, like this: "Are you comfortable enough? Is the room too warm or cool?" "Can you see the visuals?" "Did you all have a good flight in last night?" And during the body of the pitch: "Does this all make sense to you?" "Is this what you need to get out of this session?"

Get the Pace and Timing Right

More than anything else, this is where inexperienced speakers have problems. You get up there on stage, and your body and brain do an energy dump. You talk, talk, talk, fast, fast, fast. On and on, nonstop. You're afraid that if you stop, you'll forget what you wanted to say. Or the audience will lose interest, or they'll start asking tough questions. On and on you go, like a plugged-in auctioneer. What's wrong with this? Well, the audience simply can't absorb it all. They need breaks. You will also find yourself adding lots of filler material and words, just to keep up the blinding pace. Here are a few pointers about pace and timing:

- **Don't talk too fast.** Simply, slow down. If you find yourself talking faster than you do normally, you should look at this as a warning sign. Talk in clear, natural, declarative statements. Finish sentences and pronounce each word clearly. Read the audience and the situation—if everyone has a plane to catch and the session is running behind, fast talk is usually better than no talk at all. Likewise, if you're speaking to a group of Japanese businessmen just arrived from a ten-hour flight across the Pacific, slow down.
- **Don't ramble.** Speakers not in control of their pace will ramble. They will say more and more about a topic just to keep going. A better approach is to say what you were planning to say and stop. Pause. Read the audience. If the audience indicates that they need or want more, either directly or by body language, keep going. Always stick to what you were talking about. Do not jump around topics in a presentation or even on a slide. If you think of something you should have said earlier, or want to say later, hold off until the moment is right, and give the audience a pause and transition—a road sign—if you're changing direction.
- **Pause and rest.** The audience needs to rest once in a while to absorb information, to regain attention, to make a transition, or to just mentally or physically rest. Good speeches are filled with pauses. Better speeches have pauses of differing lengths, timed to give the audience time to digest or to build up anticipation for the next point. Try it yourself—stop once in a while. Do a "pregnant pause." When you stop, see how many audience members suddenly look right at you, waiting anxiously for the next thing you say. The natural tendency, when we're talking to a group, is to think we have to talk all the time, every minute of the show. Wrong. Only mothers-in-law do that. Again, lack of pauses and breaks is the trademark of the inexperienced speaker.

Transitions

This goes hand in hand with pauses and breaks. Give your audience notice—a road sign—when you're changing topics or moving forward to the next topic. "We've just talked about operational efficiency—now let's move on to the financials." Occasionally, a little more background on what you're going to talk about and why will help. "We've just talked about operational efficiency. To clearly understand the true benefit of this program, it's important to take a look at the financials."

Read the Audience

As you talk, observe the audience. You should be looking at them anyway as you maintain eye contact. But go further—try to see what they are actually saying, through body language, to you. Are faces smiling and heads nodding? Or is everyone staring out the window or at the clock above your head? People with their heads down buried in their notes or notebooks—or reading their e-mail—are probably either overwhelmed or bored. Either of the two indicates trouble. When you see this, take a pause, ask a clarifying question ("Does this all makes sense?") or even a redirect question ("Is this what you need to get from this session?"). Such an interlude can get back a lost audience, give you vital feedback, and shape the rest of the pitch for success. But reserve this silver bullet for special occasions—it doesn't help to ask "Does this make sense?" after everything you say. You should always take a quick glance to read whether the audience is ready for the next point.

Never Read Your Stuff

Don't read presentation slides or notes to the audience. They can read. Your job is to add color and talk to the main points of a slide. When you read to the audience, you send a dual negative message: first, that they can't read themselves, and second, that you don't know your stuff, so you have to read along.

Keep Track of Time

This is one of the hardest little details to handle while you have so much else going on up on stage. Most presentations have a time allotment, and it is all-important in time-crunched business settings to stick with it. Business people usually want information in short, crisp packages. When you go beyond the time allotted, chances are high you've overdone it, rambled, said too much, or given too much detail. For some audience members it is even disrespectful to go over time—it reflects a lack of consideration for their needs. And if the big boss misses a flight, you'll really be in trouble. What to do? If there's a clock in the room, watch it (but we swear there's never one in the room when we have to give a speech). Use a wristwatch—but here, be careful. It's best to put the watch down on the podium, next to your notes or laptop, where others can't see it. Rolling up your sleeve to glance at a watch sends the wrong message. The best solution is if you have a colleague or coworker in the audience, have them give you hand signals advising time consumed or time left. Some meeting planners will do time cues for you, too.

Don't Fill with Filler Words

"Um's," "ah's," and "you know's." Everybody does it. You hear these guttural pauses almost every time you hear a speech or converse with someone. But they can be really distracting in a presentation, and if overused can lead the audience to think you're not really sure what you're talking about. These filler words are borne out of a natural instinct to preserve attention while you're thinking of the next thing you want to say. The mouth/body goes "aaahh" while the brain processes. It's a subconscious reflex designed to give the brain pause and to "keep the floor" with your listener. In a nutshell, avoid filler words whenever possible. Try to consciously replace those um's and ah's with silence! Short pauses give you time to collect your thoughts and allow the audience to collect their thoughts. They also build anticipation for the next thing you say. You already have audience attention, so don't worry about losing it. Be aware that filler words often extend beyond um's and ah's—we hear "basically," "I mean," and "let's see" quite a lot. When you feel that "um" coming along, just remember to shut up!

How to Talk Through Visuals

Many practical techniques exist for managing and talking through your visual aids. As a speaker, you should connect and "synch" with your visuals. Just throwing a slide on the wall without referring to it will leave the audience wondering where you are or why it's up there in the first place. It's best, in our estimation, to walk around the projected image and use hand gestures to point to the item as you're talking about it. Don't just stand there pointing, pointing, pointing. Just point once, then walk away to get the audience focused back on you. And don't stand there staring at the visuals—your back will be to the audience.

If using an overhead projector, you can carefully use a pencil or pen on the projector surface to point to the item in review—but such pencils and pens seem to always find their way to the floor. You can also use a cover sheet to reveal

	Do's	Don'ts
Enthusiasm	Show positive, controlled emotion and good mood. Put on a happy face.	Don't be overactive or distracting. Keep enthusiasm real and genuine. Don't try to "act" it out.
Focus on others	Use "you," "yours," and "we."	Avoid excessive "I" and "me."
Pace and timing	Speak clearly, succinctly, and for many, more slowly than normal. Use pauses to rest the audience, rest yourself, and build focus for the next point.	Don't talk too fast. Don't ramble.
Transitions	Normal and natural: guide the audience to the next point as you would want to be guided.	Don't make transitions too complex or unwieldy. They shouldn't be a speech within a speech.
Read the audience	While making eye contact, also check for interest and attention. Ask a few checking questions.	Don't ignore audience cues.
Keep track of time	Use room clock, watch on podium, or helper in audience	Don't stare at wristwatch.
Filler words	Replace filler words with pauses.	Avoid all filler words, including those beyond "um" and "ah."
Visuals	Use pointers or hands, work from projected image. Hold physical visuals high but not in front of face.	Don't point constantly at visuals. Don't turn your back to the audience.

Figure 8-3. Verbal delivery do's and don'ts

items one at a time. This keeps the audience from looking ahead and getting distracted or jumping to conclusions—but again, these cover sheets also end up on the floor, helped along by the projector's cooling fan.

PowerPoint animation helps with these issues. You can "point" to items simply by revealing them sequentially in your animation. This can get a little tedious for the audience, so varying your approach might be a good idea. With projected slides, always make sure you stay out of the line of projection, and don't stand in the line of sight for sections of the audience for any length of time. For physical visual aids, hold them up high for everyone to see, but don't obscure your face. For flip charts or boards, stand at their side, and like the slides, point. Telescopic pointers are generally good (but don't point them in a threatening way to the audience). The small laser pointers are good too, but when it becomes a laser light show it's too much.

These tips and ideas, combined with your own natural gift for talk and the preparation you've done beforehand, should lead you to productive and effective conversation on stage—and an effective business presentation. (See Figure 8-3 for a summary.) Now let's move on to discuss some of the specific problems and "opportunities" you'll encounter in front of the group, such as questions, distractions, and problem audiences.

Questions and Answers

For obvious reasons, a key factor in determining success in a business presentation is your ability to handle questions. Like a basketball team that has few offensive rebounds because they shoot so accurately, you may have presented so well that the audience has no questions. But this is like having a triple-double without scoring any points. It can be done, but it's a rare bird. If an audience has no questions, it's more often because they weren't listening, didn't care, or didn't know what the heck you're talking about. If there's no sign of applause or concurrence at the end of the show, look out. The only exception is when time is a factor and *you specifically asked* that questions be excluded or saved for later.

We'll proceed with the premise that there *will* be questions from the audience. Again, how you handle them makes all the difference in the world. There is *no one single* "knock 'em dead" way to handle questions, but here are some situations and guidance.

- **Set protocol.** As we learned in Chapter 6, it's very important to set expectations on questioning—how much time will be allotted and when. You can try something like this, "You may have questions, and I will do my best to answer them. To make sure we get the maximum benefit out of the session, I would ask you to note and hold on to your questions until the end. We will have a twenty-minute Q&A session." Or: "During the session today I want you to feel free to ask questions. I'll handle them in one of three ways: first, if I can answer it then and there, I will. If it is going to be answered later in the presentation, I'll advise and field it later, and if it is off-topic or exceeds time available, I'll be glad to make time at the end of the session to talk to you personally." As a result, you'll be seen as responsive, and you can handle divergent questions without being taken off track.
- **Anticipate.** Every question is important to the questioner, and no question is easy the first time you face it. Every question is important to you because it establishes your credibility and maintains rapport. In preparation, you already should have anticipated the mainstream questions that should arise, and you may have prepared the answers with visuals. But you won't get them all, and there are some that simply don't have a pat answer and will lead to discussion.
- **Listen carefully.** Listen to the question asked. Look at the questioner and note body language, tone of voice, and degree of nervousness (or confidence). You need to identify the *real* underlying question being asked, and where the questioner is coming from.
- **Verify the question.** Verbally confirm the question with the questioner. This does three things. It clears up any misunderstandings or interpretations, it gives you time to subconsciously search for the answer while you repeat the question, and it helps other audience members who may not otherwise be able to hear it. Use the questioner's name and compliment them if possible (remember, it takes guts to speak in public, even if you're an audience member). "Lynn has a great question. She asked ________."
- **Pull unclear questions out.** Active listening goes beyond hearing. It means getting the most from an exchange by helping it along conversationally. Not all questioners are polished speakers (for one, they didn't prepare like you did), and asking questions in a large group is, frankly, hard. So give people a chance. Give them a chance to get the question out, and offer help. You cover your bases and establish further rapport with the audience.

- **Never embarrass the questioner.** Never embarrass a questioner because a question is dumb or has already been answered. Treat them with respect at all times, no matter how tempting it might be to do otherwise. This applies equally to nonverbal signals of disdain like trying to get a cheap laugh by rolling your eyes or looking bored. It's bad manners. The audience may side with the insulted colleague and stop asking questions altogether.
- **If you don't know the answer, admit that.** It happens to everyone. You just didn't research that angle. Or maybe in the heat of the moment, your mind simply goes blank. Whatever you do, admit it. Don't bluff—the odds are against you. Either someone in the audience will upstage you with the right answer, or you'll have to come forth later with a different answer, confusing everyone involved. Just say "I'm sorry, I don't know, and I'll get back to you."
- **If you're not sure of the answer, qualify it or open discussion.** Particularly with astute audiences, many questions are around gray areas where there is no unarguably correct answer. The answer may be a matter of opinion or exploring different alternatives. It's okay to give your own personal opinion, so long as you identify it as such. You may choose to give an opinion and offer to follow it up with facts later. If possible, and if time allows, it often works to throw it open for discussion. That way you can capture the audience perspective and collective opinion and have that information available for the next presentation. If an informal discussion does ensue, your job is to summarize, add insight, and finish with a concluding comment or invitation for more discussion at a later date. Whatever you do, don't let the discussion become a marathon derailing your original pitch.
- **Structure your answers.** Your answers to questions will go smoother and be more informative if they follow a similar format. Keep your answers brief and to the point, and don't allow them to take you off onto tangents (however interesting). If possible, reference your answer in terms of your presentation:
  - "As we discussed a few minutes ago . . ."
  - "Following on from my comments about ______"
  - "We could go back to the material presented last week: _______"

  A little personal or professional "touch" may help:
  - "In my (our) own experience, I (we) have found _____"
  - "Other professionals in the field have experienced ______"

Also, be alert to where a question may have been answered by a previous presenter or will be answered by someone after you on the agenda. Use visual aids where possible, and never take too long to answer a question that might be of little interest to the rest of the audience.

- **Don't feel obliged to answer all questions.** Don't evade them, but you don't have to answer them all. Otherwise, your pitch may turn into a sideshow for a completely different agenda. If a questions looks like a land mine, try to postpone it. "That's a good question, Michelle, but a good answer would take more time than we have now without disrupting the rest of the session. Let's talk one-on-one afterwards."
- **Don't get frustrated.** Often questions will throw you off track in terms of subject or time. All of your energy is tied up in making the presentation, and now you have to deal with all these questions! Simply put, the golden rules applies—do unto the audience as you would want them to do unto you. Remember your manners, and remember they are the customer. *Your job* is to satisfy the customer. That's why you're there.
- **Don't get trapped.** Every now and then a question comes along that smells like a trap. Maybe it's the tone, maybe it's the wording, or maybe it's just your primordial sense of self-preservation kicking in. Whatever it is, listen and respond to the questioner with "Tell me more." In talking further, you may reveal the true intent or agenda and get a better handle on where the question is coming from (and, maybe, from whom—remember, businesspeople work with and for others, and some like to be good little foot soldiers for their boss and boss's boss!). You can try something like, "Very interesting—to help give me a reference point, what is your perspective on the issue?" Without appearing defensive or evasive, a good tactic here also is to steer the question into the "parking lot." When you suggest taking the question offline, the questioner has both an acceptable answer and an offer of your personalized time and attention. Often the bomb will defuse itself and not ultimately be brought up at all.
- **Don't let your presentation get hijacked.** It happens a lot. Someone in the audience with an agenda of their own simply tries to take over by asking question after question. Don't let this happen. "Jack, we have limited time and must keep on track. Please help me save precious question-and-answer time for the rest of the audience. You and I can talk offline later."
- **Getting your audience to ask questions.** Most presentations are dull or uncomfortably one-sided without at least a few questions from the

audience. You will invite the audience to ask questions as you give protocol in the opener. But it is also beneficial to invite questions at various points during the talk. It serves as a pause for both you and the group, and it strengthens the audience bond. You may ask for questions, or you may simply ask questions of your own. Trolling for questions can also help deal with problem audiences—audiences that are inattentive or talking among themselves—as we explore in the next section.

The Audience Won't Cooperate

We've all been there—whether at home with our kids, with people at a party, with your friends, neighbors, spouse, family, colleagues, subordinates, superiors, customers, suppliers, human resources professionals—whomever. They just won't pay attention. They just won't stop talking. They just won't participate. They just won't cooperate. They get up and wander out of the room. Their cell phones ring while you talk. They eat while you talk. What do you do? The answer depends on the situation.

Noisy Audience

You have a noisy audience, or a couple of people holding a private conversation that distracts everyone else. The tendency is to increase your volume and speak over them. A far more effective trick used by seasoned speakers is to lower the volume of your voice. The audience will quickly quiet down in order to hear you. If the noise is coming from just a couple of people, stand right next to the offenders while continuing your presentation in a quiet voice. When they stop, which will be in seconds, smile and thank them. Then say, at normal volume, "To recap . . ." and pick up where you left off before the distraction. A pause, change of position, and change of voice also works if you perceive that part of, or all of, the audience is not listening adequately.

Audience Tired and Not Listening

They are coughing, squirming, and wandering in and out of the room. It's either late in the day and your audience is getting conference burnout, or it's time for a break. An audience's attention span bears an indirect relationship to the length of time they spend sitting in one place. Either way, they need a quick break and a change of pace. Give everyone permission to take a two-minute stretch break (know it will run to five minutes, and adjust your presentation pace accordingly).

Noise, Outside or Inside the Room

Sirens, jet planes, car alarms, you name it, they all seem designed for the sole purpose of distracting your audience and throwing you off-course. Your goal, of course, is to stay in control. If the distraction is really loud, just stop and look in the direction of the disturbance. Say something or make a joke to get the audience back ("Wasn't my car—don't need an alarm for a '63 Dodge Dart") and take up where you left off. Don't get angry or act angry, and don't try to compete with it if the situation is hopeless.

Another common distraction is when the lunch catering arrives—not only is there noise, but often people have to move, and everyone catches a whiff of today's special and starts thinking other thoughts. Some caterers are more sensitive to the disturbance they cause than others. In any event, usually it's best to try to talk through this one lest you lose the audience completely. But if it is simply too loud or distracting (say, sizzling fajitas or cherries jubilee), let the audience have a break, or break for lunch. Sum up where you are, and give a notion for what will be talked about when you resume.

Presentation During a Meal

This is another tough one. The audience is focused on food, and the clanging of plates and silverware reminds one of the factory floor. Yet the agenda calls for you to plow on, so plow on. Be especially crisp and clear with your statements, and you might need to slow down a bit. The audience usually understands your plight and will try to help. If nothing else, their hunger urges are satisfied, and if it's good food, you might get credit for that, anyway.

Audio-Visual Problems

Hopefully your preparation has mitigated most of Murphy's opportunities, but Murphy being who he is, something will happen. Your screen will go dark, the microphone will cut out or be full of static, you will get acoustic feedback, or you'll fall over the power cord and onto something vital. It happens. Summon all the help you can get (don't try to fix everything yourself—your mind is elsewhere) and try to keep going. If the slides won't work, improvise—from handouts, with flipcharts, and so forth. The audience will usually understand. If the audio-visual portion is especially important, ask the MC or meeting leader if it is possible to reshuffle events to get you on later.

Hostile Questions and Questioners

We already touched on this above as part of the section on handling questions. It happens, and the hostile party can be anyone in the audience. They can be the boss or boss's boss, a customer, an employee, a jealous colleague—you name it. Like all other situations in this section, the main thing is to keep your cool and maintain control. It is particularly important to make sure you understand the question and its intent—a hostile question isn't always what it appears to be. It can be a poorly phrased question where the nerves of the speaker give it a hostile tone or phrasing. A good first step is to repeat the question in your own words, removing any hostile phrasing or innuendo. If you capture the essence of the question, without the angst, you will be a long way toward diffusing the situation. Here are some suggestions on what to do:

- **Give the question and questioner respect.** Don't downplay their concern, and whatever you do, don't argue. Don't take the hostility personally. Any of these tactics will side the audience with them, not you.
- **Expose any hidden agenda.** The questioner may be trying to persuade others in the audience to their point of view. An answer like, "I'm sure we can go through the facts and come up with a logical, collective solution" might help defuse this bomb.
- **Demonstrate understanding of the question.** Don't blow anybody off, or give the appearance of doing so.
- **Share a neutrally phrased paraphrase with the group.** As shared above.
- **Seek audience input.** If nothing else, you'll find out who's on your side, and you can use the time to prepare an answer.
- **If you don't have an answer, say so.** And suggest when you will have one.
- **Summarize.**
- **Then, move on.**

If none of this works and the hostility is persistent, and if you have the time, consider giving the heckler the platform. "You know, it seems to me you have something really important to talk about. Rather than derail this whole session to your own end, why don't you come up here in front of everyone and say what you have to say. We'll get it out on the table, discuss it, and be able to move on." This takes guts, but most frequently they decline the opportunity, leaving you free to move on. Now if it's your boss, you want to offer the platform much sooner and with more grace.

Schedule Changes and Time Crunches

Simply speaking, do the best you can. Don't argue with the MC, the meeting leader, or the audience—if you have to cut your presentation in half, cut it in half. You know it well enough by now that you know what the important parts are and which visuals are most important. Offer to conduct a make-up session, teleconference, or one-on-ones by phone or in the "parking lot." You can even suggest an impromptu session over happy hour, if the audience really feels like it missed something.

Person Before You Said the Same Thing

Ouch. The best you can do is shorten your pitch and acknowledge the previous speaker's points and content. "As Bob already pointed out, the new Widgetcruncher will allow us to redeploy two people to other tasks." This simultaneously shows teamwork and synergy (with Bob), cuts down on some of the repetition, and gives you credit for respecting the audience's intelligence.

Miniscule Audience

What happens when you have geared yourself to present to an audience of 1,000, and there, in the vast auditorium or conference room, only 20 people show up? It has happened to every speaker, and once led one of the authors to observe after speaking for an audience of 20 in a room set up for 600, "Never, ever be the last speaker on a Saturday afternoon in San Francisco."

A drop in anticipated audience size can wrongly convince the inexperienced speaker that he or she has driven the audience away before even starting. As the presenter you have no control over audience size. You were asked to speak on your topic, and you are there to be a thorough professional for the people who did come to hear you speak and for the people who organized the meeting. As you are speaking as part of a long-term program to expand your sphere of influence, you have two important audiences there with you no matter who shows up. You have the organizers, and you have whoever does show up. You many be addressing an audience of two or ten or twenty, but nevertheless you have an audience who deserves your very best. Nothing ever changes, by word or gesture or by intimation, or by your attitude when an audience doesn't live up to its size expectations. It doesn't matter how many people are in that audience. Give the same effort for one person as you would for one thousand. Whoever attends will be thankful they got more of your attention, and the meeting planner will see you as a real trooper and someone who can be relied upon to do the job without complaint or finger-pointing.

Your Brain Takes a Day Off

Occasionally—for whatever reason—your brain just takes a holiday. You say dumb things, you say things differently than you had intended, or you completely forget just what the heck it was you wanted to say. What now? Here are some tips:

- **Motorboat mouth, rowboat mind.** We all do it. We butcher words at the wrong moments because we are nervous, and our mouths seem to be working independently of our minds. If you get flustered as a result, the mistake is only compounded. Profuse apologies only serve to focus everyone's attention on silly mistakes we all make and on your unwarranted embarrassment. The best thing you can do is to either ignore the mistake or acknowledge it in a light-hearted way and immediately move on. Some phrases that will get you out of a jam are the following:
  - "Let's try that again, in English this time."
  - "I always get tongue-tied in front of so many good-looking people."
  - "I think the chairman forgot to mention in my introduction that English is my second language."

  If the verbal bloopers become chronic—maybe after the third or fourth time—take a pause or a break. You could probably use the rest.
- **I forgot what I was going to say.** Your brain just locks up. You had it on the tip of your tongue, and now it seems gone forever. You can even hear yourself saying what you meant to say, but you just can't make out the words. The tactics are similar. Just move on. The audience never knows what you *didn't* say. Acknowledge the mistake. "I'm sorry, I had another thought on the tip of my tongue, but I can't recall it at this moment. If it comes to me, I'll be sure to share it before you leave, and if it doesn't come to me, I'll get it to you at my earliest convenience."

- **Oops, I said the wrong thing.** In the heat of battle, sometimes you'll get off an errant shot or two. You forget what that number really was, or you recall the wrong number. Was that net profit 8.7 or 7.8 percent? You say 8.7, but you realize later that it was probably 7.8. You should acknowledge this one as soon as possible. The audience doesn't know what you *didn't* say, but they will find out sooner or later if something you said was *wrong.* "I believe I told you that net profit was 8.7 percent, but now I'm not so sure. As soon as we finish this point (or topic) I'll go back to my notes and get you the correct number." And if you realize after the speech that something was misstated, a corrective memo or voicemail works. Of course, "materiality" comes into play—you need to decide how important the mistake really is in the "big picture" and to then support the validity of the message. If you stop to correct every nitpicky detail, pretty soon the audience loses faith in *all* of your facts.

Closing 'Em Down

And now, the moment you've been (desperately) waiting for. You're done with the body of the speech. You made your points, interacted with the audience, and everything seems okay. Now you have to close this baby down and get out of here, keeping everything on the up and up. You want to get that message home just one more time, to reinforce it with the audience and make your desired outcome a virtual certainty. But speakers who don't know when or how to get off the stage ruin what might have otherwise been a memorable presentation. How do we get from here to there?

Closing Pointers

Closing techniques are many and varied. Here are a few pointers:

- **Tell them what you told them.** Remember the framework: "Tell them what you're gonna tell them, tell them, then tell them what you told them"? Always keep this in mind as you head for your closer. The closer reviews what you've already said. It's a poor time to introduce more facts and information.
- **Remember that the last things you say are remembered most.** The ending is arguably the most important part of your presentation because it is what the audience takes away. The closer should be a succinct and

powerful review of your main points and message, with an exclamation point or two to set the message in the audience's mind.

- **Make a good transition.** Tell the audience clearly that you're wrapping up and that you are concluding your presentation. Otherwise, they might get confused—didn't you just talk about that point? Transition phrases can be the following:
    - "Now, let me summarize."
    - "Now, let's go over what we learned today."
    - "To restate the major points of our discussion, ______."
    - "Now, I want to pull my main points together for you."

  Note the clear statement of what is about to happen, that you are going to do something for the audience. The audience thinks "Okay, this is where I'd better listen up." You have everyone's undivided attention—make the most of it. Your audience expects you to bring the threads of your message together for them in a neat package.
- **Be succinct and clear, and don't do too much.** The closer is neither license nor the opportunity to launch into another speech. Nor is it time to apologize for your perceived shortcomings. Your closer is a summary of the substance of your presentation, a reiteration of the main points and message. It shouldn't take up more than 10 percent of your allotted time.

What Your Closer Should Accomplish

Your closer should do the following:

- **Presentation and fact summary.** Create a closing slide with the main points of your presentation. "So to recap the main points of our discussion ____, ____, and ____."
- **Complete and reaffirm the message.** If the flow of facts and path of logic has been complex, summarize it. "I said when we began just an hour ago that we would discuss tried-and-true techniques and some new approaches to _____. Our discussion led us through _____, ______, ______ (facts) and brought us to the point where we can clearly see that by applying these approaches to our daily business practices we will accomplish ______. Now you can see why I believe that is true."
- **Leave a good impression.** You serve your own goals best when the audience leaves feeling good about themselves, the way they have spent their time, and how your presentation can positively impact their future.

> "This new procedure will help you ____." "The argument runs quite clearly in favor of _____." "When you apply these techniques in your daily lives, you will benefit in the following ways: ____, _____, and _____."

Your closer can employ one or more of the following tactics.

A Call to Action

Wrap your presentation in style with any one of these effective approaches. When you tell your audience what to do, you are giving them a call to action. Every presentation should end with a call to action couched in some form. When you call people to action, when you ask their commitment to a new or changed course, there is greater chance your message will stay with them. With a call to action, you give the audience clear instructions on what to do next and on the benefits they will receive on taking your recommended course. "I want you to take this message to heart, and put it to work starting tomorrow morning. If you do ____, _____, and ____, you will see a sea change in the attitudes of your direct reports within thirty days."

Seek Commitment

Similar to the last technique, this approach is somewhat less direct and less specific, although your intent is the same. You still want to drive people to positive action. "If you take this message to heart, ____, ____, and____ will result." Or, "When you commit to apply these techniques. these will be your gains." Or, "I'm hoping from what you've seen today, it will make sense for you to adopt our new call management system." Or, "You all know these changes make sense, but will take effort to implement. Those of you who make the commitment to change will benefit as follows. . . ."

Combine Your Summary with Repetition

Simply and straightforwardly, you essentially repeat key power phrases from the body of your talk, combining them into a benefit statement. "Let me repeat. When we combine our new approaches of ____, _____, and ____, we benefit in the following ways."

Return to Your Opener

Not only is this effective, providing clear bookends to your presentation, it's easy. You've already written your opener and your main points, and this approach allows you to just restate them. "When we started, I said . . ." Or, "To return to where we began . . ." Or, "I promised you when we started that…."

Look to the Past and the Future

Here you can look to the past and to the future in two ways: what it will be like without change, and what it will be like with change. "Five years ago, we had the same problems we have today. Nothing has changed in the last five years, and nothing will change if things remain the same." After summarizing the "before and after," do a call to action or request commitment. Tables are effective visual aids for delivering this closing message.

Ask a Question

This closing technique can piggyback onto any of the others. It simply requires you to ask a question at the end rather than exhorting a call to action or seeking the audience's commitment. However, you should understand that the question you ask is itself a call to action. "Ask yourself what will happen unless you commit to this program," or "I ask you a simple question. How would things change if you implemented these changes? How hard would that be?" Or, "If you challenge yourself to improve your ____, you will find ______. So ask yourself _______."

Tell a Story

Tell a story that illustrates your point in a memorable, moving, dramatic, or funny way. Easier said than done? Yes, if you had to make up your own stories. Fortunately they are readily available already neatly bound in to books. A good place to start might be the *Speaker's Handbook of Successful Openers and Closes* by Winston Pendleton. This book has hundreds of categories of stories with two examples for each.

Exit, Stage Right

What happens when the last words have left your lips? You stand still, smile, raise your arms slightly, and quietly say "Thank you." This is the signal for the audience to applaud. In larger, more formal venues, you will most likely get real applause. In smaller, more familiar, less formal settings, you may not get "real" applause, but you'll get head nods and approving looks from the audience. You might also get a positive word or two from audience members, or better yet the audience leader or your boss. Either way, enjoy the moment. You might even join in and applaud yourself in appreciation of your audience, saying "Thanks for being such a great audience, I hope you gained as much today as I did.

But now what? Don't rush off the stage like a trapped animal just released. Ask if there are any more questions or individuals in the audience who would like to spend some one-on-one time with you. You may also want to acknowledge the MC or meeting leader and help to introduce the next speaker. "Now I'd like to turn it over to Mike, who will lead you through the financial details." Then turn off the projection equipment (some speakers like to turn it off *before* the close—to announce the transition, get total quiet in the room, and eliminate distractions), unclip your lavaliere, pack up your stuff, and walk calmly off the stage. As a courtesy to the next speaker, you want to leave the podium area neat and organized.

You may want to remain at the back of the room next to the exit. When you do this everyone will have to walk by you, and you have the chance to make a final impression with all those too shy (or otherwise too time-committed) to engage with you. You show that you're still interested in the audience and its needs. Quite a different impression is left when you rush out the door making eye contact with no one. In the more formal scenario, you might stand by the door, making eye contact with individuals as they leave, shaking hands and thanking people for coming. With so many people passing by, you will bask in a sea of praise and quick thanks from people as they pass. This is good for your ego, and it is also good to give your audience every opportunity to verbally confirm that they enjoyed your presentation.

You Mean to Tell Me I'm Not Done?

You got it done, and now you just want to pack up and go to Disneyland! Well, you're almost there, but not quite. As a good professional, you should always circle back to find out whether your presentation accomplished its objectives. As a strong collateral benefit, you will also find out things that will help refine your presenting style.

Shortly after the presentation, ask a colleague or audience member a few simple questions. "How did my pitch last Tuesday come off?" "Did you understand the points I was trying to make?" "What would have helped to make it better?" Doing this will give you the insight you need, and you will show that colleague and others around that you care.

Go back to your slides and script, and make some edits and modifications. Even without the direct feedback, you will almost inevitably find a few things to change. Some things work differently in front of a live audience than you thought they would going in. That is part of what makes presenting an art as well as a science.

In Short . . .

Your delivery can make all the difference. A smooth, natural, enthusiastic delivery—conversation on stage—where you are in control and the audience is comfortable is very important to successfully communicating your message. You need to open, close, converse, use visuals, and handle questions and contingencies with professional confidence. With sufficient preparation *prior* to walking on stage, your presentation is bound to be a "knock 'em dead" success.

Do's	Don'ts
• Remember that every speaker is nervous, and the audience doesn't know you're nervous. • Remember that the audience is on your side. • Remember that you're the expert. • Loosen up—physically and mentally—with exercises on the day of the show. • Arrive early, and arrive ready. • Always think and be "in control." • Mingle with the audience before and after. • Observe audience behavior before, during, and after. • Remember: conversation on stage. Natural language, natural body language. • Relax. • Be enthusiastic and think positive. • Handle questions—and questioners—with respect. • Exercise patient control over distractions and difficult audiences. • Circle back to get feedback.	• Don't think "they know more about this that I do." • Don't walk in at the last minute. • Don't ever rush, not before, during, or after your speech. • Don't make major last-minute changes. • Don't rush right into your speech. Walk slowly, set up deliberately, help the audience transition, and make sure you're ready. • Avoid mechanical, repetitive, or distracting gestures and movement. • Avoid "defensive" gestures or actions. • Don't bluff answers to questions. • Don't sidestep questions, but don't feel obliged to answer them all, either. • Don't get flustered or frustrated by questions or distractions. • Never argue with the audience. • Don't dart off the stage—stay engaged with the audience.

Figure 8-4. Do's and don'ts of handling yourself on stage

9 Don't Just Stand There

With modern technology, business presentations are less about speaking to live audiences. Learn to speak well with electronic media.

The advent of technology, which really started with the telephone, meant it was no longer necessary to stand face-to-face with others to carry on a conversation. Fast-forward to today's high-tech world of work, and technology has everything to do with speechmaking. Most of us will find ourselves speaking in situations and through communication media nonexistent or not widely available just twenty years ago. Indeed, it isn't just the technology. Businesses have been going ever more "national" and "global" for years. It is no longer practical to call all the employees you need into the conference room. We're often talking to meeting attendees spread across the country, and sometimes around the world, with time zones becoming a relevant factor.

As broadening business your scope works against time and travel cost, "covering the space" means using increasingly advanced technologies to communicate, hold meetings, and make presentations. For most of us, teleconferences and telepresentations far outnumber our live audience presentations. Emerging videoconferencing and Internet-based meeting technologies will make a greater portion of your presentation situations become "virtual."

This chapter explores the art of presenting in a virtual environment, where some or all of the audience is elsewhere. We'll talk about elements that are similar to and different from making in-person presentations. We'll also diverge to discuss other "nontraditional" business presenting situations, such as the following:

- **One-on-one meetings and interviews.** Quite the opposite of the global electronic conference is the "one-on-one" meeting or interview.
- **TV and the media.** Some of you may find yourselves in front of a TV camera—for videotapes, broadcast, or closed-circuit presentations.
- **You, as organizer.** If you happen to be the meeting organizer or leader, we'll take a short side road to observe important considerations for this role.

We'll actually start this chapter small and simple, with the one-on-one meeting. After that we'll explore virtual meetings, followed by media presentations, and finally, what to do when you're the organizer and planner.

I'll Be at Your Desk at 2:00

The face-to-face, one-on-one "presentation" is quite the opposite of the multinational, multiple time-zone conference described in the chapter opener. Here, you agree to share your stuff—with one or at most a handful in a generally informal environment, ranging from their desk to perhaps a small conference room. But these one-on-ones can take place in restaurants, in cars, at the gym, in the elevator—you name it. And some can be quite formal, as in the job interview.

One-on-One 101

Just like the "stage" presentation, the one-on-one should be thought of as "conversation on stage." In this case, the stage is very small, with an intimate, well-known audience. The audience is usually "one." but may be two or three or a handful of closely aligned colleagues. It is structured a little more than a typical "offhand" discussion, but essentially, it is still about listening and talking, organizing and delivering, receiving and handling questions, using appropriate visual aids, and so forth.

Like all other presentations, preparation is still the key. While you might have the opportunity to retreat to your desk for supplemental information that you might not otherwise have in a formal stage presentation, you must still have a clear message, a logical set of points, an opener, a body, and a closer. They can be less formal—certainly you don't want to distract all your coworkers and make a fool of yourself with a thunderous, pontificating opener when sitting four feet from the listener. The situation calls for a few adjustments, but all of the elements are there.

What's Different About a One-on-One?

Generally speaking, the one-on-one contains many of the same elements as an ordinary presentation: a message, opener, body with main points, closer, and interaction. It is preceded by good preparation, and it starts with good audience analysis (audience of one!), good research, organization, and practice. But there are notable differences, as the following sections describe.

Audience Analysis

You have an audience of one! What does that mean? It means that you have to get to know the needs of one and only one person. (Maybe two or three if someone else is in the office or at the desk—often the case.) That seems easy on the surface, but it's important to go deeper than you might otherwise do with a larger audience. The audience-of-one doesn't want to hear a bunch of stuff they already know. And if they don't want detail, they don't want detail. Presenting "A" when your audience wants "B" is sometimes forgiven in a larger audience, because everyone thinks "someone must need or want this stuff." But in an audience-of-one, you'll get cut off right now if you're presenting something that deviates from the listener's needs. So go deep—not wide—with your audience analysis.

You Aren't in Control!

When you speak to a large audience, you control the pace, the timing, and the stage. What goes on up on stage is largely up to you, with occasional audience input and meeting leader direction. But when the stage is yours, it's yours. This is not true in a one-on-one. You may start out in control, but your listener, especially if it's a higher-ranking manager, will quickly take charge, particularly if you're not delivering what they want. Your presentation quickly turns into an interview where your audience grills you with questions, or the topic may change entirely. Now guess who's in control? Your job is to prepare, and deliver, and respond so well to audience needs that this doesn't happen.

Two-Way Interaction

Dialog is, of course, possible in most any presentation situation. But in the one-on-one, dialog is more likely to take center stage. Your audience can—and will—ask more questions. It is simply easier to do when you're the only one there. And you can and should also take advantage of the situation to ask *checking questions.* "Does that make sense?" "Am I going too fast?" Or, "Would it help to show you Chart ABC?"

Formality vs. Informality

Generally speaking, the one-on-one is a little less formal. It is more like regular conversation with a purpose and supporting visual materials. There will still be an opener, body, and close. Frequently the opener and closer will be less formal, as in, "Hi, how're you doing," and "Hope that helps, if it doesn't, get back to me." Keep it to polite but informal language. Anecdotes and stories about last weekend's sports events or kids activities may be shared. Just the same, the body may be all business, particularly in a review presentation to a higher authority. The personality of your audience, their position, and the culture of your organization will all influence the degree of formality.

One-on-One Situations

One-on-one presentations usually occur in three situations: the normal presentation, the review, and the interview, as follows:

- **Normal presentation.** The normal presentation is just that. You are there to inform or convince someone of something you want him or her to do, agree with, or know. As mentioned above, the elements are all the same: message, opener, and body with main points, closer, and interaction. As with a one-on-one, you can tailor your talk exactly to the audience's needs, reinforcing what they know, helping them with what they don't know, and ignoring what they don't care about. The style is pure conversation, with eye contact and usually frequent interaction. Visual aids help just as they do for large audience presentations. It is a "large" presentation on a small scale. Often it is less formal, but not always. If your audience is the vice president, there may be a few more pleasantries in the beginning and end, but otherwise, count on it being all business.
- **Review.** One-on-one formats are frequently used to review your work, often with your boss or another manager in the organization. As in normal stage presentations, you need to be well organized and clear in your delivery. It's important to bring visuals that emphasize what happened versus what was supposed to happen. As with all one-on-ones, audience analysis is important. You can tailor your talk exactly to meet the audience's needs, fill the gaps in their knowledge, and avoid the unnecessary stuff. Since it is a one-on-one, you can expect more questions—perhaps more *pointed* questions—about your work than you might otherwise find in a stage presentation. Though not obviously called for, a degree of formality and seriousness is desirable.
- **Interviews.** Interviewing is an art unto itself. It is a one-on-one presentation of sorts, but with short, impromptu presentations usually prompted by "audience" questions. The job interview is a ritualized mating dance where the best partners whirl away with glittering prizes. In this type of presentation, you are in a responsive situation that requires

careful preparation to shine. You can usually anticipate and prepare for most but not all of the questions. You can't really prepare a script. You can instead prepare *pieces* of a script, like a few examples of your work and discussion of those examples, stories about experiences in school or at other jobs, and the like. But there will be no opener, body, or closer per se unless the interviewer asks for it. (An in-depth treatment of how to anticipate the interviewer's questions and respond to them in a convincing fashion is the subject of an entire book, and obviously beyond the scope in this book—see *Knock 'em Dead* for more information.) Sometimes "normal" one-on-one presentations become more like interviews—where the vice president pokes and grills you for information to see how well you understand your topic and can explain it.

Other One-on-One Issues

The following sections present a short discussion of other issues and topics as they pertain to one-on-one presentations.

Visual Aids

There are different schools of thought on the use of visuals in a one-on-one. It is usually unproductive to project slides, particularly if at someone's desk. If you have a laptop, often the two of you can look at slides this way. Or you can each work from your own slide packet or work together from a single packet. Think through what you want to leave with your audience-of-one on the day of the show. In many situations we find it easier and better to reduce the number of slides and use visuals only to show highlights. Your audience may already be familiar with many "base" concepts you might otherwise share with a larger audience. The one-on-one environment gives you a greater opportunity to "tell" your story. You can explain and illustrate with words and supplement with interactive dialog that may make complex visuals unnecessary. And you don't want to make the audience feel too much like they're being *sold* something. A perfect fifty-slide show will likely be viewed as overkill. Just take a few key slides and be ready to show the rest if needed.

Interruptions

Absolutely without fail, the telephone will ring just as you're about to nail your biggest point. Whether or not your audience-of-one is inclined to answer it, inevitably there will be some loss of concentration and degradation of the "golden moment." If the meeting is interrupted, make a note on your pad of the point under discussion at the time of the interruption. Once it is over, help your audience get back on track. "Jane, before you had to take that call, we were discussing _____, and you had just asked me to clarify a couple of points… Would you like me to pick up were we left off?" In doing this, you show yourself to be in control of the situation and as someone who keeps his or her eye on the ball, which is not a bad reputation to have in any company. If you're doing the talking, you should react as if nothing happened. Try to reinforce where you are ("As I was saying…") and recapture the moment. Other types of interruptions will happen too, particularly in an "open" office environment. One person sitting and talking to another is almost viewed by others as an invitation to come "chat," so you'll have to deal with that—politely, gracefully, and always willing to help your audience get back on track.

Reading the Audience

Nothing is more important in a one-on-one than reading the words—and especially the behaviors—of your audience. If they look bored or disinterested, they probably *are.* If they look angry, they probably *are.* If they look distracted, they probably *are.* And so forth. You must read these cues and tactfully respond to them. If they look bored, speed up, cut stuff out, and by all means, ask checking questions. An audience treated as a customer is a better audience.

Out of Sight but Not out of Mind

As we covered in the chapter opener, the ever-broadening and decentralizing business base presents certain challenges and needs to the craft of communicating and presenting in business. Many, probably *most,* business meetings within large corporations are either virtual or have a virtual component. *Virtual component?* That means there may be a group of individuals in a conference room working a normal meeting format, but another individual, single group, or multiple groups are joining in using electronic media (usually teleconferencing). And more and more, customers, clients, and suppliers are joining meetings in similar fashion. Technology has provided a lot of the means and media for making these meetings *feasible* and *possible.* You as presenter have to learn to use these technologies and their features. You have to adapt your presentation techniques to make these virtual communications *effective.*

In this section, we'll give an overview of the different virtual media, their advantages and disadvantages, and "best practice" techniques for using them. Developing expertise on advanced technologies and feature sets is beyond the scope of this book. Each one is different and changing every day, anyway. We'll summarize adjustments you may want to make to both preparation and delivery to use these media most effectively.

Virtual Meetings

In a virtual meeting, some or all participants are connected electronically, either through audio (phone), video, an Internet connection, or sometimes a combination of these. Following is a brief overview of today's virtual meeting media and a discussion of some of the basic challenges you'll encounter in a virtual meeting.

Teleconferencing

Teleconferencing is essentially an electronic meeting place established by connecting individual or group ("speaker") phones into a common node. Teleconferences can be composed of individuals at different locations all dialing into a central node, or they can consist of a group in a room with a speaker phone talking to another group in another room with a speaker phone, or a combination of the two. We've seen the "gamut," from three-way individual teleconferences all the way to two or three large meeting rooms all hooked together using speakerphones with dozens or *hundreds* of individuals all dialing in to the central node. Teleconferences obviously suppress visual communication, particularly in body language and expression. Without special preparation, the use of visual aids is more difficult. Phone "hardware" can be designed for the purpose or can be somebody's desktop phone used in speakerphone mode. The good instruments are easy to use, and they pick up and distribute sound quite well, while the desktop varieties work about as well as a three-dollar transistor radio and may require you to shout into them to be heard. If you are with a small business or are a sole practitioner, you may not have sophisticated teleconferencing facilities at hand. Your telephone service provider has conferencing capabilities that can put the same sophistication of a GE or Hewlett-Packard at your fingertips. You can get dedicated service with your own personal teleconference node and number, or you can get a "one-time" setup—just call customer service and ask for teleconferencing services.

Videoconferencing

Videoconferencing technology—just like picture-phone technology—has been around for a while, but it is being only rather slowly adopted in the workplace. Cost, poor quality, complexity of use, and the need for special rooms and studios have hampered its acceptance. Videoconferencing technology comes in two basic modes: studio and PC-based. Studio videoconference setups require rooms to be specially outfitted with cameras, monitors, and controls. Typically these rooms are connected to other videoconference studios with dedicated high-bandwidth communications lines. If they are not, the transmission will be slow, voice and visuals will be out of synch, and visuals will be jerky and distracting. So if your company has multiple, large, geographically distant facilities, you may run into such setups. Obviously a disadvantage is that you can't just connect to anyone anywhere or anytime. Someday these may be as simple and standard as telephones, but we're a long way from that today.

PC-based videoconferencing takes the videoconference idea to the desktop. PCs are outfitted with special cameras and linkable to other PCs with similar technology. But again, you can't link to someone who doesn't have compatible technology, and while the PC-based system works for individuals sitting at their desks, it doesn't work for groups or conference-room settings. The technology has become neither pervasive nor easy to use. If you find yourself videoconferencing in a group of experienced videoconferencers, meetings will be as similar to stand-up presentations as you'll get in the virtual world. You'll have to learn to talk "on camera" (see page 225). But for now, videoconferencing is still at the fringe, though the September 11, 2001, terrorist attacks and resulting reluctance to travel may give this medium a boost. If you are a small business or sole practitioner needing teleconferencing services, you can access them just by visiting your local full-service copy shop.

Internet-Based Meetings

Microsoft, Oracle, and other companies are working hard to develop shared meeting technologies using the Internet. Microsoft NetMeeting allows users to "dial in" to a central node on the Internet just as phone conferencers dial in to a central phone node. NetMeeting users all use their desktop PCs, and a group in a conference room can participate with an Internet-connected laptop and projection system. Essentially the NetMeeting combines the use of a telephone with an Internet-based system to show presentation slides to each "client" desktop. In background, there is also a real-time "chat" utility to allow participants to dialog with each other or log questions for the presenter. Some NetMeetings may be configured to show a "window" with live camera images on the desktop, but this, like PC videoconferencing in general, is still on the fringe.

NetMeeting offers a presenter a way to do a teleconference while delivering visual aids—usually a PowerPoint or similar PC-based set of visuals—onto each participant's desktop in real time and with live animation. This overcomes one of the major limitations of the teleconference (no "live" visual aids) and is becoming more standard on corporate desktops. But NetMeeting is still hard to use for all but the seasoned user, and it requires exceptional meeting leadership and control skills from the presenter.

Virtual Meeting Challenges

It seems that with all that's good, there are also challenges. Virtual meetings allow you to reach larger audiences in real time without enduring endless travel and delays. Some corporate staffs literally never see each other. They simply get together for their weekly teleconference and use teleconferences for whatever meetings are required along the way. They may use a mix of media, such as teleconferences for the short, routine update meeting, and more elaborate Internet-based meetings for major project or department reviews. Use of virtual media is a function of cost, organizational preference, the types of meetings and presentations given, and, obviously, geographic challenges. But with its benefits, virtual media present some basic challenges to even the seasoned presenter, including the following:

- **Live, or Memorex?** As you're no longer "face-to-face" in a virtual meeting, electronic media will to some degree suppress or eliminate some channels of communication. Certain communication barriers and filters will come into play. If you're teleconferencing, then body language, facial expression, and eye contact are lost. Subtle voice inflections and intonations may also be lost, particularly if you talk too fast or too far away from sound capture devices. The very rich nuances of face-to-face communication can be lost, in the same way that an electronic reproduction falls short of a "live" performance. As a presenter, you must be aware of these inhibitors and work to compensate for them when necessary. Here are some tips:
- **Familiarity.** Virtual meetings are supported by technology, and we all have different levels of understanding and comfort with technology.

What might seem like a simple sequence of mouse clicks in Microsoft NetMeeting for some is horrid complexity for others. Some presenters just never get comfortable with a speakerphone. Ever seen someone hunched over a speakerphone as if they were about to throw up on it? To the extent that you or other meeting participants are less than totally familiar and comfortable with the technology, there will be snares. You, as the effective business presenter, will have to help others get through them.

- **Meeting dynamics.** Keeping discussions and dialog under control in a virtual format is challenging. In a teleconference, we cannot pick up visual clues (such as raised hands) when someone wants to talk. It is common for more than one person to try to talk at once. It is easier for meetings to get off track. As the speaker, you can't tell when someone has a question. So as speaker or meeting leader (which you are, since for the time you own the virtual stage), you must exercise stronger leadership and play "traffic cop" to manage all the dialog. You can't "read" the audience as well, and you don't know if they're "getting it"—or even listening. Sitting at your desk while engaged in a telemeeting provides meeting participants a fantastic opportunity to "multitask"—to do other work, surf the Web, read e-mail, check stock quotes, or talk with others at their desk. As presenter, you need to "go the distance" on key points. You must make sure the audience knows you're making them and recapture wandering mindshare. More frequent breaks and checking questions are required to see if your audience has any questions or feedback. These adjustments may not be as necessary in a videoconference, but the issue is still there. You must—more than ever—think about what the audience needs and what it is getting at every moment.
- **Distractions.** Corollary to the technical challenge, the opportunity for distractions is greater in virtual meetings. Many of these distractions originate from the technology itself—glitches, static, poor visual images, cutoffs, and so on. But many more emerge from the nature of the media itself, such as people entering and exiting virtual meetings, outside noise, and our favorite—dentist office music invading the teleconference when someone presses the "hold" button. As an experienced virtual presenter, you will learn to prevent—and deal with—such distractions. Mr. Murphy always lurks as a digitized file, ready to boot up and run at the worst possible moment.

Tips and Tricks for Virtual Meetings

In some companies and organizations, virtual meetings are a way of life. Like public speaking itself, you'll find over time that you tend to get used to the nuances and differences that crop up in virtual meetings. You begin to develop a style, and soon you'll have a checklist to adapt your presenting style to the medium. "Learning curve" progress may seem slow at first, but over time, both you and the organization get better and better at using virtual media.

To help "jump-start" your virtual meeting skills, here is a list of things you might do differently. As in business presentations themselves, there are two major phases—preparation and delivery—and we'll offer some pointers for each. The focus will be on what's *different* in the world of virtual meetings.

Preparation Tips

Following is a short list of considerations in preparing a virtual presentation:

- **Prepare to go slower.** Virtual meetings simply take longer. You will have to talk slower and repeat certain points. People may get lost during the presentation, multiple conversations may break out, or distractions will take you off track. Prepare to cover 25 percent less material in a virtual presentation than you do in a standard stage presentation. If you end up not using this time, it doesn't hurt to end early. We don't know many people who like to be on the phone longer than they have to, and some communication setups, especially teleconferencing, are expensive.
- **Simplify visual aids, and organize them extremely well.** Since you won't be there to point the audience to what you're talking about (although some videoconferencing and Internet conferencing tools may let you point to specific items within images), it's imperative to keep your visuals simple. Complex visuals tend only to lose the audience. Mark each visual clearly so if you say "Refer to Slide 3.1," your audience will be able to follow without delay.
- **Send visuals in advance.** Where possible, make sure everyone has a copy of your visuals. It will help them get familiar with your topic and how the visuals are organized.
- **Confirm everyone's calendar.** Attendance glitches are one of the chief reasons for virtual meeting "stalls." A key audience member doesn't show up because of a calendar mix-up, and guess what: you have to put everyone else on hold while you track them down. Not only will that consume gobs of your valuable "on stage" time, it doesn't do wonders

for your credibility or give you the appearance of being organized either. Another common source of trouble is lost or confused "dial-in" numbers or other connect procedures. To make sure everyone can reach the meeting in the first place, it's a good idea to call in advance to confirm calendars and reiterate access information.

- **Analyze your audience.** Just because you can't see them, it's no less important to know who your audience is and what they need. In fact, the availability of virtual media has a tendency to expand audiences and the diversity of audiences because virtual meetings are easier to attend, especially for teleconferences. Know your audience as customers—who they are, what they need—and be prepared to meet those needs. And be prepared to take a more active role introducing certain parts of the audience to other parts.
- **Check apparatus.** If you're using equipment that you're not completely familiar with, it's a good idea to become familiar *in advance* with its operation. Becoming familiar with it *while* you're trying to deliver your speech is an obvious setup for failure. Learn how to turn it on and off, dial in to networks and meet-me numbers, adjust volume, put people on hold, and how to work the mute buttons. Locate a second phone so you don't have to use your conferencing apparatus to locate other attendees or find help. (You can cut off your conference and lose your "meet-me" line altogether—never a recipe for success!) And if it's videoconferencing or Internet conferencing, spend practice time getting familiar with the media—and how the media handle your presentation. Do a dry run with someone in another location if it's a really important show.
- **Plan for setup time.** More complex virtual media, such as videoconferencing and Internet conferencing, will require setup. You will have to hook everyone in. Invariably there will be small glitches and audience members that may need some coaching. Conference phones must be checked to get their volume and placement right.

Delivery Tips

There's no other way to put it. On the day of the show, you must be a cool, organized, collected cucumber. Your brain will be on multitask mode—managing the presentation itself, delivering the talk around the ideas, staying with the structure, dialoging with the audience—but now you have the additional task of managing the media and making sure the message is getting through to people you can't even see. The task is particularly challenging when you're doing a mixed virtual meeting—where you have an audience in front of you and another audience connected virtually. The following sections present a few tips.

Set the Stage

Perhaps this is part of preparation, but make sure the apparatus is set effectively to pick up and convey the communication. Too often, speakerphones are placed too far away from you or key audience members, and projectors and fans are set up too close, drowning out the sound. Remember that microphones pick up many sounds differently than ears do. At the beginning of your talk—especially if you're the first speaker—you should check acoustics and conveyance. Ask if everyone can hear you clearly, and have a few audience members say something back to you.

Welcome and Introduce Everyone

Go around the "virtual" table and have everyone identify themselves and, if necessary, what organization or department they're from. If someone joins late, identify yourself and have him or her identify themselves. You may also want to inform them who else is attending.

Be Especially Precise with Opening

Tell them what you're going to tell them, and pay special attention to protocol. Set the tone, set the stage, and tell the audience what to expect. Remember that your virtual audience can't see as much, if anything at all, and it is harder for them to interrupt to figure out what's going on. "We are going to go through the slide package I sent you yesterday. The slide set has three parts. On the bottom right-hand corner, I've included numbers that will help you identify the part and page number we are talking from. In general, I will be covering just the first three slides from each part, but if further discussion is needed, we will make time for it. As questions arise, please feel free to interject—identify yourself and then ask your question. If I can answer it then I will. I'm planning for a twenty-minute Q&A session after the presentation, so if you can hold your questions until then, that might be better. Also I understand that Bill, Bob, and Mary are planning to join us at 3:00. Before going further, are there any questions?"

Virtual Meeting Protocol

- Introduce yourself.
- Identify other attendees, or have them self-introduce. Identify their department and job function.
- Establish agenda and timetable, including breaks.
- Identify visual aids.
- Establish questioning and dialog protocol.
- Identify who may be arriving late or leaving early, and other possible interruptions.

Figure 9-1. Establishing protocol in a virtual meeting

Go Slowly

You prepared to go slowly—now stick with it. Going too fast will simply lose people, especially if they are new to the medium. You don't have visual cues, and the audience can't so easily "raise its hand" when it gets lost. As it is impolite to interrupt, audience members may stay silent—and confused. You don't want to go so slow as to be unnatural—this will also lose people. Your best bet is to find a happy medium—a deliberate but not unnaturally slow pace. Keep the pace even, and ask the audience occasionally if the pace is right.

Enunciate

No matter how sophisticated the technology, some members of the audience will find you harder to hear or understand. Speak slowly, clearly, and evenly—as a newscaster would on the evening news. Be especially careful when talking across language barriers and international long distance—technology is great, but it doesn't conquer everything.

Remember, There's No Eye Contact and Body Language

People won't so easily show whether they are interested or bored, getting it or lost. When you hear people typing away in the background on their keyboards, that's a sign of trouble, but otherwise you're not sure if they are there or not. You must make it as easy as possible to stay with you—and ask checking questions every now and then. Plan also to pause a little more frequently.

Be a Strong Leader and Moderator

The success of your presentation will often be determined, not directly by your presentation, but by how well you manage the session. You must stay in control and keep the floor—it's easy for a telemeeting to degenerate into a series of endless sidebar discussions. You must manage the interchange between attendees, repeat and answer questions, step in to set aside distractions, set certain things aside for later, and recapture attention when necessary. Without eye contact, sometimes you must overcompensate verbally—it's a good idea to ask checking questions at certain times to certain parts of the audience. But remember that the risks are magnified of losing an audience in virtual meetings—and also remember that an ounce of prevention is worth a pound of cure. It's hard to get someone back when they've already started a side meeting with someone else or have started reallocating their 401K at their desk.

Remember, Not Everyone Is Comfortable with the Medium

Perhaps you've overcome your shyness with the camera or microphone, but remember that not everyone in the room may have done the same. You may have to encourage some audience members to participate or to participate effectively. Be prepared to coach. This is particularly true if you're using Internet conferencing—you may have to give a little course on using the features with every pitch, unless your work group is totally "into it." Make sure you plan time to accommodate such coaching. If you are really comfortable with the medium, you can achieve recognition in your company by coaching others and making the new medium more effective throughout the business. At the same time, you can benefit your own presentations by making your audience more "functional."

Give Plenty of Road Signs

With all we've said, this is by now fairly obvious. It is important during the body and close of your presentation to give appropriate cues and indicators of where you are and where you're going. A pause and cue, such as "That's it for Part 2. Now let's move into the final part of the presentation to cover the financials, starting on Slide 3.1. We'll spend approximately fifteen minutes on this." Note this isn't too different from our transition recommendations in earlier chapters, but in this case you go into more detail, and perhaps you take a longer pause to let everyone get caught up. More than in normal standup presentations, a pause will serve to get audience members who are "behind" or not fully engaged back on track. But be careful not to let the pauses go on too long, for it's easier for virtual audiences to drift away once the listening imperative appears diminished.

Don't Forget Breaks

People in virtual meetings have biological needs, just as people do in "face-to-face" meetings. Allow time for bathroom breaks and even to take care of routine work issues such as voicemail. Remember to keep the media connections open, at least on your end, otherwise you may lose your audience altogether.

Do Follow-Up

Follow-up is important with all presentations, but it can be even more important with virtual presentations. By doing follow-up, you'll get an idea if the audience "got it." Additional valuable questions and discussions may surface, and you may also uncover technical glitches that may have "blacked out" certain portions of the audience temporarily. Since building rapport is a bit more challenging in a virtual setting, a little follow-up can help enhance rapport and build a more personal relationship.

Manage Distractions

Distractions are an issue with all presentations. When technology is involved, and people are "out there" somewhere and not in the room with you, the opportunities for distractions grow exponentially. Anticipate the distractions—for example, people coming in or leaving. Keep your wits about you, and keep your antennae up to capture potential problems and head them off at the pass. We could go to much greater length talking about virtual presentations, their strengths, weaknesses, and consequences. We firmly believe these media will become more pervasive in business life as the "speed" of business increases, the geographic reach expands, and the importance of controlling travel costs increases. As a successful "knock 'em dead" business presenter, you should always work to sharpen your virtual presenting skills.

Multimedia Megapitch

Peter once had to give a project launch presentation to a large in-person audience, including a company vice president and her entire management team. There were about fifty people in the room. Another roomful of managers and employees, probably twenty-five or so, were conferenced in from another site in a common room. Perhaps twenty more were conferenced in from their desks, with a few more calling in from Europe and Asia. The project launch was for a new Web tool. The presentation included about twenty-five slides showing the basic features and benefits of the Web tool. In addition, there was a live seventeen-page Web demo to be handled by trained agents and made visible by Internet browser.

The audience ranged from the company vice president to call-center agents to system administrators. The main communication medium was teleconferencing, with accompanying Web browsers and projection in the two live rooms. The meeting was about two hours long. The amount of preparation and exactitude required in the delivery were enormous. Peter followed most all of the steps outlined above and prepared for nearly a week. He had to pay attention to the slides, the demo, the live audience, and the virtual audience all simultaneously. He succeeded, but it was clearly one of the most stressful moments of his business-presenting life! Boy, did those refreshments afterward taste great!

Smile, You're on Camera!

Occasionally in the business world, you may find yourself in front of a television camera. It may be in a "standard" context if you get an opportunity to be interviewed or show something on normal broadcast television. Or, as is increasingly common, you may find yourself in front of a video camera, filming a closed-circuit broadcast, making a Webcast, or doing some other television-based communication internal to your company. In many businesses, the visual media is an increasingly important tool to gain visibility among the masses.

For some people, standing in front of a camera is like having a Howitzer aimed right between your eyes—few things could be more intimidating. There's an audience of who-knows-who and who-knows-how-many lurking out there watching for your every misstep. And hard as you try to make it respond to you, that doggoned camera will not move, flinch, bat an eyelash or provide any other "human" response to you or your talk. We've seen some of the most polished, relaxed, dynamic individuals go to pieces when that red light goes on. What do you do? We won't go into the detail here—Chapter 10 has more on handling TV and other external media.

	Advantages	Challenges	Best Practices
Tele-conferences	Inexpensive. Fast, easy setup. Can be done at desk; requires minimum travel. Becoming familiar and pervasive in most businesses.	Establishing rapport. Keeping attention, focus. Incorporating visual aids. No body language or visual cues. Audience participation. Discussions can become disorderly. Access problems cause large distractions.	Introduce everyone, or have them self-introduce. Clearly identify protocol. Make visuals simple and easy to identify. Go slow, ask checking questions, and give audience chance to talk. Exercise strong, assertive leadership. Listen to audience. Make sure pre-conference communication is effective—visual aids, phone numbers.
Video conferences	Body language, eye contact restored. Easier-to-use visual aids. Warmer, more personal.	Expensive. Usually requires special facilities. Not available to everyone. Hard to set up, unfamiliar.	Thoroughly familiarize with setup. Only use when necessary. Use teleconference if facilities are good enough.
Internet meetings	Solves visual aid problem in teleconferences. Can do at desk.	Complex, hard to use, unfamiliar. Not available to everyone.	Make sure beforehand that everyone has capabilities and knows how to use it. Keep visuals simple.

Figure 9-2. Virtual media comparisons and best practices

When You're the Meeting Planner

You never thought it would happen, but—guess what—you're in charge! You may have volunteered or you may have been volunteered. It doesn't matter. Either way, you have to plan a meeting, secure the presenters, and run the meeting. The outcome of the presentation depends as much on you to organize and deliver it effectively as it does on the success of the individual presenters. You have a lot to think about. Really, it isn't altogether unlike planning your own individual presentation. There is a preparation phase, where you must determine the desired outcome, analyze the audience, decide what will be presented, and do the "little stuff" required to make the flow as smooth and effective as possible. Next comes the "delivery" phase—the day of the show—only now you are mainly the stage *manager,* not the lead actor. You still need to make sure things happen as planned and that the desired outcome is achieved. This isn't a book on meetings or meeting management, but we suspect you will be involved sooner or later as a meeting organizer or leader in a business presentation setting, so a few tips are in order.

Surprise—It's All About Preparation

Once you say "yes" to the job of running a meeting (regardless of what *made* you say "yes"), the clock starts ticking. Your job is to put together a good show to achieve a desired outcome. Only this time, you get to delegate the main speaking chores to others. Yes, that makes it easier, in a way. But you still need to plan and organize. You need to get a venue (real or virtual). You need to get the right audience and set their expectations. And you need to get the right speakers and get them to do the right thing. You can't forget those little details that, if you don't think them through in advance, can derail the entire process. It's like managing a work group. Create the right environment, find the right people, set the right objectives and expectations, and get out of the way to let them do their thing. Everything should work right with only minor course corrections. Here are a few specifics:

- **Determine the desired outcome.** Just like in your individual speeches, the first step is to figure out the desired outcome for the session. By the end of the day, what do you want the audience to do, think, or know? Put yourself in the audience's place. What would best drive that desired outcome? Set some goals and objectives for the day as a framework for selecting speakers, topics, audience members, and venue.

- **Decide who should be there.** Selecting the right audience is important. You don't want people who have no interest or connection with the topic, or people who have so little involvement that attending would be a waste of time. On the other hand, you want to include those with significant involvement, decision-making capacity, or "need to know." Typically, you will have an "A" list and a "B" list of attendees—those who really should be there and those who "opportunistically" might want to attend. Use your judgment, but for each potential participant, you should be able to explain *why* they should be there.
- **Determine topics and presenters.** From the desired outcome and the audience makeup, you should be able to outline at least the tentative topics and presenters you'd like to see. Identify the presenter, and then state themes ("in a single sentence," as we did in Chapter 3) for each presenter. Make sure you cover all angles. If it is a new program, talk about operational, marketing, and financial aspects if they are appropriate. If it is a more specific topic, think through what depth and detail might be required. Again, keep the audience's needs in mind. Once you have your list of topics and single-sentence themes, plug the presenters in as you see fit.
- **Structure the day.** How much time to set aside for the whole meeting—and each presenter—is a judgment call. You must weigh the importance of the meeting and each topic with the amount of attention the audience will be willing to allocate to it. If it's an all-day meeting, you'd better have a pretty good reason to make it an all-day meeting. You need to respect your audience's needs to keep up with their "day jobs" outside your meeting. For most business meetings, other than training sessions or major planning workshops, half a day or less is a good guideline. If you can get it done in an hour or two, all the better. But it's generally not a good idea to force people into speaking segments of any less than half an hour. For each speaker and topic, you'll want to set a guideline in advance for how long it should take. Be prepared to negotiate with the presenter. Build a rough schedule and have it ready to discuss with your presenters.
- **Contact presenters.** Meet with or call your presenters (a personal touch is usually better). Tell them what the meeting is all about, what the desired outcome is, and how they fit into the day. Show them a tentative agenda or structure. Tell them who the audience will be. Share the

single-sentence theme with them. Tell them how much time you had in mind, and, if appropriate, give suggestions for what and how much they should say. Help them help you, and do your best to get their commitment. Be as flexible as possible. If you wanted them in the morning, but they're available only in the afternoon, go with it if possible. And if they can only teleconference in, go with that, too.

- **Plan the venue.** As we've seen, whether real or virtual, venues done right are an asset. Venues that are done wrong or that are not thought through create problems. If it's a "real" venue, get a good room in a convenient location. Make sure it is big enough and that it has the right audio-visual facilities. If it doesn't, work with those in charge to *get* the right equipment. Some presenters just won't be effective if they do laptop projection and all you have is an overhead projector. If they want dry-erase pens to use on a white board (or if you *think* they might)—make sure in advance that they are available. Think about things like food, drinks, access to telephones, parking, chairs, tables, microphones, podiums, screens—and so forth. Set up the venue just as you would want it set up yourself to deliver the kinds of presentations you're asking for. Remember that one path to an audience's heart is through its stomach, but don't make food and refreshments so elaborate as to be distracting.
- **Develop a kickoff.** You may not be "on" for a presentation slot yourself, but by virtue of your role, you are on the hook at least to perform the meeting kickoff. A meeting kickoff is not unlike a presentation opener. Your goals are to establish rapport, establish the theme and message for the day, and tell them what you're gonna tell them. Thank them for attending, and explain what they will get out of the day and how they will *benefit* from it. Go through the schedule. Advise the audience who will speak and about what. Again, the single-sentence themes—with maybe a little more elaboration—will work. Go through protocol. Tell them where the restrooms are and when the breaks are planned and so forth. Get them prepared and "psyched" for what follows.
- **Reminder message.** Many business meetings require careful advance planning. The meeting may be so far in advance that a quick reminder will help to make sure both your audience and presenters are still "hooked in" to your day. Advise what, where, when, and why the meeting is happening. If it is a virtual meeting, remind folks of meet-me numbers and passwords. You may recapture a few "strays"—given that people *do* forget or get called into other things—and it shows a greater degree of

passion, interest, and involvement on your part. Of course, if you just planned the meeting two hours ago, which sometimes does happen in today's fast-paced business world, reminders probably aren't necessary.

And Now—It's Showtime

Just as with individual presentations, handling the meeting should follow a path—*your* path. It is important to keep presentations on track, to keep the audience on track, and to deal with contingencies. Just as it's hard to recover from a derailed presentation, recovery from a derailed meeting may be even more difficult: the difficulty compounds with the number of speakers and the length of the session. A meeting gone asunder usually reflects badly on *you.* Successful meeting leadership and execution usually requires the elements discussed in the following sections.

Deliver a Strong Kickoff

Much of what happens during the rest of the session depends on how effectively you lead, or "kick off," with an opening presentation. Clearly articulate the desired outcome and all the steps you envision to get there. Tell people what will happen during the session, and set their expectations. Tell them who will present, and give an idea for what they will present. Get them motivated—*excited*—to be there, to the point they forget they have jobs outside the door. And don't forget to discuss protocol—restrooms, food, breaks, and general guidelines for questions and discussions. Identify the materials they will receive. Ask a few checking questions to make sure the audience—particularly key audience members—are "on board" with your program and the time allocated to different activities. The kickoff should be short and sweet—the audience isn't necessarily there to hear *you.* Keep it to fifteen or twenty minutes at most, and make it shorter if the session itself is a few hours or less.

Introductions

You may choose to introduce presenters and key audience members during the kickoff, or you may save presenter introductions until they speak. That's your choice. Keep in mind that not all presenters may be present in the beginning. Share a few words about their credentials, their work, and why they have been chosen to attend.

Transitions

Providing effective transitions between sections of the meeting is one of your key roles as meeting leader. When one speaker's presentation ends and another is about to begin, you should step in, thank the earlier speaker, summarize a few nuggets from their pitch, introduce the next speaker, call breaks, and take care of other announcements and housekeeping items. This helps the audience make the transition and helps keep the meeting on track. Without good transitions, people tend to drift away. The next speaker may not start on time. You can help the current speaker wrap up on time by stepping forward in the room to signal that the presenter should move to close.

Wrap-Up

A meeting without a wrap-up is like a book missing its last page. The audience is left hanging without closure. A good wrap-up summarizes the day's events and outcome. Really, it's an expanded version of "Tell them what you told them." In the wrap-up, recognize and thank your participants for their achievements. Recognize your audience as well for their time, learning, patience, and good dialog.

Stay Positive

Many things can go awry and get "under your skin," but it's your job as meeting leader to deal with them and stay positive. Frustration over schedule changes, interruptions, and distractions will infect the audience and, eventually, your presenters. These frustrations can make you lose control. Stay upbeat and positive. Be flexible, and try to appreciate what presenters and the audience do even if it isn't what you had in mind.

Be Assertive

While being positive and flexible, it is important at the same time to be assertive, gently, quietly—but relentlessly. You're in control, and the outcome of the meeting depends on you. Manage the flow, the schedule, and your people to deliver the outcome. Don't be afraid to interrupt or step in to change something that needs to be changed. If a presentation appears headed to go a half-hour long, jump in and ask the presenter to speed up (politely and helpfully, of course!). If something needs to change and you don't "step up," your credibility will rapidly disappear and your meeting will slip away toward chaos. But don't be too assertive. Meeting leaders shouldn't completely take over or upstage the participants.

In Short . . .

In today's rapidly changing and increasingly fast-paced business environment, you are sure to run into frequent situations where presentation skills are required, even if not in front of a live audience. Just as you learn and grow into the art of presenting itself, you will learn and grow into the special capabilities and nuances of alternative presentation media and special presentation situations.

Do's	Don'ts
• Plan and organize your talk much as you would for a live audience. • Be aware of the limitations of the medium, and adjust for them. • Stay patient and calm. Be flexible and adaptable during delivery. • Pay special attention to introductions, protocol, and setting expectations in the opener. • Exercise strong, patient, active listening and leadership. Don't let control slip away. • Ask checking questions, and reach out to the audience.	• Don't leave preparation and setup to the last minute—it will invariably interfere with delivery. • Don't try to do too much. Keep it simple. Reduce your content by 25 percent or more. • Don't forget to take breaks and pauses. • When on camera, don't act. Be yourself.

Figure 9-3. Do's and don'ts of presenting using alternative media

10 Build on Your Excellence

Build your professional "brand" by speaking more effectively and more often.

Your business presentation skills are a springboard to new levels of professional success. Throughout this book, we have talked about making business presentations in the larger context of long-term career management. The skill sets you use to make good business presentations can work to your benefit throughout your career. The ability to express your professional competence will increase your professional credibility and widen the sphere of influence in your professional life. The dedicated professional can learn to nudge this process along to his or her advantage.

Building Your Professional "Brand"

All professional fields and fields of creativity share some common ground in the nuts and bolts of their creative processes. In all fields, creativity is only recognized when it is fixed in a communication medium and shared with a larger audience. Increasingly in the modern world, creative people can experience a degree of success in one medium only to learn that they can apply their creative drive to expression in other media. You are one of these creative people. You create and fix your ideas in a recognizable medium, and it is only logical for you to learn to apply your creativity in a different communication media. You can take your message to a wider audience, whether it's through the printed word or through the glamour of radio or television. What you learn in this chapter will maximize the impact of the lessons in the rest of the book. It will also give a sound introduction to the underpinnings of both "external" and "internal" public relations. This is another much admired professional competence, whose acquisition will only serve to increase your satisfaction with your work life.

External and Internal Public Relations

As a professional, your goal is to become more widely recognized and to build greater credibility in whatever you do in your profession. Greater recognition leads to bigger assignments and more important undertakings. Ultimately, building your "brand" leads to promotion opportunities within your business. It can also improve your visibility outside your organization. What builds your "brand recognition"? Solid performance is a big part of it, to be sure. Style without substance nets only temporary gains—if any at all. But substance without style, while normally enough to get by or even to bring modest success, may well stop short of producing the big career wins you're looking for. Certainly, some people are happy to do a good job, and that's that. The upside is that they continue to get to do that good job. They may be rated highly enough to get paid well and achieve all the comforts and recognition accorded to a true expert. But that's the upside. Without a little good public relations, or PR, even the best job done can sometimes result in misunderstood results or in someone else with inferior talents getting the plum assignments—or even *your* job. You need to do a little marketing—*marketing of yourself.* Remember that PR and personal "branding" are good *offensive* career tools, but they can also be important *defensive* career tools in many organizations.

Let's make the distinction between "external" and "internal" PR. In some situations, the distinction is clearer than in others. Here is the essential difference: External PR involves building your name and recognition within the industry and in external media—essentially outside the four walls of your organization. External PR means getting involved in outside organizations such as trade and industry associations, public interest groups, and the media.

Internal PR, on the other hand, refers to getting your name and talents into important places *inside* your organization, such as the company president's task force, certain high-visibility job assignments, project assignments, foreign assignments, and so forth. In doing so, your name gets recognized more widely in the organization. You get recognized for your versatility, diversity of talents, and leadership. And if you've figured out by now that success with external branding leads to internal branding success, you're getting it. Give the headline speech at the trade association in your field, and you're bound to get some recognition in your own organization.

As you may have guessed by now, your ability to deliver good business presentations is a vital ingredient in the personal "brand development" process. Being important requires you to let others know how important you are.

External PR Secrets

External PR is all about getting yourself into public forums, whether within or outside your profession, and in front of the public at large. There are many ways to accomplish this. Just like speaking itself, external PR requires identifying potential audiences, understanding them, building a message, and delivering it. As there is plenty of competition for most external PR venues, there is an additional element: *getting noticed.* For that, we offer some additional tips and tricks for getting the PR opportunities you crave.

Finding External PR Opportunities

In the beginning, when you start to deliver presentations for audiences bigger than your department, you might well spend weeks or even months developing a program, which subsequently runs a mere forty-five minutes. While this is professionally worthwhile in and of itself, you will benefit far more from your efforts if you can find venues where you can repeat that same performance.

If you develop a presentation for one particular event, the chances are that it can be given in countless other venues as well. You may have to customize it (as discussed in Chapter 6), but most of the work will nevertheless have been done.

The number of different audiences for your work depends on its applicability. The wider its general appeals, the greater the likelihood that you can find speaking opportunities.

Beyond speaking opportunities, there are fringe benefits. The benefits and advantages of *networking* are there to be had. You will gain more knowledge and insight about what you do, what others do, and how they do it. And networks also furnish resources. There are people to hire, merchandise to buy, and—just maybe—jobs to be had as you move up in your industry and pursue your career.

Outside of your own company, there are opportunities at the local meetings of professional associations. Every working professional should be an active member of at least one professional association. As a speaker, you should seriously consider membership in multiple associations. You will benefit from the ongoing professional development programs, from a much greater professional network, and from more speaking opportunities and the myriad ways they will impact your credibility and visibility. Even small towns have dozens of speaking opportunities going begging every month. Look close and far, narrow and wide for the multitude of possible speaking venues and audiences, such as the following:

- **Professional and trade associations.** Most professions have some kind of trade group or association. Even if the association doesn't fit exactly, it's likely to be close. Some are nonprofit associations and interest groups. Others are for-profit enterprises that host paid-for conferences in your field. Even if you're in an hourly labor type of situation, chances are there's a union, club, or organization for people in similar positions. The list is endless. If in doubt, ask your colleagues or manager. A quick Web portal search will usually find you an organization or two. Here are some examples:
    - AMA (American Management Association)—for general business and management.
    - IIR (Institute for International Research)—for-profit organization sponsoring trade seminars and conferences in the field of marketing.
    - ASME (American Society of Mechanical Engineers)—and others covering all engineering and technical professions.
    - APICS (American Production and Inventory Control Society) for materials and inventory management.
    - SWE (Society for Women Engineers)—for female professionals.
- **Community service organizations.** Your town has numerous groups that run meetings on an ongoing basis, and those meetings require speakers. Apart from local chapters of national associations, such groups include the following:
    - Chambers of Commerce.
    - Church groups.
    - Youth groups.
    - PTA and other family-oriented groups.
    - Fraternal groups, such as Kiwanis, Rotary, and other organizations.
    - Charities.
    - Libraries.
- **Other public venues.** As book authors, we often find ourselves giving talks on our books in local bookstores. There may be a retail shop or some other commercial establishment interested in hearing about you and your work. And don't forget local schools. Students are always

excited to hear about things that come from the "real world," no matter how mundane they might seem to you. (We can't all be firefighters or astronauts, can we?) Speaking to students is a delightful way to practice your pitch. You must keep your points short, sweet, and simple in that kind of audience. And you had better build rapport early—or else! The kinds of questions you get may really show a different perspective and will keep you on your toes. Each of these will serve to further build your speaking and credibility base.

Building a Speech Synopsis

To get yourself in front of one of these audiences, it is important to develop a summary of your pitch, including why it will interest that group. Building the synopsis is much like stating a theme and message, but the synopsis may go just a bit deeper into the topics you cover and the style of your pitch.

> *Sparing the Children in Divorce.*
>
> Michelle Lilt, attorney with the firm of Lewis, Banks and Larson, talks on the topic of how to minimize the negative impact of divorce on a couple's children. The talk goes for an hour, sharing numerous experiences from a legal and emotional perspective on how to deal with this delicate situation. A question-and-answer session follows. Recently, Ms. Lilt was the guest at the library's Tuesday night lecture series, where she held the audience spellbound.

Figure 10-1. Sample synopsis

The speaker here was a regular divorce attorney who developed a presentation that promoted her practice with an angle that had wide consumer appeal. The presentation positioned her as a caring and decent human being in a profession not always known for its compassion and decency. This is an almost totally overlooked PR technique that serves not only to increase awareness of your speaking availability but also of your professional availability. This can only serve to increase your long-term employability.

A more detailed synopsis of your presentation might also be developed for wider, more "national" distribution. Develop a synopsis that contains some of the real substance of your presentation. Short pieces like this are easier to do and are therefore less intimidating to attempt than bona fide articles (which we'll address shortly). They also provide a good steppingstone into the world of print. Because the target publications are less formidable, they are likely to be good confidence builders as you take your message into new media.

. . . But Don't Expect to Be Paid

Few of these situations offer much opportunity to generate income from your speaking efforts. However, with a couple of years of conscientious effort at company and local venues, you can become a competent and respected professional speaker. When this happens, other opportunities open up for you. All those local association chapters are part of national groups that hold regular conferences and trade shows. Every one of these events requires speakers. As they say, "No man is a prophet in his own land": meeting planners are always on the lookout for a speaker from out of town.

You will hear about upcoming conferences and conventions as you become connected to your community and profession through your speaking activities and by keeping your ear to the ground. As a rule of thumb, the bigger the conference, the longer the development lead-time you will need. Big associations book venues three and sometimes five years out. However, speakers are usually booked in the twelve to six months before the event.

If you develop topics with broad enough appeal, your fame as a speaker can extend far beyond your profession and industry segment. It can take you literally around the world. As audiences get to know you and as your reputation spreads, more and bigger speaking engagements can come to you gradually over time. This process really does take time to develop, so think in terms of calendars, not clocks. Encourage the development of your reputation by approaching the types of organizations we have addressed in this section. Additionally, you can seek representation from speaker's bureaus and lecture agents.

Presentation "Recycling"

One presentation given once will give your credibility and visibility a little bump, but it won't make a significant change in your professional life. The more you stand up and are heard, the more you will build your reputation. The best way to achieve your long-term goals is by building presentations around more topics and then recycling those topics into other media will. A particular presentation and body of work around your speaking topic makes you, in the eyes of the world, a bona fide expert. And as an expert you can take your ineffable wisdom into other media. You can use it to recycle your knowledge by doing the following:

- Getting quoted in a newspaper or magazine as a subject-matter expert.
- Writing articles for newspapers and magazines in your area of expertise.
- Using your presentations, articles, and body of knowledge as the basis for a book.
- Getting interviewed on the radio as a subject-matter expert.
- Getting interviewed on the TV as a subject-matter expert.

Meeting the Press

Few things have more impact than a couple of well-placed mentions in the press. A wide audience reads them. Most people immediately assign great credibility to whatever they read, almost by virtue of the fact that the material appeared in the press in the first place. Occasionally the audience is narrower, as in a trade or industry "rag." In that case, you know a greater portion of the audience is aware and interested in the topic. In any event, you can exploit the power of the press to your advantage. It is amazing to see jaws drop and eyes go wide when you circulate a newspaper or magazine story that includes you or, better yet, is *about* you or something you did.

There are two paths to media coverage. First, you can issue a press release. (You might also have your company's PR department do this for you—sometimes a better idea.) The other path is to get actual press coverage, where members of the media—journalists—seek to interview and cover you.

Issuing Press Releases

Getting into print is much easier than you think. Newsletters, newspapers, and magazines all have a voracious appetite for news, and short announcements come in very useful for filling in odd blank spaces on the page. There's a newspaper, magazine, or newsletter to support every organized activity in modern life. Every group with whom you are active will have a reason and interest in publishing the noteworthy activities of its members.

Press releases do more than get you better known to those aware of your existence. They bring your name and capabilities to an entirely new public, some of which will one day be looking for a speaker or a professional for their team who knows how to handle herself in public! The committed professional will make every effort to connect to his or her profession via association membership and to his community via volunteer, fraternal, social, and church activities.

And again, remember that the press is *always* looking for something to print. For some reason, people feel that getting press coverage is a once-in-a-lifetime opportunity, an honor and a privilege. That's not usually true. Behind most published material, there's a journalist or editor hungry to fill space with something. They win by getting your material to publish, and you win by getting your material *published.*

Make the press release short and to the point, and be sure to include contact information for the publication so it can gather more information, if necessary. The following example of a press release isn't very grand or on its surface memorable in any way. It appeared in a village news bulletin on the activity calendar.

Wednesday. Local employment expert talks about job hunting. Church Hall 9 PM

Figure 10-2. Sample news bulletin

The actual press release gave the speaker's name and intimated that he could walk on water and swallow fire, all of which mysteriously disappeared by the time the press release reached print. Why would we show you such an innocuous example? Because these things start small and must be pursued over time. The release in question is framed and sits on the wall in Martin's office as a reminder of small beginnings. Since the publication of that release, he has earned hundreds of thousands of dollars from speaking engagements in countries around the world. A life-changing activity, it all started when he determined to improve his business presentation activities. Getting into the village newsletter was hardly the greatest PR coup of the last twenty-five years. It is important only because it speaks of what PR is really about, raising public awareness with lots of small actions applied consistently over time.

Letters to the Editor—and to Journalists

Another approach is to write letters to the editor of broad or industry-specific publications. You can take the topic of your presentation and reposition it as a matter of interest to the readership. (Think carefully of the readership to give yourself the right angle of attack.) You send this as a letter to the editor, either in response to a published piece from that organization on a related topic or as an issue that you feel might be of interest to the readership.

Getting Published

Just as you must address the needs of an audience in a presentation, you must meet the needs of journalists to get published. It helps to understand *that* audience.

Journalists get paid by the word and by column inches. They are assigned an area of specialization and are required to produce product in that area on an ongoing basis. They have to take topical ideas in their area and turn them into stories, and they have to do it every day. In newspapers and magazines, the use of subject-matter experts is seen to give substance to the topic. Journalists are always on the lookout for expert testimony. Some of these references are quite brief—perhaps just a one-line quote with your name on it—but effective for you nonetheless. The first step is to identify the publications that speak to your area of expertise. In the next step, you get to know the needs of those publications.

Magazines have calendars that identify ongoing needs for different times of the year. While each publication has a specific focus, and therefore somewhat unique needs, they do all work to a calendar. Let's take women's consumer and fashion magazines as a broad example, one with which we all are able to identify. These magazines follow the fashion cycle of the seasons, but they are also an ongoing source of advice and inspiration to women about their health, finances, love life, entrepreneurial, career, and other important issues. Their calendar for business-oriented articles and columns is easy to understand.

For example, the months of December and January are always times for career planning. New Year's is the time for professional resolution and "start your own business" pieces. Why? Because that is what we all think about at this time of year. Such pieces strike a chord with the readership. By the same token, issues from March through May—graduation time—always have pieces on career choice and breaking into the world of work for the first time. September often finds pieces on returning to the workforce or to education and learning venues.

This same kind of logic applies to all publications. Start reading the press. Look for themes that follow the general calendar or the topics that apply to a particular profession at a given time of year. Another good example is journals for accounting and finance, which are guaranteed to need pieces on tax planning, especially in the early months of the year. You can approach the editorial departments of magazines and ask for their calendars. A good resource for this is *Writer's Market*, published by Writer's Digest Books. You can buy this book, check it out at your local library, or access its information at *www.writersdigest.com*. *Writer's Market* identifies the vast majority of U.S. magazines. It gives information about editorial needs and contact information. For both magazines and newspapers you should also start clipping articles and columns that carry bylines. File these by month, and over a period of time you will begin to see the ongoing needs for certain types of articles at different times of the year. You will also begin to build a database of journalists who write about topics in which you have subject matter expertise.

Another thing to remember is that while ego has us thinking about *US News and World Report* and the front page of the *New York Times,* common sense tells us that we might start with the local "Business Journal" or some similar publication. Realism tells us that any press is good press. We not only have a better chance of getting into smaller publications to begin with, but it will give us valuable experience in dealing with journalists and the confidence to deal with bigger publications down the road. Journalists want to gain knowledge that they can use to beef up the piece they are working on and quotes they can attribute to a bona fide subject matter expert. But most of all they want sources who can be succinct and to the point. This is where your development as a speaker pays big dividends. Learning to share your knowledge in a concise, succinct, and entertaining manner in front of an audience is excellent training for dealing with the press.

Building a Media Relationship

It helps to have a consistent relationship with members of the media. You want the relationship so that they *call you* when they need something. But that can take a while. Building that kind of relationship starts with really understanding what a particular media resource or journalist needs. You can study this over time. Eventually, you'll understand what they need as well as they do. Collect articles and columns that address your areas of expertise. Build an awareness of the "beat" a particular journalist covers by analyzing their subject matter and approach, and attempt to identify trends and recurring themes.

It's a two-way street. Journalists are like other mortals, at least in that they are susceptible to a little judicious flattery. Just as you and I appreciate a round of applause after a presentation, the journalist always appreciates a compliment and a thoughtful comment on a recent piece. Building bridges to journalists is as easy as dropping a note about the quality of a recent piece.

You can write occasional notes saying you liked a piece, or you can suggest an idea yourself. "If you ever consider doing a piece on ______, I would be happy to be a resource for you."

One day that journalist will quote you. What you can achieve with one journalist in a local paper, you can multiply by your energy level. Being quoted in the press gives you tear sheets to send out with your speaking proposals as supporting evidence that you are a bona fide subject-matter expert, recognized by the press. Your press clippings also add to your personal credibility and visibility within your profession. It can even add a line to your resume.

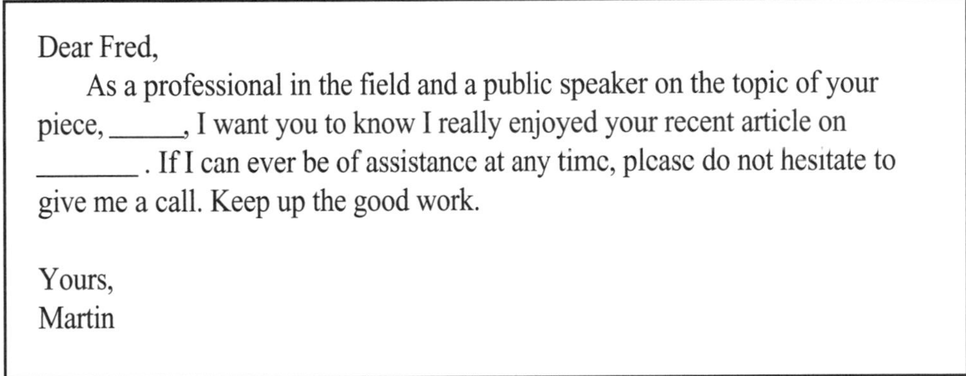

Dear Fred,

As a professional in the field and a public speaker on the topic of your piece, _____, I want you to know I really enjoyed your recent article on _______ . If I can ever be of assistance at any time, please do not hesitate to give me a call. Keep up the good work.

Yours,
Martin

Figure 10-3. Sample letter of appreciation to a journalist

Make Your Credentials Known and Available

Some people are incurable egotists, walking billboards bragging and advertising every feature and virtue of their existence wherever they go—whether true or not. Others, probably the majority of us, don't realize just how many credentials and valuable experiences we really have. If you plan to get involved in the media, it helps to take a complete inventory of everything you've done, learned, and experienced. Well—maybe not everything—the summer job twenty-five years ago at the local drive-in theater just might be perceived as irrelevant. But take inventory and be sure to include all the professional stuff—jobs, degrees, licenses, and accreditations. Hit on any media experience, whether large, medium or small. You may also include a few things outside your profession as well, especially if they reflect leadership, achievement, or unique and special interests. The fact that you lead the church choir may well pique the interest of someone. Here's an example:

Education and Professional Credentials

John Smith

M.S., INFORMATION SYSTEMS ENGINEERING
Polytechnic University, Brooklyn, NY
B.S., BUSINESS ADMINISTRATION
Pennsylvania State University, State College, PA
AFFILIATIONS
Member IEEE, NASD Series 7, 63, 3, New York Academy of Sciences, NYSSA
MEDIA
CNBC, CNNfn Digital Jam, CNN Your Money, CNN Nightly Business Report, Bloomberg, MSNBC, CNBC Smart Money, *Wall Street Journal,* Dow Jones

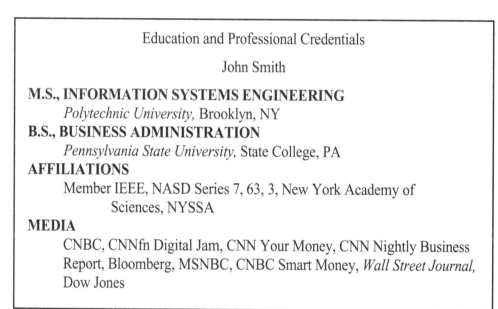

Figure 10-4. Sample summary of expertise and experience

Remember "Freedom of the Press"

Here's a word of caution to heed. You have no control over what is ultimately printed in a newspaper or magazine. You can be misquoted, so be careful with what you say. Everything you say to a journalist is on the record. Don't for a moment think you can get away with off the record quotes because you can't. Controversy and ill-considered remarks are godsends to journalists always looking to inject a little excitement into their stories. Don't let it be at the expense off your reputation. You can do worse than adopt the Hollywood ethos in this regard: speak no ill of your colleagues, profession, or competition. Speak well of all at all times, and if you must criticize, be sure you decline to give concrete examples that name names. Ignore this advice at your peril.

If at First You Don't Succeed . . .

When you read the papers and trade magazines, you see fellow professionals quoted all the time. Sometimes the press sought them out for interviews, but that doesn't happen very often. When it does, it is also invariably the result of that person's having consciously made himself or herself visible to that press as part of an ongoing personal public relations program. These programs are carefully integrated into their long-term career management programs, in just the ways we are discussing here. These things don't happen by accident. The people you see quoted in the press, the professionals with their bylines attached to an article or a book or who you hear on the radio and see on the television, have all worked to get there. In the instance of the press, they took the time to understand a particular publication's needs and they made themselves known. They invested themselves in this activity over time, understanding how valuable third-party public endorsements can be to a career.

Writing Articles

There's usually a logical development to your PR program. Taking your expertise and speaking abilities into new arenas happens by logical steps. However, each of these media presents its own challenges. It is better to start with the easier steps, and that is why we have talked first about getting your name in the press. Now we'll address turning your presentations and other professional expertise into articles that you write for magazines, trade journals, and other publications.

The hardest part of any writing is getting the nascent idea down on paper. Rewriting and polishing what you have written isn't nearly as exciting a task as capturing the ideas in the first place. That's why the true definition of creativity is not so much having good ideas in the first place but rather having the ability to manifest those ideas in a communication medium and then to take them to a larger audience. With all the work you did in preparing your presentation, you have the raw materials for one or more articles. You are simply taking the hard work you have done for one medium and transposing it to another.

One presentation can become an article for a company or association newsletter or even a series of shorter pieces. The trend in the press is for shorter and shorter pieces. It is conceivable that you can take each section of a presentation and turn it into a brief article. This way you can get your name out there to a professional public a number of times. While there is much to be read and much to learned about the form and style of short nonfiction, the biggest assets you need are the following:

- Subject-matter expertise.
- The desire to make the effort.
- The will power to rewrite, until you get it right.

Having gone through the process of building and giving a business presentation, it should be quite clear that you already have these assets. You also have the structure and the content of the article already in place. Journalistic writing basically follows the familiar presentation format: *Tell 'em what you are going to tell them, tell them, and tell them what you told them.*

The editorial standards of a national magazine are much higher than that of a company newsletter or association journal. However, you don't need that national exposure to benefit from people seeing your name in print. Any publication that gets your name and work in front of a reading public will add to your professional stature.

If you try turning a presentation into an article, or even just part of it, you'll be pleased to discover that your graphics and handouts provide all the information you need to write a publishable article. In effect, you are at least halfway there. If you try your hand at writing an article, be prepared to do a number of rewrites. Most people will struggle through a piece and at the end experience elation at having actually written something for publication. Then the next day, when they come back to read their words of deathless prose, they realize that overnight it turned into the total gibberish. Don't despair. Like fine wine, writing gets better with time and gentle, persistent work.

If you complete the process, you will also likely come to a realization. While a presentation can readily be recycled into an article, an article idea can just as readily be developed into a presentation. The message here is that when you take subject-matter expertise out of your head and share it with the world by fixing it in a communication's medium, the options for recycling are almost infinite. You are capable of creating in many different media.

You Really Could Write the Book

It's an oversimplification to say that a book is nothing more than ten big articles strung together. But at the same time, the statement contains a whole lot of truth. In fact, over the coming years, you will probably see many chapters of this book recycled into articles in professional journals as part of our ongoing PR campaign to increase and maintain awareness.

Everything you learn in building and making presentations helps you prepare to share your knowledge in these other mediums. If you can write and make a presentation, you can write an article. If you can write one article, you can write ten articles. In its simplest form, a book is nothing more than ten thoughtfully developed "articles" linked together as chapters. In fact, the content of every chapter of this book has also appeared in presentations by one or another of the authors over the last twenty-five years.

Your presentation might have enough content to support a book all by itself, although this is not usually the case. It's more common that a combination of presentations and articles within your area of expertise will coalesce into the larger scope of a book. A book may seem beyond you now, but in reality it is within your grasp. Bear the lessons of the book in mind as you develop presentations and perhaps turn those presentations into articles. There are few more satisfying achievements—or ones that enhance your credibility—than writing a book in your field of expertise. It is the same power of having your name in print, only this time your name is on two or three hundred printed pages that are distributed nationally or even internationally. It speaks better than almost anything else for your credibility and ability to present your facts and your topics for the benefit of others.

Appearing on Radio and Television

Taking your message to the electronic media is another way of recycling your professional expertise. This method requires you to compact and distill your expertise into just a few moments. It presents some challenges but offers some very exciting opportunities for exposure.

Working in the electronic media is a challenge. You usually have just a few minutes of airtime, and that time will be driven by the host's agenda. You will be fielding questions. You are expected to come up with concise, meaningful answers, literally on the spur of the moment. Only a deep, wide body of knowledge on your subject will give you the ability to distill complex ideas into the succinct expression necessary with electronic media.

Live or Tape

You may be live or taped. This is actually the least of your challenges. With live broadcast it all happens in real time. The interview goes out over the airwaves as it occurs. With tape, the interview may happen weeks beforehand. But it will have been recorded "live" and the interview will be treated as such to give your segment the immediacy that makes radio and television so gripping.

Your typical airtime on television is going to be just three or four minutes (a little longer on radio). In that time, the anchor will introduce the segment and start firing questions at you. You are expected to give short, smart answers that allow those three or four minutes to sound like a genuine impromptu conversation. You usually won't know in advance exactly what the questions will be (though we do have some tips to stack the odds in your favor). Then, at the end, the anchor has to wrap your segment and transition to the next part of the show. This leaves no time for rambling or thinking out loud. You have to be on top of your game to work in these media, but it is a skill you can develop and master and have for the benefit of your long-term career management.

If this sounds stressful, that's because it is. Why would you want to strut your stuff on the radio or television? Because it is great PR: for you, for your company, for a product or service you might be promoting (say your upcoming presentation, or the book you'll write one day), or for a professional association with whom you are associated.

You will never experience another four minutes that goes by as quickly as it does when you're on the air. Time seems to compact in a frightening way, and it is all over before you get going.

Getting "On the Air"

Getting "on the air" requires many of the same efforts and techniques we discussed with print media. First, you need to understand your role within the medium. You are on the air to entertain the audience between commercials. If you manage to be entertaining between the commercials, the host gets to keep his or her job, the commercial sponsors sell their product, and everyone is happy. The radio or television station needs to entertain and retain its listeners and watchers. That makes you the centerpiece of the station's effort to obtain and maintain audience interest. You must make your host successful, too. Do it well, and you're likely to get chances to appear over and over—even to discuss topics derived from or removed from the original. As an example, Jennifer Basye Sander, wife of coauthor Peter, appeared on a local television morning talk show to discuss her book *The Complete Idiot's Guide to Getting Published.* Six months later, when Bill Clinton took a multimillion advance to write his memoirs, she was asked back by the station to comment on this transaction.

The TV and Radio "Pitch"

You get on the air by pitching radio and television stations to have you on as a guest. Radio and television audiences are made up of the general public. They are not fellow professionals. They come from all walks of life. While they watch or listen to your performance, they are engaging in every conceivable activity known to man. This means that you must have a topic with wide consumer appeal. The broader the appeal of your topic, the greater the likelihood you will get a booking. This means looking at your professional expertise in a different way. For example, a certified public accountant (CPA) may feel that her profession has little to offer in the way of consumer appeal. That may be especially true if her latest presentation was about the recent changes to corporate tax law S34567 H. She would be right in this thinking, but she also has a wide body of knowledge that could be of value to the man and woman in the street. As with all presentations, she only has to *think about the customer and what they would want.* A CPA likely has a body of knowledge that encompasses the following topics of interest:

- **Tax preparation.** In the months coming up to tax season, the CPA could well get a producer's attention by suggesting segments about deadlines for various deductible activities. She could talk about the different deadlines for deductions. For example, charitable contributions have to be made by the end of the calendar year, but IRA contributions can be made up to the time of your tax filing on the fifteenth of April.
- **Retirement planning**. The same accountant could well get a producer's attention by suggesting segments about the benefits of starting a retirement plan sooner rather than later. She could describe how to start a retirement plan on a budget and how to fund a retirement plan no matter your age or income level.
- **Getting out of debt.** Well, you get the idea.

The same thinking applies to any profession. Because of your profession and industry, you have special knowledge with wide consumer appeal. If your business presentations don't immediately translate to the wide consumer appeal necessary to access the electronic media, you just have to work out what the consumer angles are.

Internal PR

Internal PR refers to the art and science of building yourself as a "brand" within your organization. Indeed, you are marketing *yourself,* and there are many ways to do this. The idea is to create visibility for *you* and *what you do.* The end result is that your achievements are recognized. You become the more likely candidate or selection for special assignments, promotions, and job opportunities. Toil away in silence, and you might be quite happy, but like a product placed on a shelf with no marketing investment, not even a package, you are less likely to get noticed and sold.

Building Internal PR

We could probably write an entire book on building your own internal brand identity. This is a book on business presentations. The importance of business presenting to brand building is obvious. Become a good speaker and the obvious authority on any topic, and your internal "brand equity" is bound to increase. And as we mentioned in the beginning of the chapter, building your external brand will carry over into the internal workplace. If you've written the articles, written the book, spoken at the trade show or conference, or appeared on TV, you become almost instantly more known and credible inside your organization.

Internal branding opportunities may not *directly* involve speaking, but they probably will involve some speaking along the way. Get yourself assigned to special projects or task forces and you'll invariably bring back results or updates to your workgroup in the form of presentations. More than likely, you'll present ideas and items from your workgroup to the task force. In larger companies, you'll be called on to "evangelize" the results of the task force to the rest of the organization. Few things can make your "stock" go up like being called upon to play one of these roles. Special task or geographic assignments can also produce the same results. You can also write for internal company media or newsletters, which not only results in internal PR but also provides practice, experience, and collateral valuable toward acquiring external PR opportunities. It's a career "must" to let your managers know you're open to such things (demonstrating initiative among other things), and then to make the most of the speaking opportunities that inevitably result.

A Few Final Thoughts

In these pages, we have tried to give you the result of many years of accumulated practical expertise in the field of speaking in public. However, nothing is cast in stone. Presenting is an art form rather than a science. The medium through which the message is expressed (you) will give your work a quality all its own.

If the speaking bug bites you, and it might, considering all the long-term benefits it has to offer. You must continue your education. You might want to join Toastmasters International or the American Society of Training and Development. Both organizations have local chapters all over the country. Membership will help you develop your craft and allow you to make contact with like-minded professionals.

Put this in the context of long-term career management, and it means you will be developing relationships with other committed professionals. If you

Toastmasters

Toastmasters is a wonderful venue for developing and practicing your public speaking and business presentation skills. Founded in 1924, the Toastmasters mission goes beyond public speaking into general communication skills and leadership. Small Toastmaster chapters, usually consisting of twenty to thirty members, meet in most locales about once a week. As a member, you get an opportunity to deliver prepared presentations and impromptu speeches. You also get to do speaker evaluations and to develop meeting management skills by helping to run meetings. Toastmasters's meetings also provide a good opportunity to "network." Membership is only $40 per year, and attendance can be tailored to your own work schedule. Toastmasters's membership is a great way to practice, learn techniques, try new things, and observe other speakers, and it is a solid credential inside and outside your organization. For more information, including local chapters, check out *www.toastmasters.org*.

become connected to and involved with your profession, you will receive some very special benefits over the years. Successful people in every profession will tell you that they are probably only a few phone calls away from almost anyone they could ever wish to speak to. Just as they have become successful, the people they have gotten to know became successful, too.

When you personalize and apply what we have shared with you in these pages, you will increase your credibility and visibility within your company and your profession. More than learning how to make a successful business presentation, you have learned career-management techniques that will benefit you for as long as you apply them. This was why we wanted to add this book to the *Knock 'em Dead* line of career management books.

Speaking effectively in public is not a God-given gift. It is a skill-set that is learned, developed, and honed over time. In this information age, over 100 million professionals attend over 100,000 meetings and conferences every year. The demand for people who can express interesting ideas to an audience without boring or embarrassing that audience to death is well nigh insatiable. When you learn to speak, you will find eager audiences waiting to hear your words, whether that is in the department meeting, the boardroom, or the convention center. But the reasons for speaking don't end with an enhanced career. Everyone wants to feel fulfilled. They want the sense that their life has meaning and that they are making a difference with their presence. And the reasons for speaking can be quite personal. Everyone wants to overcome the fear—or the perceived fear—associated with public speaking.

Professionals who make a difference by their presence in different communities receive great personal satisfaction from their efforts. The opportunities are endless for you to put your skills to work outside of your professional milieu, in church groups, community organizations, charities, self-help, and civic action groups. While your involvement will be a reward unto itself, by doing the right thing, for the right reason, you will reward yourself in two final ways. You will be polishing the very skills you need to become more influential in your professional life. And the people you meet in your ad hoc activities will be active dedicated professionals committed to making a difference in both their professional and personal lives as well. They, too, will have wide professional spheres of influence, which will expand your own by the association.

The authors wish you well in your speaking career and look forward to hearing from you at *www.knockemdead.org*. Now get in front of an audience and knock 'em dead!

Index

A

B

C

D

E

F

G

H

I

K

L

M

Q

R

S

T

V

W